The Soldiers' Peace

The Soldiers' Peace

Demobilizing the British Army 1919

Michael Senior

First published in Great Britain in 2018 by
Pen & Sword Military
An imprint of
Pen & Sword Books Ltd
Yorkshire - Philadelphia

ISBN 9781526703040

A CIP catalogue record for this book is
available from the British Library

Typeset in 10.5/13.5 Ehrhardt MT l
Printed and Bound in the UK by TJ

Pen & Sword Books Ltd incorporates
History, Fiction, Maritime, Military,
Select, Wharncliffe Local History, W
Wharncliffe Transport, Leo Cooper,
White Owl, Seaforth Publishing and

For a complete list of Pen & Sword titles please contact
PEN & SWORD BOOKS LTD
47 Church Street, Barnsley, South Yorkshire, S70 2AS, England
E-mail: enquiries@pen-and-sword.co.uk
Website: www.pen-and-sword.co.uk

Or

PEN & SWORD BOOKS
1950 Lawrence Rd, Havertown, PA 19083, USA
E-mail: Uspen-and-sword@casematepublishers.com
Website: www.penandswordbooks.com

Contents

For
May, Peter and Margaret

Acknowledgements

I would like to thank the staff of The National Archives, the Imperial War Museum and the British Library for their courteous and efficient support. It is always a pleasure to visit these wonderful institutions. Throughout the book I have quoted from numerous articles and monographs and I have endeavoured to make the appropriate acknowledgements. My thanks go to all the authors concerned and in particular to the contributors to *Stand To!*, the journal of the Western Front Association and to the authors of the memoirs held by the Imperial War Museum.

I have received considerable help from Malcolm Allen, Jane Perkin, Ann and Bev Risman and Jim Spence. John Newton and Colin Picton deserve a special word of thanks for the time and trouble they have taken trawling through local papers in pursuit of relevant news items. I am indebted to Professor Ian Beckett who kindly read the draft text and gave many useful suggestions. My wife, Jenny, has contributed to this book in many ways and she has my heartfelt thanks.

I am grateful to the following for their permission to use their photographs in this book: the Socialist Health Association (Dr Christopher Addison); the History of Economic Thought (E. Llewellyn Smith); Carolynn Langley (the Stoke Hammond War Memorial); and David Brooks and Jeremy Harte of the Bourne Hall Museum (Police Sergeant Thomas Green and his Funeral Cortège). Other photographs are courtesy of the Taylor Collection (Asquith; Lloyd George; Churchill; Sir William Robertson; Sir Henry Wilson; Sir Douglas Haig, Haig and Plumer; Nursing Sister; the Big Four; *Evening Standard*; Horses; 'Nobody Wants You'; the Aberdeen tank; Peace Celebration) and from Wikipedia where there is no known copyright restriction (Sir Reginald Brade; Edwin Montagu; Bonar Law; General Smuts). Every effort has been made to avoid using photographs restricted in any way and my sincere thanks to the various sources.

It has been a pleasure, as ever, working with my editors, Rupert Harding and Alison Miles of the Pen & Sword Books Ltd team. I am grateful for their encouragement and practical advice.

Any errors that might be found in this book are entirely mine and I offer my apologies in advance.

Abbreviations

AIF	Australian Imperial Force
ASC (later RASC)	Army Service Corps (Royal)
BEF	British Expeditionary Force
CGW	Comrades of the Great War
C in C	Commander in Chief
CIGS	Chief of the Imperial General Staff
CO	Commanding Officer
CQMS	Company Quarter Master Sergeant
CSM	Company Sergeant Major
DLI	Durham Light Infantry
DSO	Distinguished Service Order
GHQ	General Headquarters
GOC	General Officer Commanding
HLI	Highland Light Infantry
IRA	Irish Republican Army
IWM	Imperial War Museum
KOYLI	King's Own Yorkshire Light Infantry
MC	Military Cross
MM	Military Medal
MP	Member of Parliament
MT	Motor Transport
NADSS	The National Association of Discharged Soldiers and Sailors
NCO	Non Commissioned Officer
NFDDSS	The National Federation of Discharged and Demobilized Soldiers and Sailors
POW	Prisoner of War
QMAAC	Queen Mary's Army Auxiliary Corps
QMG	Quarter Master General
QMRAC	Queen Mary's Royal Army Corps
RAF	Royal Air Force
RAMC	Royal Army Medical Corps

RAOC	Royal Army Ordnance Corps
RASC	Royal Army Service Corps
RE	Royal Engineers
RHA	Royal Horse Artillery
SAA	Small Arms Ammunition
TNA	The National Archives
VAD	Voluntary Aid Detachment
VC	Victoria Cross
WAAC	Women's Army Auxiliary Corps
YMCA	Young Men's Christian Association

Introduction

The Consequences of Peace

At 5.15am on Monday 11 November 1918 an Armistice was signed with Germany in a railway carriage in the Forest of Compiègne. It signalled the end of the First World War. After four-and-a-quarter years of fighting the combined forces of France, the British Empire, Italy and America had defeated the Central Powers led by Germany, Austria-Hungary and Turkey. Most men on the front line received the news of the Armistice in a mood of subdued relief. Gunner Stokes of the 13th Battery, New Zealand Field Artillery, wrote:

> We moved on 11 November and we heard the announcement of the Armistice when we were still in the Forest of Mormal on a cheerless, dismal, cold, misty day. There was no cheering or demonstration. We were all tired in body and mind, fresh from the tragic fields of battle, and this momentous announcement was too vast in its consequences to be appreciated or accepted with wild enthusiasm.[1]

Major J. Ewing, in his history of the Royal Scots Guards, recorded that the Armistice was 'welcomed by our troops in France in a spirit of sober gratitude'.[2]

In London there was a different mood. The British Prime Minister, David Lloyd George, announced in the House of Commons: 'The armistice was signed at five o'clock this morning, and hostilities are to cease on all fronts at 11 a.m. today'.[3] At that hour Big Ben on the Tower of Parliament chimed for the first time since August 1914. Winston Churchill, then the Minister of Munitions, recalled: 'The bells of London began to clash. Almost before the last stroke of the clock had died away, the strict war-straitened, regulated streets of London had become a triumphant pandemonium'.[4] King George V marked the occasion by opening a hundred-year-old bottle of brandy thus ending his wartime abstinence. The *Daily Mirror* of 12 November described the scene in London: 'Bells burst forth into joyful chimes, maroons were exploded, bands paraded the streets followed by cheering crowds of soldiers and civilians and London gave itself up to wholehearted rejoicing'. It was noted at a meeting of the War Cabinet that a bonfire had been lit in Piccadilly Circus and that 'it had been impossible to circulate the War Cabinet boxes owing to the crowds'.[5] The weather in London was cloudy and grey with some drizzle, but it could not dampen the mood of general exuberance.

The outpourings of jubilation were no less evident outside London. In Buxton 'it was round about noon that the wires came through, then the mid-day papers arrived, splashed with big headlines ... The people flocked into the streets laughing, joking and singing'. A parade was quickly organised. It was led 'by a large officer upon a small horse, which, putting in a timely appearance from somewhere, was pressed into service ... From the church towers happy peels rang out. Immediately the news arrived S. Mary's bell was pealed.'[6] Ernest Read Cooper, the Town Clerk of Southwold, noted:

> I went to the office and at 11 was rung by the County Adjutant, who told me that the Armistice had been signed and that guns were firing and bells ringing in Ipswich ... Flags soon came out, the Bells began to ring and a few of us adjourned to the Mayor's house and cracked some bottles of Fizz.[7]

In the small village of The Lee in Buckinghamshire the news of the Armistice was greeted with a mixture of relief and elation. The Vicar, Canon Phipps, went immediately to the local school: 'He said a few words, the Flag was saluted, the National Anthem sung and rounds of cheers were given'. The church bells were rung and a service of thanksgiving was organized: 'How can we adequately describe that wonderful assemblage of joyful people ... Everyone who could be there was in attendance and right gladly did we sing'.[8]

When the Armistice was announced, Winston Churchill was overlooking the crowds in Trafalgar Square from his offices in Northumberland Avenue: 'I was conscious of reaction rather than elation ... My mind mechanically persisted in exploring the problems of demobilisation. What was to happen to the three million Munitions workers? What would they make now? How would the roaring factories be converted? How in fact are swords beaten into ploughshares?'[9] By 23 November Lloyd George was of a mind to take a practical approach to these challenges of the peace. Referring to the ubiquitous ringing of bells during the previous week, he cautioned: 'Don't let us waste this victory merely in ringing joybells. There are millions of men who will come back. Let us make this a land fit for such men to live in'.[10] This was a worthy objective for any government and Lloyd George was well aware that the people of Britain required to see evidence of the benefits of their victory. With economic hardship at home and ¾ million dead abroad it was clear that measures were required that might compensate for the years of deprivation and, in many cases, of painful personal loss.

Such measures could only be devised and implemented by a strong government and Lloyd George, immediately after the Armistice, decided to call a General Election, the first for eight years, and solidify his position as Prime Minister. It was a shrewd political move. After all, he was popularly acknowledged as 'a man of the people' and 'the man who had won the war'. Demonstrating his forward-looking credentials, Lloyd George had, in August 1917, set up a Ministry of Reconstruction to review every aspect of British life in preparation for the eventual peace. Moreover, he had introduced two major pieces of legislation in 1918 which aimed to establish a more just and liberal society. The Representation of the People Act trebled the electorate. It gave the vote to all men over 21, instead of confining it to householders. For the first time, certain groups of women were enfranchised – those over 30 who were married, householders and university graduates. In addition, the President of the Board of Education, H.A.L. Fisher, who had been appointed by Lloyd George, brought in the 1918 Education Act. The Act provided, among other things, for free elementary education up to the age of 14 (the minimum school leaving age had previously been 12), provisions for nursey and higher education, and an increase in teachers' salaries. Not all the improvements contained in the Education Act were, for financial reasons, implemented, but they were at least an indication that the government was intent on making social conditions better than they had been before the war.

Lloyd George based his election campaign on issues guaranteed to appeal to public sentiment: punishing the Kaiser, making Germany pay reparations, improving social conditions in Britain, ensuring fair treatment for the troops and bringing the army home as quickly as possible. The outcome of the December 1918 election was a land-slide victory for Lloyd George and his Coalition Party, made up of Liberals and Conservatives, who won 478 seats giving an overall majority of 266.[11] The Labour Party with 59 seats became the official Opposition. Sinn Fein, the Irish Republican Party, won 73 seats which would have made them the second largest Party in Parliament. However, they refused to come to Westminster.

This action of the Irish Republicans was just one of a range of problems that faced the new Coalition Government. The issue of Home Rule for Ireland had been deferred for the period of the war, but with the coming of peace, the voters of Ireland gave clear evidence of their frustration at the lack of progress. As Sir Henry Wilson, the Chief of the Imperial General Staff (CIGS), was later to write: 'Ireland goes from bad to worse'.[12] Another issue that had been left over until the end of hostilities concerned the Disestablishment of the Welsh Church. It was argued by those supporting Disestablishment that the Church of England had misused the resources of the Welsh Church for its own benefit rather than for the people of Wales. The matter was complicated since a number of English Conservatives had land rights in Wales which they feared would be lost. It was by no means as important a problem as that of Irish Home Rule, but it was a cause of strong feelings and had to be dealt with.

Lloyd George faced other problems. A major issue was the need to re-gear and redirect industry and commerce away from the production and distribution of goods related to war towards the manufacture and trade of goods and services related to peace. The Treasury had serious challenges. The British government had made loans to allies during the war that amounted to £1,825 million, mainly to Russia (£586 million), Italy (£412 million) and France (£434 million). These loans were largely off-set by loans from America to Britain of around £1,000 million. The trouble was that it was highly unlikely that the loans made by Britain would be fully repaid. Britain's international balance of payments had been favourable for most of the war, mainly because of shipping services, but in 1918 there was a deficit of £107 million. The National Debt was fourteen times greater than the pre-war level and servicing it took almost half the yield from taxation as compared to 14 per cent before the war.

Britain's infrastructure had been neglected during the war years. The railways had been over-used and much of the equipment had been worn out. Roads had fallen into disrepair and it was estimated that £60 million would be required to renew them.[13] The building of private houses had ceased at the end of 1914 and in 1918 some 600,000 new houses were required.[14] In June 1917 a Commission of Enquiry had reported on housing conditions in Wales: 'the workers feel deeply discontented with their housing accommodation and with their unwholesome and unattractive environment generally ... houses are scarce and rents are increasing ...'.[15] It was not a problem confined to Wales; most large cities had areas with similar problems.

The number of trade unionists had increased from 3.4 million in 1913 to 5.5 million in 1918. Many trade unionists had resented the introduction of women workers during the war and the consequent effects of 'dilution' whereby skilled work could be performed by semi-skilled or unskilled labour. As Lloyd George later wrote: 'The Unions had accepted such measures, I will not say grudgingly, but with misgivings and only because they were forced by the extremity of the war emergency'.[16] Implicit in the union concessions on dilution was that they should apply only while hostilities lasted. Even before the end of the war a draft parliamentary Bill made 'provision with respect to the restoration … of certain trade practices … whether or not the practice was one tending to restrict production or employment'.[17] Britain had a poor labour relations record during the war. In the four years 1915–18 Britain lost 17.8 million working days. In the same period France lost 2.7 million working days.[18] Industrial unrest was widespread. The new government faced strikes and threats of strikes particularly in the mining and transport industries, either of which could paralyse the country.

In foreign affairs there was a range of important matters to be dealt with. Should an army be sent to North Russia to support the White Russians and overthrow Lenin, particularly at a time when Britain was committed to providing armies of occupation in both Germany and Turkey? There was already intervention in Russia by French, Italian, Czech, Rumanian, Serb, Japanese, Latvian, Finnish and American forces in support of the anti-Bolsheviks and the Russian Cossacks. How far was Britain prepared to risk lives and incur considerable expense on this far-off venture? Churchill, who was appointed Minister of War in January 1919, was vitriolic in his condemnation of the outcome of the 1917 Russian Revolution: 'Russia had fallen by the way; and in falling had changed her identity. An apparition with countenance different from any yet seen on earth stood in place of the old Ally. The old Russia had been dragged down, and in her place there ruled the nameless beast'.[19] Churchill supported intervention in Russia and on 14 February 1919 he put the issue starkly during the peace negotiations: 'Was it peace or was it war?' Woodrow Wilson's response was enigmatic: 'Russia was a problem to which he did not pretend to know the solution'.[20] The British government faced foreign policy problems in parts of the world other than North Russia. Intervention in South Russia was strategically more appropriate than involvement in the North since the Caucasian and Transcaspian republics bordered on India. In the Near and Middle East there was a power rivalry between the British and the French and national unrest was growing in the Arab world.

Relationships within the British Empire were changing. The pre-war Liberal government had made proposals that gave India some control over provincial and municipal affairs, but these minor changes were seen as unsatisfactory by the Indian nationalists. Independence for India was not a popular idea in Britain. It put at risk the existing trade arrangements with a country that had an immense market – not least for the cotton products made in the mills of Lancashire.[21] However, in 1917, in the face of increased unrest, Britain conceded that, at some point in the future, India would have an elected government with control over domestic issues.

The contribution of the Dominions to the war effort had provided them with grounds for greater independence. It was significant that South Africa, Canada, Australia and New Zealand were represented separately when the peace negotiations began and they signed the final treaty as individual countries. Australia and South Africa insisted on retaining the ex-German colonies of New Guinea and South West Africa.[22]

Lloyd George devoted much of his time and energy to the Paris Peace Conference. If President Wilson of the United States, President Clemenceau of France and President Orlando of Italy were personally involved, then it was necessary that the Prime Minister of Great Britain should be personally involved also. The treaty negotiations were mainly concerned with deciding the new frontiers in Europe, disposing of the German colonies and, crucially, arriving at the amount that Germany should pay in reparation to the victors. Lloyd George was less concerned with the new frontiers than with the redistribution of colonies and the potential inflow of cash from reparation and he was determined that Britain should receive an appropriate share of whatever became available. Lloyd George had promised in his electioneering speech in Wolverhampton on 24 November to make Britain a country fit for heroes. Money from Germany was seen by many as the way to fulfil that promise. The peace negotiations dragged on with an apparently endless number of meetings and the Treaty of Versailles was not signed with Germany until 28 June 1919.

Much discussion at the Conference centred on the establishment of a League of Nations – a worthy effort to safeguard the peace and resolve international disputes without the need to go to war. There were, inevitably, different views as to the aims of such a league and Lloyd George found himself at odds with both Clemenceau and Woodrow Wilson. Lloyd George was in favour of a body whose function was to conciliate and arbitrate, whereas both Clemenceau and Wilson, in their different ways, wanted the League to have powers of armed intervention.

As a terrible backdrop to these many problems, the world-wide influenza epidemic struck Britain in the winter of 1918. Three-quarters of the population were affected to varying degrees, among them Lloyd George who was obliged to spend ten days in bed. The peace celebrations were said to have caused a marked increase in 'flu' victims. An estimated 1,000 Londoners died of the 'flu' on Armistice Day.[23] The dire situation was not helped by the shortage of doctors, many of whom had enlisted and were still serving abroad. In November 1918 the National Health Insurance Committee reported that there was a 'depletion of doctors in the civil community whilst the serious epidemic of influenza is still occasioning great havoc in many parts of the country … The civilian doctors in many places have broken down under the strain'.[24] In Britain more than 150,000 people died during the epidemic.[25]

In addition to these many problems was the issue of the demobilization of the armed forces. It was a problem that was both immediate and acute. Churchill later recalled that on the morning of Armistice Day, shortly after 11 a.m., among the questions uppermost in his mind were: 'How long would it take to bring the Armies home? What would they do when they got home?'[26] Churchill's self-questioning focused on the problem of employment. Many of the 3 million munitions workers, now that the demand for their products had disappeared, would be seeking new work. At the same time, there would be about the same number of men who, when demobilized from the army, would also be looking for employment.

The issue was one of continuing concern for the government. After only three months of war, in December 1914, a memorandum from Sir Hubert Llewellyn Smith, the Secretary of the Board of Trade, clearly outlined the problem:

> The disbanding of an Army of over a million men, together with the simultaneous cessation of the demand for labour for the purposes of arming and equipping troops, will have results on the Labour Market of a kind and of a scale for which there is no precedent. However carefully the problem of demobilisation and of the transition of the army from military to civil employment is thought out before-hand, and however wisely and skilfully it is handled when the crisis comes, the economic reaction is certain to be very severe. Without careful preparation and suitable organisation in advance it will be impossible to avoid an industrial catastrophe.

This somewhat doom-laden memorandum concluded:

> The war may of course last for years; it may on the other hand come to an end sooner than is generally expected. It is very unlikely that we shall have sufficient notice that peace is about to be signed to enable suitable arrangements to be devised thereafter and before demobilisation actually begins, to ease the transition and to mitigate its effects.[27]

In 1916 the government received warnings about the likely effects of demobilization from a variety of sources. A joint memorandum from the

Secretaries of the Board of Trade and the War Office on 'The Labour Market' spoke of 'the serious problems that will arise when the labour market is flooded after demobilisation' and suggested to the Prime Minister, Asquith, that 'an outline scheme' should be prepared 'to minimise the dislocation of the labour market on demobilisation'.[28] In July of the same year, the London banker Huth Jackson wrote to the Army Demobilization Sub-Committee of the Reconstruction Committee:

> The problem to be faced is not merely a question of finding work for the men who return from the war, but the arrangements for such employment in conjunction with that of munition workers and other civilian workers who will be thrown upon the labour markets at the same time as our returning soldiers, and who will include a large number of women and even juvenile workers who have proved themselves to possess special aptitude for work which was performed by men only before the war.[29]

Again in 1916, a report by a group made up of members of the Parliamentary Liberal Party and trade unionists stated: 'To resettle all these millions into productive labour, without widespread unemployment and without causing a disastrous fall in the Standard Rates of Wages, will tax all the capacity of our administrators'. The report continued: 'One large employer is said to have declared that he would lay off a thousand women within 24 hours at the Declaration of Peace. It is to be expected that within three months, some two or three million will have been turned off.'[30]

There was certainly a marked chauvinistic attitude to the women who had contributed to the war effort. In March 1917, in a speech to the Royal Philosophical Society of Glasgow, Lieutenant Colonel D. M'Ewen put forward a view in relation to women munition workers:

> a considerable proportion is drawn from classes not usually earning their living. These may be dismissed at once without hardship … In the case of married women, it will be both in the social and economic interests of the nation that they return to their homes … Domestic Service has been largely depleted and women … will be quite willing to revert to their old occupations.[31]

As regards the army, the 1916 Report of the Parliamentary Liberal Party and trade unionists was of the opinion that:

> The Army cannot be got rid of so summarily. In the first place the troops cannot be instantly withdrawn from all the various territories

> they are occupying … there will be problems of settling accounts, dealing with clothing and equipment, civilian clothes, transportation, etc. … It is calculated that the disbandment cannot take place at a greater rate than 5,000 per day. At that rate it would take over six months before even one million men could be released.[32]

As it turned out, the problem was not restricted to a million men. There were, in November 1918, around 3.8 million men in the army who would demand to be demobilized. Many were based in Britain, but others were spread across various parts of the world: 1.7 million in France; 149,000 in Salonika; 73,000 in Italy; 11,000 in Mesopotamia; 8,000 in East Africa; and 3,500 in Russia.[33] Only a few of the original Regular soldiers remained. The great majority were volunteers or conscripts who considered, with the cessation of hostilities, that they had carried out what had been required of them and should be allowed to leave the army. Many soldiers subscribed to the view that: 'The war was over and all that had held it together had gone'.[34] The President of the Board of Agriculture and Fisheries considered that:

> Our army in its highly trained and organised sense will cease to be an army in spirit – its mind will be directed solely to its civilian future. The army as such will be transformed, becoming absorbed in non-military thought – it will be motionless as an army; such movement as there is will be directed to the re-establishment of its civilian status – indeed the army as such will die.[35]

Captain Charles Carrington, who was serving in Italy with the 48th Division when the war ended, was aware of similar feelings: 'Until the armistice, we had been "with it", willing to accept discipline, indeed welcoming it … On armistice morning the surface tension broke. Whatever cohesion had held the army together, "like a great machine", worked no longer. My five hundred or six hundred comrades … were mine no more but living their own lives.'[36] Major J. Ewing described the mood of the Royal Scots: 'now that the work to which they had dedicated themselves was accomplished, the great majority of officers and men began to find the yoke of military discipline irksome and were anxious to return to civilian duties'.[37]

Demobilization was uppermost in the minds of most soldiers and this had been anticipated long before the end of the war. A document from the President of the Board of Agriculture and Fisheries to the Army Demobilization Committee, dated September 1916, read: 'With the declaration of peace an incalculable reaction will overcome our army … The obsession of the army is to get home'.[38] In 1918, true to this prediction, Sergeant Arthur Vigurs of the 6th Battalion, Somerset Light

Infantry, wrote home on Armistice Day: 'The question on everyone's tongue is "When shall we get Home?"'[39] Captain J.C. Dunn of the Royal Welsh Fusiliers noted on 27 November that, following a series of lectures on future employment possibilities 'the men were quite indifferent; to get home, not to prepare for some nebulous job on getting there, was all they cared about'.[40] One soldier recorded the feelings of the great majority of his comrades: 'And of course, everybody but everybody wanted to be demobbed – immediately.'[41]

There were, however, more thoughtful views expressed. Tom Bromley of the Army Service Corps wrote philosophically: 'They knew, the authorities knew, that there would be a sort of difficulty in organising demobilisation in an orderly fashion instead of being a free-for-all, which would have been terrible. It would have been absolute chaos, everybody going home at once … It was very difficult.'[42] At the March 1917 meeting of the Royal Philosophical Society of Glasgow Lieutenant Colonel D. M'Ewen, said:

> There is need for much intense and continuous thought, as well as discussion, on this subject … We were unprepared for war … unpreparedness for peace would be nothing short of criminal madness. We owe it to the men who have fought our battles so to plan that on leaving the forces they may, without hardship, get promptly back to independent subsistence.

A second speaker, Mr John Dallas, added: 'Millions of men have to be redrafted into the civilian life of this country. Such immigration could never be permitted in any country without regulation'.[43] The government was well aware of the potential difficulties. Lord Milner, the Secretary of State for War, outlined the problem as he saw it in a speech in December 1918:

> To put back an army of millions of men, scattered over 3 continents, into civil life is just as difficult as it was to raise that giant army. In fact, in some ways, it is more difficult. It involves – quite inevitably – just as many complications, hardships, inequalities … the difference is that while the war is on, people mind less. The sense of national danger, national necessity, submerges complaints … But when the danger is over, or thought to be over, there is at once a reaction. Men are, quite naturally, less patient and more exacting.[44]

There were other important factors to be dealt with in repatriating Milner's 'army of millions'. How quickly would the soldiers be demobbed? In 1916 the Cabinet had predicted that 'the demobilisation of our troops from France will take twelve months and responsible persons have anticipated even longer'. The Trades Union Congress had urged that 'demobilisation should not be hastened, in order to prevent a sudden accession of labour upon disorganised markets'. On the other hand, however, a demobilization period of twelve months could well be considered by the troops as 'not only a cruel hardship, but as a frank injustice'.[45]

To complicate matters a proposal was advanced in July 1917 in a note from Sir Reginald Brade of the War Office to Vaughan Nash, the Secretary of the Reconstruction Committee, which, if implemented, would delay demobilization even when an armistice was declared. The note emphasized 'the importance of securing an armistice or an interval between the moment when we can take overt measures for demobilisation and that when actual demobilisation can commence'. Brade's thinking was concerned with post-war industrial competition with Germany:

> With their highly organised systems and their armies concentrated in great measure within or close to their own country, the Germans can get back into their places much quicker than we can. They may thus get a good start of us in the industrial and commercial race when the flag falls. We ought not to let the flag fall until our preparations at least are complete for a start and I think we might manoeuvre – as far as we can – to keep the German armies standing idle for as long as possible after actual hostilities cease.[46]

Even in late 1918 the Reconstruction Committee was purposely vague as to the rate of repatriation once an armistice was agreed. In answer to the question: 'At what rate is it expected that demobilisation will be carried out?', it responded: 'The estimated daily rate is a high one, and there is no intention of keeping any man in the Army longer than is absolutely necessary'. And, once these soldiers had been repatriated, what financial obligations did the government have? After the South African War a sliding scale of gratuities had awarded officers from £2,500, for a Field Marshal, to £30 for a Second Lieutenant. Other ranks had received from £20, for Warrant Officers, to £5 for a Private. In 1918, given the possibility that many soldiers would be unable to find work, Lloyd George and his government had to consider the precedents set in 1902 to plan for possible unemployment and hardship benefits as well as clothing and travel allowances for demobbed soldiers.

The government's fears following the Armistice were therefore two-fold: could mass unemployment be avoided and, if it could not, would it lead to widespread social unrest? A Reconstruction Committee document of July 1917 showed just how deeply engrained were the concerns of the government. The document referred back a hundred years to the period following the Napoleonic Wars – 'one of the darkest chapters in British History'. A main cause of 'the disastrous decline in the general standard of life' at that time, was the 'disbandment of some three hundred thousand soldiers and sailors without any kind of plan'.[47]

Alongside these fears of unemployment and possible social unrest was the spectre of extreme left-wing activity – that the malign influence of Bolshevism would spread among British troops and British workers. In June 1917 a gathering in Leeds of 1,100 members of the Independent Labour Party and the British Socialist Party had welcomed the revolutionary developments in Russia and passed a resolution calling for the establishment of Workers' and Soldiers' Councils.[48] An effort to set up one such council was attempted in Newcastle on 28 July 1917. One of the leaders was Charlotte Despard, a suffragette and the sister of Sir John French who had commanded the British Expeditionary Force in France in 1914 and 1915.

In May 1917 a conference for all socialist parties, regardless of whether or not their home countries were at war with one another, was convened in Stockholm. The purpose was to support a Russian peace proposal. It was a proposal that was considered by the British government as being inappropriate both in content and timing. The Labour Party, to the dismay of the War Cabinet, voted to send delegates to this conference, but none attended. The government refused them passports and, in addition, the British merchant seamen's union refused to carry them.[49]

Long before the Russian Uprising of 1917 an element of anxiety existed among the leaders of both the British government and the British Army as to the possibility of revolutionary activity. Even the introduction of conscription, through the Military Service Act of 1916, had raised concerns. Britain had previously relied on volunteers to fight its wars – men considered to be of upright patriotic sentiment. Conscripts were thought by many to be of a lesser calibre. The then Commander in Chief of the British Expeditionary Force, General Sir Douglas Haig, expressed his concerns about conscripted soldiers: 'The influence of these men and their antecedents generally are not such as to foster any spirit but that of unrest and discontent, they come forward with compulsion and they will depart the Army with relief. Men of this stamp are not satisfied with remaining quiet, they come from a class which like to air real or fancied grievances'.

There was a feeling that conscription had changed the relationship between the soldier and the State. The author J.L. Hammond, who had been the Secretary to the Civil Service Commission, made a lecture tour of army camps and YMCA centres in France and England during spring 1916. His stated main objective was to 'investigate … the mind of the soldier', and he later reported on the comments he had heard from the YMCA organizers and the soldiers:

> One YMCA official said that he had often heard men remark that if the State was entitled to demand a man's life, it was under far greater obligation than it had recognised hitherto … that is assumed in all conversations in the camp … There are rankling memories of Military Tribunals, bullying methods and gross inequalities. I am told that in many cases the men talk openly of violent reprisals in the future.

The report also touched on the expectations of soldiers concerning conditions of work:

> There is a general demand for a widely different life in the future … there will be a demand after the war for shorter hours, more recreation, and more education. One YMCA official had seen a great deal of the Lancashire Regiments, and he said it was a common thing for textile workers to say that they were going to have an 8 hour day if they went back to the Mills. A Huddersfield worker made the same point.

Hammond summed up his experience:

> I was struck by the tone of the discussions after my lectures [on the French Revolution]. One man said that if there was going to be any dragooning or sweating of the working classes after the war, there would be a French Revolution in England and his words were endorsed generally. The Secretary in one of the fighting areas was very emphatic on this saying that it was important that people at home should realise the temper of the Army and not imagine that the soldiers would come home in a mood to be grateful for patronage or benevolence.

Hammond concluded: 'It is my duty to record these representations, too numerous and general to be due to local accidents, because the temper of the men will no doubt be affected by this atmosphere when they leave the Army'.[50] Whether the gist of Hammond's report was truly representative is uncertain. Nevertheless, some of the extreme comments would have made unwelcome reading in government circles.

There was no doubt that the government wanted to learn more about what Hammond called 'the mind of the soldier'. A memorandum dated 25 September 1916 from the Reconstruction Committee to the Army Council read:

> in connection with several questions which will arise on the conclusion of peace [the Reconstruction Committee] are anxious to obtain some information concerning the general desires and intentions of the rank and file of the Army in regard to the resumption of their pre-war occupations ... The Committee have received from various sources somewhat contradictory accounts of the mental attitude of the men on such questions as the return to sedentary or ill-paid work, settlement on the land, and emigration. It is obviously of the first importance to ascertain what is the general trend of feeling among the men on such matters, so far as any general trend is discernible; and the Committee would be much obliged if the Army Council could assist them in this object.

The memorandum then suggested a means by which such information might be collected:

> the subject scarcely seems one with which it would be appropriate to deal at present by means of official enquiries addressed to the men themselves. It has, however, occurred to the Committee that valuable results might be gained by means of a confidential enquiry addressed to the Chaplains of the Army, asking them to record and summarise the impressions which they have gathered in the course of their conversations with the men: and I am to suggest that if the Army Council concur in this view steps might be taken to address such an enquiry ... It seems probable that results so procured might be both easier to obtain and more generally trustworthy than if a formal investigation were set on foot.

The reply from the War Office to this suggestion, dated 5 October 1916, was brief and unhelpful:

> I am to inform you that it is not considered advisable to place any reliance upon information on this subject which is obtained from other than official sources. With reference to the proposal to address a confidential enquiry to the Chaplains of the Army ... I am to inform you that the experience of the Council leads them to believe that the information to be obtained from the Chaplains would not be of a nature to assist the Committee in their enquiries.[51]

Considering that the memorandum from the Reconstruction Committee was received by the War Council during the twelfth week of the grinding Battle of the Somme, such a response can hardly be regarded as surprising. Even an eminent member of the clergy, Canon E.H. Pearce, the Archdeacon of Westminster, had doubts about the use of chaplains for this purpose. In September 1916 he wrote to the Secretary of the Reconstruction Committee saying that the chaplains would be 'only too glad to help', but asked 'are they the ones that know the Tommies most intimately and truthfully?' The idea was quietly dropped.

Of more immediate concern to the government was the establishment of a number of servicemen's associations. The National Association of Discharged Soldiers and Sailors (NADSS) was formed in September 1916; the National Federation of Discharged and Demobilized Soldiers and Sailors (NFDDSS) followed in April 1917; and the Comrades of the Great War (CGW) was created in August 1917. The CGW was conservative in character, but both the NADSS and the NFDDSS were radically inclined. Between them, NADSS and NFDDSS put forward twenty-nine candidates in the 1918 election and one was elected. Their purpose was to apply pressure on the government in the areas of employment and pensions. As far as the government was concerned, any agitation was suspect – were they straws in the wind of pending revolution?

In the mind of the government there was good reason to be suspicious of organizations set up to agitate for those out of work. Demobilization after the South African War had led to an upsurge in unemployment which had doubled from 2 per cent in 1899 to 4 per cent in 1902. The Independent Labour Party had formed a National Employment Committee which pressed for a government department specifically to deal with finding work for the unemployed. Another body, the Social-Democratic Federation, had organized a demonstration in Hyde Park in June 1902 and again in February 1903 to raise public awareness of the plight of unemployed ex-servicemen. The government took little action, but the demonstrations were regarded as threats to public order.[52] Lloyd George's government of 1919 did not want a repeat of such disturbances.

Understandably, because of the numbers involved, the government was primarily concerned with the orderly demobilization of soldiers. But other groups were also important – not least the women who formed part of the British Army. Over 50,000 women joined the Women's Army Auxiliary Corps (WAAC), later officially renamed Queen Mary's Army Auxiliary Corps (QMAAC), after its formation in 1917. They carried out useful work, mainly in Britain, as cooks, canteen helpers, clerical workers, transport drivers, ambulance drivers and storekeepers thus relieving thousands of men for the front. By 1918 there were some 6,000 QMAACs, known to the French as 'Les Tommettes', who were serving with the BEF in France.

Women were particularly well represented in the various medical units. Over 7,000 nurses and Voluntary Aid Detachment members (VAD) joined the RAMC. In addition, over 1,000 nurses and VADs were part of the British Red Cross Society which included members of the St John's Ambulance Brigade, the Friends Ambulance Unit and the First Aid Nursing Yeomanry. The Queen Mary's Army Auxiliary Corps accounted for 7,800 nurses and the YMCA, the Church Army, the Salvation Army and the Soldiers' Christian Association contributed a further 1,000.[53] The women of these organizations served their country well. By 1919, they had made it possible to release 11,000 men for military service. Seven had received the Military Medal.[54]

The nurses who were stationed abroad all had to be repatriated. Many had volunteered from well-to-do families and it was likely that they would return to their pre-war way of life. Some could expect to be absorbed into hospitals and nursing homes on their return to Britain. Others, however, would be looking for work and their future was unclear. Women munition workers were expected, at least in certain quarters, to quietly resume their former domestic lives. Would the returning women in the army and the medical units be content to act similarly?

The government also faced the problem of dealing with the returning prisoners of war. The number of British prisoners of war totalled 167,555 of whom 161,287 were in Germany. Others were in Mesopotamia (2,726), Egypt (1,245), Turkey (304) and East Africa (67). Between 17 November 1918 and 23 January 1919, 162,650 POWs (7,176 officers, 150,847 other ranks and 4,627 civilians) were returned to Britain. Around 160,000 came from Germany.[55] Many were in a poor physical state and they required hospital attention. This further exacerbated the burden placed on the doctors and nurses already caring for the tragic cases of soldiers who had been mutilated both physically and mentally and who needed to be placed in hospitals and nursing homes on their return to Britain. These men had the sympathy of the government but they also needed work. Moreover, to the State they represented a major financial commitment both in terms of the cost of care and the cost of pensions. The number of pensions granted between August 1914 and March 1919 to the disabled, both permanent and temporary and including allowances for dependent children, amounted to 1,156,330.[56]

The requirements of 'total war' demanded the employment of many resources. Although the internal combustion engine had made possible various forms of mechanized transport, the movement of goods and equipment during the war relied largely on the horse and the mule. In November 1918 there were 735,409 horses and mules in the British Army. They had been acquired not only from Britain, but from South America, Canada, the United States, Spain and India. Now that the war had ended, what was to be done with them and the 18,766 men who looked after them in the various remount depots?[57]

There was also a staggering amount of army equipment and ordnance strewn around the various theatres of war. Spare boots, shirts, socks, trousers, caps and pantaloons were available in their thousands. A survey of artillery pieces dated 17 November 1918 showed that in France alone there were 3,144 18pdr guns with over 8 million rounds of shrapnel and heavy explosive shells; 984 4.5in howitzers together with 2.3 million shells; 1046 6in guns with 2.6 million shells and 456 60pdrs with around 679 million shrapnel and high-explosive shells. In addition, there were 46,638 machine guns, 2.6 million grenades and 60,865 unused rifles. There were no fewer than 325 million .303 bullets stored in dumps ready for distribution to the army. Such a list, far from exhaustive, was a testament to the massive efforts of the British munitions industry.[58]

Mechanized transport was spread throughout the various theatres of war – France, Italy, Salonica, North Russia, Malta, Egypt, East Africa and Mesopotamia. In August 1914 the BEF had 827 cars (all except 80 were requisitioned) and 15 motorcycles.[59] It is quite remarkable, and indicative of the move to increased mechanization in the British Army, that, on 16 November 1918, the number of serviceable vehicles, with the great majority again in France, included 46,565 lorries, 33,845 motorcycles, 10,614 cars and an unspecified number of tanks.[60] All of these had some value and needed to be disposed of or allocated to the military units that were to remain in occupied areas.

The various demobilization committees frequently raised a question central to the issue of demobilization: how many men will the army require following the peace? Sir Reginald Brade of the War Office raised the issue at a meeting of the Demobilization Sub-Committee of the Reconstruction Committee on 2 September 1916:

> it was essential that the Government should decide as soon as possible what was to be the size and composition of the standing army after the conclusion of peace. The question would have to be decided whether it would be necessary to employ compulsory means of enlisting a standing army, or whether it would be possible to get sufficient numbers by voluntary methods.

The response to Brade was that 'It will be desired to retain with the Colours 200,000 – 750,000 men at the end of the war and that will be the number of the permanent army'. The range of the numbers given was so wide that they could be regarded as a vague guess. At the same meeting the chairman of the Demobilization sub-Committee, E.S. Montagu, asked Brade: 'What would happen if the Government were to decide that all men who had enlisted for the duration of the war should be at once disbanded on the conclusion of peace?' Brade answered: 'That would mean that Egypt and India would be left without garrisons'.[61]

To give a precise estimate of the size of the army after the war was just not possible. As a December 1914 memorandum from the Board of Trade commented: 'No precise forecast can as yet be made of the Trade, Politics, Military or International situation at the close of the war'.[62] What applied in 1914 applied also in autumn 1916. The outcome of the war was far from clear and even if the Allies won the war the outcome of the peace negotiations, where a standing army might be employed and in what numbers, could not be predicted. It was not until a White Paper dealing with this issue was published in March 1919 that a definitive figure was given. One thing was certain. If there were no battles to be fought and considerably fewer soldiers to command, then the need for the senior officers seriously diminished. The generals themselves – Haig, Allenby, Plumer, Byng, Horne, Rawlinson, Wilson, Birdwood – and many others who had spent the past four years at the centre of the British Army would need to consider their futures.

In autumn 1918, when peace had become a real possibility, the Reconstruction Committee published a series of pamphlets for the British public, the aim of which was to 'outline in general terms the main problems of reconstruction' that faced Lloyd George and his government. The list of problems was formidable. First, shipping – 'until we know roughly how many ships we are going to have at our disposal we cannot go far in our arrangements either for bringing home the armies abroad or for bringing in the raw materials in order to provide the men with work'. Second, transport – 'When the raw materials have been apportioned, how shall it be carried to the place where it is needed?' Then, industrial organization – 'we cannot carry the war debt, still less improve the conditions of the workers, unless we increase and improve our production'. Health, housing and education were also listed among 'the social questions which will face the country at the end of the war'. There was 'the all-important question of finance. The war has made enormous demands upon our financial resources, both national and individual ... we shall have to reduce our imports to the barest needs and so stimulate our production as to pay for our imports and for the interest due on foreign loans'. However, the subjects that received most attention in these pamphlets were those of demobilization and employment: 'at the end of the war we hope to see the soldiers and sailors demobilised as soon as possible ... The transition from a war to a peace basis will cause, at the very least, great dislocation in industry and finance, and at the same time there may be considerable unemployment'.[63]

Following the December 1918 General Election a cartoon appeared in *Punch* headed 'The 1919 Model'. It showed Lloyd George dressed as a pilot standing next to a bi-plane carrying the sign 'Coalition Majority'. Mr Punch is addressing Lloyd George with the words: 'They've given you a fine new machine, Mr Premier, and you've got plenty of spirit, but look out for bumps'.[64] Whether demobilization and the general dismantling of the British Army was to be one of those 'bumps' was yet to be seen.

Chapter 1

Plans for Demobilization, 1914–18

The plans for demobilization developed during the war years were a serious effort to organize an orderly reduction in size of the British Army. They were aimed at minimising the possibility of social and economic disruption and this was to be brought about by a controlled and systematic release of troops in a way that would avoid unemployment and support the regeneration of key sectors of British industry and commerce. The more effective the regeneration, the more opportunities there would be for the returning soldiers to settle back quietly into civilian life. Given the daunting size of the demobilization task, and bearing in mind the disruptions that followed both the Napoleonic Wars and the Boer War, it was a formula that commended itself to politicians and civil servants alike.

In their memorandum of 14 December 1914, Sir Hubert Llewellyn Smith (Secretary of the Board of Trade) and Sir Reginald Brade (Secretary of the War Office) proposed that the 'the whole question needs as thorough and prolonged study and preparation as the question of mobilisation received from the Military Authorities and the Defence Committee before the war'. Considering the ad hoc and random recruitment pattern of 1914, which had the effect of stripping skilled and urgently required men from industries important to the war effort such as mining and ship building, the comparison was unfortunate. Nevertheless, Llewellyn Smith and Brade were the first to raise the subject of demobilization as an important and pressing issue. In the opinion of Llewellyn Smith it was 'by no means premature to begin this study at once ... I have accordingly conferred on the subject with Sir Reginald Brade and we have provisionally agreed that a scheme shall be prepared at once by the two Departments jointly for consideration by the Government'. Brade was to seek authority from Lord Kitchener, the Secretary of State for War, and Llewellyn Smith requested the President of the Board of Trade to ensure that 'the Prime Minister [Asquith] ... is aware and approves of the course which we propose to follow'.[1] On 16 December Llewellyn Smith received a reply from Colonel

Hankey, Secretary of the Committee of Imperial Defence, saying that 'the Prime Minister has approved of the course which you propose to follow'.[2]

By January 1915 Llewellyn Smith and Brade, with commendable speed, had put together an outline proposal on demobilization and this went before the Cabinet in April 1915.[3] The main provisions of the proposal included a furlough (leave) with full pay and allowances; a free travel warrant from the place of demobilization to home; money gratuities for war service; assistance in finding employment; and free insurance against unemployment. It also proposed that the local labour exchanges and the Territorial Force Associations should be used to help soldiers into employment. The provisions were very broad-brush and lacked detail, but they were approved by the Cabinet. And then, 'in view of the paramount necessity of secrecy', they were pigeon-holed.[4] It was not until mid-1916 that they received further attention.

Britain had entered the war in 1914 essentially to preserve its world position in the face of the threat of German expansionism. All the attacks and all the battles that took place during the four-and-a-quarter years of war were aimed at destroying Germany and its allies. But even before that aim was achieved it was clear that a return simply to 1914 conditions, socially and economically, was just not acceptable. Many millions of men and women, both at home and abroad, had worked hard for victory. Everybody knew somebody who was either killed or wounded in the war. The British government may have entered the war to maintain the international status quo but expectations domestically had risen. Numerically, the greatest contributors to victory had been the 'lower classes' who had formed the ranks of the armed forces or who had worked in industry or on the land. They were the mass of the people and, with peace, they awaited their reward. The acquisition of some additional territories to enlarge the Empire was irrelevant to the bulk of the British population. Their hopes for the future were set on improved living and work conditions at home – education, housing, a steady job and good pay. As the 1916 report from J.L. Hammond on 'the mind of the soldier' had pointed out: 'They think that by their hardship in the trenches they have earned a real stake in the country'.[5] Lloyd George's election pledge to build a land fit for heroes had certainly caught the mood of the time, but was he able to make good his promise?

The politicians were well aware that the generality of the population expected an improved standard of living once the war had ended. They were also aware that countless significant problems would arise in industry and commerce as the country moved from war to peace. It was with these matters in mind that on 18 March 1916 the then Prime Minister, Herbert Asquith, announced the creation 'of a body for the organisation of British post-war reconstruction'. The announcement read: 'In accordance with the decision of the Cabinet, I propose to set up, on the analogy of the Committee of Imperial Defence, a Committee over which I will preside, to consider the advice, with the aid of Sub-Committees, upon the problems which will arise on the conclusion of peace …'.[6] Apart from Asquith himself, this Reconstruction Committee was made up of seven members of the Cabinet: Andrew Bonar Law (Colonial Secretary), Arthur Anderson (President of the Board of Education), Austen Chamberlain (Secretary for India), Lord Crewe (Lord President of the Council), Edwin Montagu (Chancellor of the Duchy of Lancaster), Lord Selbourne (President of the Board of Agriculture) and Walter Runciman (President of the Board of Trade).

While this was the first national body to consider post-war problems, certain government departments had of their own volition started to discuss and make plans on issues relevant to them. It was because of this that Asquith, in his minute constituting the Reconstruction Committee, specifically referred to 'the aim of co-ordinating the work … done by the Departments in this direction'. And it was clear, at the first meeting of the Committee on 24 March, that much work had indeed already taken place.[7] Runciman 'made a statement of the Committees appointed by the Board of Trade to deal with post-war problems'. Apart from the Llewellyn Smith-Brade Committee on Demobilization and the Labour Market there were committees dealing with Trade Relations, Commercial Intelligence, and 'the position of certain important British industries after the war' including iron, steel and shipbuilding and textiles. In response to a question concerning the terms of reference of this last group of committees, Runciman replied that the terms were 'to consider the position of the Industries after the war, especially in relation to international competition, and to report what measures, if any, are necessary or desirable in order to safeguard that position'.

The discussion that followed Runciman's statement at this first meeting illustrated some of the concerns held by certain members of the Reconstruction Committee. A major issue was whether the committees should remain secret. Montagu considered that the names of the committee members and their reports should not be publicized. Bonar Law agreed that the reports should not be publicized, but that the composition of the committees should be made public. Such were Montagu's feelings on this subject that he later wrote:

> I would submit … that the existence of, the terms of reference of, and the personnel of the different sub- Committees should be secret. This is essential. It will not do to let the public or the enemy know

> what the Government is considering. On the other hand, I think it will be desirable that the Prime Minister should announce that he has appointed and is chairman of a Reconstruction Committee which is appointing sub-Committees … The announcement should state that the sub-Committees are secret because it is not desirable in all cases, and therefore not desirable in any, to say what we are considering, but that the public may be assured that nothing will be forgotten and that the sub-Committees contain among their members not only politicians and officials but men and women drawn from the widest possible sources.[8]

This policy was adopted by Asquith who, on 10 July, responded to a question in Parliament: 'The Reconstruction Committee is a Committee of the Cabinet, and, as my hon. friend [a Mr Whitehouse] is probably aware, it is not the practice to give the names of the members of such Committees'. On the same day Asquith, in a reply to a question from an MP, Mr MacCallum Scott, stated:

> I do not think that it would be convenient at the present stage to make any announcement as to the character of the inquiries which are being undertaken by the Reconstruction Committee. The Government are making every effort to deal with the whole range of questions which in their judgement will call for immediate treatment at the close of the war[9]

An article in *The Times* of 30 June repeated the government policy: 'It is not expedient in the public interest to specify the nature of many of the inquiries which are being undertaken, and no announcements will be made concerning them; but it is hoped that the entire range of subjects which will call for immediate treatment at the close of the war may be covered …'.[10]

Another major issue concerned the confidentiality of information and the role of employee representatives. Lord Crewe thought that 'the employers were very nervous about letting the details of their business be known to everyone concerned, including the representatives of labour'. Runciman 'did not see how a Committee could possibly include representatives of labour owing to the number of different classes and trade unions of operatives concerned'. Chamberlain thought that 'the workmen were more inclined to co-operate with employers at the present time than they were before the war'. Asquith intervened saying that 'Mr Runciman might communicate with the Board of Trade Committees, expressing the view that Committees should include representatives of labour'.

A wide range of topics was discussed at this first meeting of the Reconstruction Committee. Apart from industrial and commercial matters, these included fiscal policy, imperial trade and the role of the

Dominions. Asquith took the opportunity to summarize the purpose of his Reconstruction Committee which was: 'to deal with post-war commercial and industrial policy, with reference not merely to the penalisation of the enemy, but also to the recovery of markets, the maintenance of former industries, finding new markets, the establishment of key industries, etc.' It was at this point that Colonel Hankey, attending in his capacity as Secretary of the Committee of Imperial Defence, made a significant observation: 'nearly all the discussion had been concerned with the period of peace and very little with the transitional period or on demobilisation'. Hankey was immediately supported by Montagu who considered that 'there ought to be a special sub-Committee to deal with demobilisation. This was a question for the Reconstruction Committee'. When a summary of the matters agreed at the meeting was circulated to the members of the Committee there was no mention of a Demobilization sub-Committee and this caused Montagu to write to the Secretary, Vaughan Nash: 'I thought that the Committee was with me when I suggested we wanted at once a Demobilisation Committee.' It was therefore as a result of Hankey's telling intervention and Montagu's support that a sub-Committee on Demobilization was established and Montagu became its chairman.[11]

The membership of the sub-Committee was published on 21 August with the terms of reference: 'To consider and report upon the arrangements for the return to civil employment of officers and men serving in the land forces of the Crown at the end of the war'. Apart from the chairman, Montagu, the Committee had thirteen members with representatives from the Board of Trade, the Treasury, the War Office, the Board of Agriculture and Fisheries, and the National Health Insurance Commission. Among the members were Hankey, Brade and Llewellyn Smith.[12]

When the Reconstruction Committee was set up on 18 March, Asquith referred to the work that had 'already been done by the Departments in this direction'. Vaughan Nash, the Secretary of the Reconstruction Committee, followed up this point and on 28 March sent a circular letter to all government departments: 'You will favour me as soon as may be convenient with particulars of the work falling within the terms of the Committee's reference which has already been done by your Department, is in progress, or is contemplated, together with copies of any relevant documents such as reports of Committees, draft Acts of Parliament, etc., which may have been prepared.' Vaughan Nash, apart from being the Secretary of the Reconstruction Committee, was also the Secretary of the Demobilization sub-Committee and when that Committee began its deliberations in May 1916 it had access to the April 1915 proposals of Llewellyn Smith and Brade.

The Demobilization sub-Committee met on five occasions between May and September 1916 and its First (Interim) Report to Asquith's Reconstruction Committee was published on 9 October of that year. The Report focused on the terms under which the soldiers would be demobilized and the arrangements to help ex-soldiers find employment. As the minutes of the various meetings indicate, the members of the sub-Committee often disagreed as to how these issues should be dealt with.

Two of the Llewellyn Smith-Brade 1915 provisions for demobilized soldiers were accepted without debate. Each soldier 'released from service with the colours at the termination of the war' would receive 'a working furlough … on full pay and allowances for a period of about four weeks' and also ' a travelling warrant for his railway fare from his place of his disbandment to his home district'. Three other matters were not so easily dealt with. They were, first, the provision of free unemployment insurance for those demobilized soldiers who were unable to find work – a matter that Llewellyn Smith and Brade had referred to in their 1914 memorandum as something that might only 'possibly' happen; second, the granting of service gratuities to those who had been involved in the war; and, third, the arrangements for finding work.[13]

During the discussions of the 1916 Montagu sub-Committee, the two issues of gratuities and unemployment insurance became inter-related. A member of the sub-Committee, Mr H.P. Blackett of the Treasury, took the view that the amount of money available to the government for the payment of gratuities and insurance would inevitably be finite. Therefore, the 'good' soldier, i.e. the soldier who was in employment, would receive a lesser gratuity since he would 'have to pay out of his own pocket (for this is what it comes to) considerable sums for insuring his less worthy or less fortunate fellow …'. Blackett considered that the solution to the problem:

> will be found in dropping the notion of insurance. Let the ex-soldier be granted a bounty of 100x, of which he will be paid 50x on disbanding, and the remainder either in two quarterly instalments of 25x (or in ten monthly instalments of 5x), with the right when unemployed, but not otherwise, to draw weekly in advance at the rate of (say) 2x.

Not only would all soldiers be treated alike, argued Blackett, but the 'expense to the State will be defined instead of indefinite … and with insurance against unemployment out of the way, the State can concentrate on what is, after all, the vital point, viz., the provision of work for the soldier'.[14]

Blackett's views were discussed at the August meeting of the sub-Committee. The chairman, Montagu, put it to the sub-Committee that it 'must now decide the question whether free Unemployment Insurance policies should be granted to the returning soldier … it was desirable that the sub-Committee should at once settle whether Unemployment Insurance policy was regarded in any way as affecting the question of gratuities given at the end of the war'. Montagu then went on to make clear his own opinion: 'they were entirely different questions. A gratuity was in the nature of a payment for services rendered and was concerned only with the past, whilst Unemployment Insurance was a provision against future distress which might arise as a result of the dislocation occurring after the war'. When asked by a member of the sub-Committee whether gratuities would be reduced because of unemployment payments, Montagu answered that 'he did not think that this would happen'. Montagu was supported by Brade who considered that Blackett's proposal was unworkable: 'In 1901–02 we tried in the soldier's interest to induce him to accept payment by instalments. We failed, and I see no reason to suppose that we should succeed at the end of this war.' Brade went on to say: 'If trade were good after the war, and many sound judges believe it will be, and employment were plentiful, Mr Blackett's plan would undoubtedly be very costly'.[15] Llewellyn Smith also supported Montagu: 'the great advantage of Unemployment Insurance was that the assistance from the State was given as and when needed to the ex-soldier – namely, when he was out of work'.

There was then some discussion as to the amount of benefit that should be paid during a period of unemployment and the number of weeks that would be covered. Llewellyn Smith thought that the amount should be the same as that given to work people in general, i.e. 7*s*. per week. Others thought that 7*s*. was too low. Montagu proposed a benefit of 15*s*. for the first four weeks and then 10*s*. thereafter. The usual rate paid by trade unions to their unemployed members was 10*s*. per week and this prompted a sub-Committee member to point out that 'many men would be receiving benefit from their trade unions in addition to that granted by the State, and that the total amount received by them might be such that it would not make them particularly eager to take employment which might be available'. Yet another member said that 'in agricultural districts 12 shillings would be too much, as it was too near to the actual amount of wages usually received'. The discussion ended when the sub-Committee agreed to: 'A free unemployment insurance policy, valid for one year from a month after the date of discharge from the army; the rate of unemployment benefit to be 10*s*. per week for a period of not exceeding twenty weeks during the year'.[16] The sub-Committee estimated that around 500,000 soldiers would be unemployed for an average of 6 months each and that the total cost would be within a figure of £5,000,000. This proposal was put to the main Reconstruction Committee in October 1916. Blackett signed the report, but appended a reservation stating that in his view 7*s*. per week unemployment benefit was quite adequate and that a rate of 10*s*. per week 'might give rise to abuses'.

The second issue that caused much discussion in the Demobilization sub-Committee was concerned with gratuities that might be paid to soldiers at the end of the war. At the fourth meeting of the sub-Committee in August 1916, Montagu started the discussion: 'the questions before the Committee were: should there be a present in money to men who had served during the present war and, if so, should it be confined to those men who had been in theatres of war'. Montagu would have been well aware that, following the Boer War, soldiers who had remained in Britain did not receive a gratuity.[17] He added that 'no precedent exists for granting a gratuity to a man who had not been in one of the theatres of war'. Brade put the War Office point of view that there should be no proposal 'to grant any gratuity in addition to the service gratuity to men who had only served in the United Kingdom. The service gratuity of £1 for each year's service is part of the State's ordinary contract with each soldier, both in war and peace time, and could not therefore be touched'. The Right Hon. Arthur Henderson, the leader of the Parliamentary Labour Party, thought that 'it should be considered whether the circumstances of this war were not peculiar, and whether it would not be desirable to grant a gratuity to all soldiers who had enlisted'.

Montagu himself thought that there should be a 'differentiation between men who had been and men who had not been in theatres of war'. Llewellyn Smith considered this to be an 'artificial distinction' and was in favour of 'a gratuity to all men, but a higher scale should be given to men who had 'smelt powder'. Further discussion in the sub-Committee showed that that there was a strong feeling that men who had not 'smelt powder' should receive some gratuity in addition to their ordinary service gratuity. The recommendation that went to the main Reconstruction Committee therefore proposed that every enlisted man should receive: 'A special war gratuity in addition to the ordinary service gratuity; the amount of the war gratuity to differ, if the Treasury and the War Office think it desirable, according to other distinctions in the character of the service rendered, but so that every man receives some war gratuity'.

The actual amounts of the gratuities were therefore left in the hands of the Treasury and the War Office, but, as Montagu wrote in the sub-Committee report: 'Whatever may be the total expenditure required for an adequate scale of gratuities, unemployment insurance, and other benefits to the army and navy at the end of the war, we are confident that Parliament and the nation will face it cheerfully'.[18]

The third issue that caused some controversy was concerned with the administration of unemployment pay and the task of finding work for the unemployed soldier. It seemed appropriate that the existing labour exchanges had an important role to play. Llewellyn Smith and Brade assumed that this was so in their 1915 proposals and also suggested that, since the Territorial Force Associations had obligations that included 'the care of reservists and discharged soldiers', they should also be involved 'acting probably through a special committee for the purpose'.[19] A variation of this proposal, involving local committees, was included in the sub-Committee's report to the Reconstruction Committee.

The use of labour exchanges did meet some opposition. Lord Derby, then Under-Secretary of State for War, attended the July 1916 meeting of the Demobilization Sub-Committee and made it clear that he had strong reservations. He was 'disturbed by the proposed use of Labour Exchanges in connection with demobilisation as he thought they would be unpopular with ex-soldiers, especially with the class of men who composed the new armies'. Instead, Lord Derby suggested a new organization made up of a central co-ordinating committee and a number of local committees which would be funded voluntarily. It was a point taken up by Brigadier General Auckland Geddes, a member of the Montagu sub-Committee:

> I think that it is necessary to realise that the Labour Exchanges are not popular, and that they are associated in the minds of the majority of people with the unemployable and the dregs of the labour market. It is very necessary to remember that the soldiers when they go back to civil life will still feel that they are part of the army, and I am inclined to believe that there will be much less friction if they see the hand of the army in the organisation through which they draw their unemployment insurance money.[20]

In the First (Interim) Report to the Reconstruction Committee of October 1916 Montagu argued that the unpopularity of the Labour Exchanges would:

> be removed if ex-soldiers of all classes can be induced to use Exchanges freely during the period of demobilisation ... the Exchanges must in any case deal with the unemployment insurance and ... they are bound for that reason alone to come into close and regular contact with most ex-soldiers. It is obviously a sound arrangement, and convenient to applicants themselves, that the same organisation should pay them employment benefit and assist them to find employment.

Referring to Lord Derby's suggestion of a new local committee structure, funded voluntarily, to deal with the employment of ex-soldiers, Montagu firmly dismissed the idea: 'There would be numerous practical difficulties arising from the fact that it would be the function of the one body to pay unemployment benefit to an ex-soldier out of work and refuse it if he declined suitable employment, and of another body to find him work of that character'. As far as Montagu was concerned: 'The final and perhaps most important consideration is that, in our view, the State cannot and should not abdicate the control of so large and important an operation, conducted at the cost of public funds, and transfer it to unpaid committees under no direct responsibility to Parliament and the nation'. The trade-union movement put forward its own view about Lord Derby's proposals:

> None of these proposals would be acceptable to Organised Labour because (a) it would never do to make the getting of situations a matter of charity or favouritism (b) such bodies could not be trusted to keep in view the paramount importance of maintaining the Standard Rates of wages and (c) it would be impracticable to duplicate the efforts of Employment Exchanges.[21]

The eventual recommendation of Montagu's sub-Committee to the main Reconstruction Committee was that 'the State should use the already existing machinery of the Employment Department of the Board of Trade and the Exchanges. The Board of Trade should … strengthen and extend the machinery of the Exchange administration'. Further, a Central Committee and local committees, made up of equal numbers of employer and worker representatives, should be appointed 'to assist the Employment Department of the Board of Trade' for each town or area where there is a Labour Exchange. Montagu thus established the labour exchange, despite Lord Derby's intervention, as the prime organization to deal with employment issues with the support of local committees whose function would be to 'undertake propaganda work by press appeals, circulars, personal canvassing, etc., with the object of inducing all employers to notify their demands for labour to the local Exchange …'.[22]

Llewellyn Smith and Brade, assuming that labour exchanges would be involved in the demobilization process, had proposed in 1915 a simple scheme that would help the exchanges in their task of finding work for ex-soldiers. The scheme was based on two forms:

> Every soldier to be required, one or two months before the date of disbandment … to fill up a form (Form A) as to his occupation and last employment before enlistment, whether his employer made any

> arrangements to keep a place open for him, and, if not, whether he would like his last employer to be asked to re-engage him if possible.

Copies of this form were to be distributed by Commanding Officers (COs) and it was compulsory for every NCO and private to complete them. Men who had not been in work before enlistment were to return their forms with a statement to that effect.

These completed forms would be sent to the central Labour Exchange Department who would then communicate by letter (Form B) with the employers asking whether they would be prepared to re-engage the soldier and any additional soldiers. The replies would enable the local labour exchanges to compile a register of all soldiers returning to the locality with details of work places available. The demobilized soldier would also be issued with an Identification Certificate. When he presented this certificate to his local labour exchange he would receive information about possible employment together with a statement on unemployment policy.

A further recommendation by Llewellyn Smith and Brade concerned those soldiers who would be demobilized and who would not be regarded as an employee – for example, those who were self-employed and owned their own business: 'The Civil Liberties Committee should be kept in existence for a period of at least two years after the war, with a view to considering on their merits applications for State assistance from men now serving in the army who were not and will not hereafter be employees'.[23]

Three other important matters were touched on during Montagu's sub-Committee meetings. One concerned the rate at which soldiers would be demobilized. A member of the sub-Committee, Sir Sydney Olivier of the Board of Agriculture and Fisheries, wrote to Montagu in September 1916:

> It was announced at the last meeting of the Cabinet that the demobilisation of our troops from France will take twelve months, and responsible persons have anticipated longer … Assuming twelve months to be necessary, the War Office is estimating that as regards France, it will only repatriate at the rate of 5,000 to 6,000 men a day.

Olivier considered, 'in the interests of our army', that these numbers were 'insignificant' and unacceptable. Olivier then argued that more French ports should be used for embarkation and 'our existing transport must be supplemented by Admiralty ships and German mercantile marine must be freely commandeered. In short, there is nothing whatsoever to prevent the daily embarkation of 20,000 men, which would complete demobilisation within four or five months'.[24] At the September meeting of the sub-Committee Brade accepted a figure of 20,000 men per day, but 'stated that he did not think it was possible that this figure could be exceeded'. A further proposal that the demobilization rate should be 40,000 men per day – 20,000 from France and 20,000 troops based in the UK – brought a strong objection from the Ministry of Labour. Even 20,000 per day would create 'a very much more difficult problem for the Employment Exchanges than the original figure of 5,000 per day … The proposal now made that the rate should be not 20,000 but 40,000 a day would, in the opinion of the Ministry, create such a serious situation that they cannot see their way to accepting it …'. This view was supported at the September meeting when two members of the Committee from the Ministry of Labour, Mr Butler and Mr Rey, pointed out that 'the prospect of having such a large number of men thrown on the labour market in such a short time must be viewed with serious alarm'.[25]

Montagu raised the second important issue during the August sub-Committee discussions: 'How will the order of demobilisation be settled …?' However, there was little discussion about this matter. Brade said that he would 'endeavour to obtain answers, but it would be difficult as everybody at the War Office was very busy and it was very difficult to get people who could give time and attention to prepare the answers'.[26]

The third important issue discussed during the sub-Committee meetings was clearly difficult to resolve. How large an army would be required after the war? W.H. Beveridge of the Board of Trade made an estimate that 500,000 men would be 'retained with the colours'.[27] The question was highly relevant since the number of soldiers that remained in the army after the war would affect the number to be demobilized, but in 1916 the war was far from over and it was impossible to predict with any accuracy either the size of the army at the end of the war or the requirement for a standing army when peace did eventually arrive. At the end of his report to the Reconstruction Committee Montagu could only raise the question and make a plea for information: 'In order for us to make any great progress with the task entrusted to us it is essential that we should obtain from the War Office a draft scheme of demobilisation embodying and based on the information now available concerning probable military requirements and facilities at the end of the war'. Montagu then requested specific information about 'the number of the Standing Army to be maintained for the first few years after the war, its composition, and the manner in which the requisite number of men is to be obtained on the conclusion of peace'.[28]

These three important questions were substantial and, before peace arrived, there was no doubt that they would require practical and well-thought-through answers. In October 1916, however, this was not possible and none of the three issues was addressed in Montagu's report to the

Reconstruction Committee. In any event, the involvement of the Asquith government with reconstruction and demobilisation was, because of imminent political events, soon to end.

Asquith's position as Prime Minister and leader of the Coalition had, towards the end of 1916, become precarious. In military terms 1915 had been a disappointing year with little to show for the series of British offensives – Neuve Chapelle, Aubers Ridge, Festubert, Loos – on the Western Front. In addition, GallipolI had been a failure. In 1916 the Battle of the Somme had not proved a strategic success and had resulted in massive losses. There was widespread belief that in order to win the war, Britain needed to conduct it in a more energetic and effective fashion. Lloyd George, who thought that Asquith 'was devoid of vigour and initiative', had shown, as Minister of Munitions, that he could produce results and carry the people with him.[29] He now wanted to lead the war effort and proposed to Asquith that there should be a War Council of three, outside the control of the Cabinet, and that he, Lloyd George, should chair it. Asquith insisted that he should chair any such Council and that it should report to the Cabinet. After much political manoeuvring Asquith resigned. Lloyd George gained the support of the majority of Members of Parliament and on 7 December 1916 he became the new Prime Minister.

Where did that leave Asquith's Reconstruction Committee and its twenty sub-Committees?[30] Vernon Nash, the secretary of the Committee, discussed the matter with Maurice Hankey of the Committee of Imperial Defence in late December. Hankey's opinion was that 'we should carry on'. Nash then asked Hankey to let him know 'through whom communications should be made to the Prime Minister as there are questions accumulating which call for decisions'[31] It was, however, several weeks before these 'questions' received any attention. There was clearly frustration among the various sub-Committees because of the delay in communication from the War Cabinet. Nash informed Hankey on 7 February 1917, two months after Lloyd George had become Prime Minister, that 'pending the decision of the Cabinet, the Chairman of the Army Demobilisation sub-Committee [Montagu] does not feel himself in a position to summon meetings of the sub-Committee, which are urgently required in order to complete the military side of demobilisation'.[32]

Lloyd George eventually decided that he did wish to continue with a Reconstruction Committee and, on 15 February 1917, he announced the names of the members.[33] The Prime Minister was to be the chairman with Edwin Montagu as vice-chairman and Vernon Nash as secretary. The first meeting of the new Committee, which took place on 16 March, was addressed by Lloyd George:

> Under the late Cabinet the Reconstruction Committee was a Committee of Ministers. Much was to be said for that arrangement, but the balance of advantages were against it. In particular, Ministers were too busy to give full attention. The present Government has therefore determined to set up a Committee of men and women of wide experience to survey the whole field of Government.[34]

Lloyd George then went on to describe the work to be carried out by the Committee: 'There are two main kinds of questions – first, those which would arise immediately at the end of the war and would require settlement without delay. Secondly, those which looked to laying the foundations of a new order'. By 'new order' Lloyd George referred to 'conditions before the war' which were 'often impossible and stupid'. The role of the Committee was to advise 'what steps could be taken to make a repetition impossible'.

Among the questions that would arise 'immediately after the end of the war' was:

> the demobilisation of the Army – the return of two or three millions of men to civil life. The problem would be urgent the actual moment the war came to an end ... what steps should be taken, whether by way of public maintenance, public works, unemployment insurance, or other means? He could not say when the war was coming to an end, but the Committee must proceed on the hypothesis that it might be soon.

Lloyd George ended his address: 'No such opportunity has ever been given to any nation before – not even by the French Revolution. The nation was in a molten condition.' He then added that, since 'he had so much to do', Montagu was to be vice-chairman and he urged members to 'keep in touch ... so that he might know how matters were progressing'.[35]

The organizational activity that followed Lloyd George's endorsement of the concept of reconstruction was frenzied. A list of sub-committees of the main Reconstruction Committee was published on 17 February 1917. They were to 'consider problems that would arise on the conclusion of peace'. In all there were twenty-three sub-committees ranging from Commercial and Industrial (Number I) to the Physiology (War Committee) of the Royal Society on the Food Supply of the United Kingdom (Number XXIII). Some of these sub-committees found it necessary to have their own sub-committees. The Engineering Trades (New Industries) Committee, for example, had sixteen branch committees which, between them, had 138 members. The Army Demobilization Committee, which continued to be chaired by Montagu, itself had sub-committees including one concerned with the 'Demobilisation and Resettlement of officers in civil life, and also of men belonging to classes to which in the main officers belong'. This sub-committee was chaired by Sir Reginald Brade.[36]

Lloyd George's statement that Asquith's now-defunct Reconstruction Committee had 'the balance of advantages against it' gave rise to a potentially awkward issue. At the second meeting of the new Reconstruction Committee on 22 March, Montagu stood in for Lloyd George as chairman. A question was raised about the status of the reports that had been issued by the old committees. Mr Leslie Scott MP pointed out that 'the Prime Minister had invited the new committee to consider *de nove* every report of every sub-committee' and that they should not 'tie hands as regards criticism'. As far as Montagu was concerned, such an approach would simply mean wasting time going over arguments that had already received careful attention. He no doubt had in mind the recommendations contained in the 1916 Interim Report of his Demobilization Committee which had been 'considered by the former Reconstruction Committee and adopted practically without alteration'.[37] Montagu's response to Leslie Scott was that: 'He did not support that the committee should re-investigate the problems investigated by sub-committees, but should use these reports in sending in any further reports to the Prime Minister' and that the new committee 'should not entertain the idea of knocking the sub-committees on the head'. Montagu closed down the discussion by stressing that the existing Demobilization Committee, with a few changes of membership, would be carrying on as before.[38]

And so it did. Between April and August 1917 it held five meetings and delivered a Second (Interim) Report in October. While the First (Interim) Report had considered the personal measures relating to the demobilized soldier – length of furlough, a travel warrant, a gratuity and free unemployment insurance – the meetings leading up to the Second (Interim) Report discussed the key issues of the sequence and rate of demobilization and the method of finding work for the returning soldier. A further issue, the proposed size of the post-war army, was raised, but as had happened during the 1916 discussions, no firm figure was forthcoming. When asked by the War Office to give some guidance 'as to the size and composition of the future standing army' the government responded that it was not in a position to give such guidance and that the question 'was to be deferred'.[39]

The Demobilization sub-Committee meetings of 1916 had been numbered One to Five and the sequence was carried on into 1917. At meeting number Six on 4 April Montagu reported that, since the acceptance by the Asquith government of the First (Interim) Report, 'both the War Office and the Ministry of Labour had made great progress with the technical side of demobilisation'.[40]

The War Office Demobilization Committee, chaired by Sir Reginald Brade, published their report in April and it set out the main principles that would govern the sequence in which soldiers would be returned home.

> The Committee have based their scheme on the idea that the selection of men for return and the rate of disbandment are to be governed by the requirements of the nation as a whole, from the point of view of the principal industries and the maintenance of services of public utility, and not by the wishes or even necessities of the individual. Nor have they built their plan on any consideration that classes or groups of soldiers have prior claims to release by reason of the length of their military service or the conditions on which they enlisted.

As an example of this approach the report continued: 'Agricultural labourers will come home first, if the Government so order, whether they are Regulars, Territorials or New Army men, or whether they were early or late voluntary recruits or conscripts.' The report went on: 'Nor have they thought it necessary for them to make any special provision for hard individual cases. The Committee feels that concessions in such cases should be discouraged as much as possible. Nothing but adherence to the broad general principles, justified by the national necessities, seems likely to allay private dissatisfactions.' Apart from certain 'cadres' designated by the War Office to maintain and guard equipment, buildings and stores 'the rest of the men will be considered as a mass of individuals. They will be dealt with by occupations and trades and will be sent back to civil life in trade groups in the order dictated by the Government according to trade and labour requirements at the time'. The idea that soldiers might be demobilized by army units was accepted for troops in distant theatres of war – Italy, Palestine, Mesopotamia, Salonika – for logistical reasons, but was dismissed for the large concentration of men serving in France and the UK, 'since the men would then be returned to civil life indiscriminately, without regard to the fundamental trades required first ...'.[41] The trade unions also gave their support to this approach: 'to supply the kinds of labour most urgently required for the revival of peace production, and prevent any congestion of unemployment'.[42] Such were the principles that determined future discussions on the sequence of demobilization and also the events that followed when hostilities came to an end.

The mechanics of demobilization proposed by the War Office Committee were reasonably straightforward.[43] Army Order 93 of March 1917 required every soldier to have his occupation and trade noted in his pay book. Officers responsible for releasing soldiers would be instructed by the War Office as to the priority of occupations required and the numbers required in each draft. The drafts would then be sent to Reception Camps, probably five in number, situated near railheads and adjacent to Continental ports. When leaving his unit the soldier would receive a Dispersal Certificate detailing his personal information, his Industrial Group number and the articles of equipment and clothing in his possession. Once across the Channel a soldier would travel to a dispersal station (also referred to as a 'concentration camp') which would be in his home area. Twenty-four such stations would cover the various areas of the UK and it was estimated that each station could process up to 1,000 men per day. After returning his rifle and equipment and being given an advance of pay for immediate needs, the soldier would then be allowed home to begin his one month of paid furlough. He would receive a Protection Certificate in exchange for his Dispersal Certificate which would entitle him to free travel to his home and enable him to claim his weekly pay while on furlough. He would travel home in his uniform which he would keep. He was to return his greatcoat or buy it for £1 and an allowance would be made to buy civilian clothes It was expected that a soldier would spend no longer than 24 hours in a dispersal station.

The War Office Report also identified four groups whose demobilization would be given priority. First, those men who intended to re-enlist. Sir Reginald Brade explained that this was important because, until the re-enlisted men became available 'it would be impossible to release territorials and other troops at present serving as garrisons in India and elsewhere'.[44] The second priority group would be those who were 'required for the actual process of demobilisation such as the necessary officials of the War Office and Ministry of Labour, the police and probably a certain number of the staffs of the Railway Companies'. These men were referred to as 'demobilizers' and 'arrangements will be made for those men to come home in advance of the general process of demobilisation'. The third group, 'pivotal men', were those required immediately for the regeneration of essential 'priority' industries and the fourth group would be those whose employment on leaving the army was guaranteed by a previous employer. These men became labelled 'slip men' since their release was triggered by a tear-off slip. The process of releasing slip men required the man to record on a Civil Employment Form, a variant of the original Llewllyn Smith-Brade Form A, that he would be re-employed by his previous employer. If this claim was confirmed by the local labour exchange a tear-off slip at the bottom of the Civil Employment Form would be sent for action to the man's CO. Self-employed men were to be dealt with as slip men. It was estimated that there would be a total of 150,000 demobilizers and slip men.[45] The priority sequence of demobilization, therefore, was:

men wishing to re-enlist; demobilizers; pivotal men; slip men; then men according to occupation. Should there be more slip men available than required for a particular draft, then priority would be decided by occupation. It was estimated that many soldiers, about 40 per cent 'of the men serving with the Colours' were not priority men and would not have jobs waiting for them.[46] In such cases, when, eventually, they were demobilized they would rely on their local labour exchange to find them work.[47] Within all the groups, married men would be given preferential treatment, not particularly for family reasons, but, as Sir Reginald Brade put it, 'to avoid continued payment of separation allowances as much as possible'.[48]

The five meetings of Montagu's Army Demobilization sub-Committee, held between April and August 1917, discussed the issues connected with Brade's War Office Report and also matters left over from the First (Interim) Report of October 1916. Clearly, a key area to clarify was the priority list of trades and occupations which was central to the War Office proposals. At the April 1917 meeting of the Army Demobilization Committee Montagu raised this topic stating that 'classification by trades was the first essential …' and suggested, 'that the Ministry of Labour should prepare a priority list of occupations in the order in which soldiers are to be discharged from the Army. It would be recognised that, except in broad outlines, this priority list must be provisional; it would require and should be capable of adjustment from time to time'. The Second (Interim) Report of the Army Demobilization sub-Committee to the Reconstruction Committee in October 1917 made some suggestions as to the main trades and occupations: 'The first class might for example consist of agriculture, shipbuilding, railways, and coal-mining; the second of employees of public and local authorities, seamen and fishermen, iron and steel manufactures, and so on'.[49] Mr Rey of the Ministry of Labour supported this proposal but added that 'he feared that every trade would claim priority and it would be extremely difficult to differentiate between different occupations'.[50] To some extent, Rey's 'fear' was well-founded. Even the tentative suggestions of the Demobilisation Committee resulted in a strong objection from the Building Materials and Building Trade Employers: 'It is desirable to urge upon the Ministry of Labour the extreme importance of the early demobilisation of workers in the building trades and allied trades.' The memorandum went on to stress that housing was an 'acute problem' and all other trades 'will depend upon an adequate supply of houses being proceeded with at the earliest possible moment … it is therefore urged that brick-workers, quarrymen, cement-workers and others engaged in the manufacture of building materials should be included in the first class to be demobilised'. The memorandum ended with a barbed comment: 'Attention must also be called to the fact that seven out of the eight Commissions on Industrial Unrest specifically referred to housing as a cause'.[51]

It was not until March 1918 that the Demobilization Priority Committee of the Ministry of Labour published the principles upon which a priority list of industries and occupations would be arrived at. The list would be based, first, on those industries necessary for 'the reconstruction of industry in general and restoration of normal conditions of life'. These would include shipping, shipbuilding, agriculture, transport and coal production. A second group of priority industries would be those 'in which special activity is required in order to make good loss or deficiencies which have accrued during the War'. Building and allied trades were placed in this group as being essential for a re-housing programme. And a third group would be 'the staple export industries on which our commercial position in the world mainly depends'.[52] Every soldier had in his pay book (AF B 103 if at home or, if abroad, AB 64) a list of forty-one industrial groups and he was classified in one of them according to his past experience. The equivalent document for officers was AB 439. The final industry priority list, to be decided just before demobilization took place, would be a ranking of those forty-one industries based on the above principles. (See Appendix II.)

The problem of the rate of demobilization, discussed in 1916, was revisited several times during the 1917 meetings. Everyone agreed that soldiers should return home as quickly as possible and that morale and discipline might well suffer if they were not. But what was a practicable plan? At the meeting of 4 April Sir Reginald Brade repeated his view that 'the utmost speed with which men could be passed through the Dispersal Stations would be at the rate of 40,000 a day: 20,000 from France and 20,000 from home forces'. Brade emphasized that the numbers to be demobilized from France and from the home forces should be equal otherwise 'discontent might be created amongst soldiers abroad if soldiers at home were to get the first pick of the jobs'. Mr Rey's response to the demobilization rate of 40,000 per day was much as it had been in 1916. He considered that such a rate of discharge 'would be a terrible thing from an industrial point of view. It would be impossible to absorb them at that rate'. Rey received support from the Minister of Labour, George Roberts, who wrote to Montagu on 21 May: 'The proposal now made that the rate should be not 20,000 but 40,000 a day would in the opinion of the Ministry create such a serious situation that they cannot see their way to accepting it …'. Roberts then suggested that 'to prevent widespread unemployment and the serious troubles which are certain to ensue from it' the one-month furlough period on full pay and allowances 'should be extended to every man for whom work cannot be found at the end of that period up to a total of six months'.[53] Brade's response was unsympathetic: 'I do not think that the War Office could entertain this suggestion ... The proposal would not prevent widespread unemployment, but only unpaid unemployment'. Brade added that the demobilization rate proposed was a maximum figure and not a daily average and that many men 'were required in France for handling stores, etc. and could only be demobilised many months after demobilisation had begun'.[54]

A recurring issue during the Army Demobilization sub-Committee discussions of 1917 was the level of unemployment insurance. Montagu raised the matter again at the April meeting: 'The Reconstruction Committee were particularly anxious that the rate should be increased because of the great rise in the cost of living. He understood that the Trade Unions were considering the question of raising their own unemployment rates and that the railway men proposed to make grants of 15*s*.' At the June meeting maximum figures of 20*s*. and 30*s*. per week were proposed and it was agreed that while 10*s*. would be a minimum amount, the Ministry of Labour, together with the Treasury, would have the power to increase the flat rate to a maximum of 30*s*. per week.[55] At the August meeting there were some second thoughts about the maximum figure. While Mr Leith Ross proposed 20*s*. as the maximum since 'this was almost as high as the full employment wage', Sir David Shackleton favoured 25*s*. because the unemployment benefit for munition workers 'would be likely to follow that fixed for soldiers'. The Committee agreed that the decision should be left to the ministries concerned taking account of the circumstances at the end of the war.[56] The final figure agreed at the time of demobilization was 24*s*. per week with supplementary allowances for dependent children.

Another important matter to receive attention in the Second (Interim) Report of the Committee on the Demobilization concerned 'officers and men of like standing'. As regards demobilization, officers would accompany drafts of soldiers as 'conducting officers' back to the UK and be themselves demobilized. The conditions of their demobilization were dealt with by two sub-committees of the Demobilization Committee, one chaired by Sir Clarendon Hyde and the other by Sir Reginald Brade.[57] There was a concern for 'a certain number of Officers and men whose reasonable claims for assistance would not be met by unemployment insurance'. These 'reasonable claims' would include rent, rates, insurance premiums and school fees. On this point Sir Clarendon Hyde's committee decided that: 'It would be inadvisable to have anything in the nature of two schemes of Unemployment Insurance, one at a much higher level than the other, based on the fact that the recipient came from a different class.'

The proposed solution to this problem was that officers should approach the Civil Liabilities Committee for specific assistance 'probably for a maximum of six months after their return'.

Sir Reginald Brade's committee, which had co-opted representatives of the Inns of Court and Artists Rifles – units that had been a source of officer recruitment – considered the arrangements that might be made to resettle officers into civilian life. Their main recommendation was the establishment of an Appointments Board, organized by the Ministry of Labour which would work alongside the University Appointments Board. University entry qualifications and the length of courses would be relaxed for officers returning from active service.

On 17 July 1917 Sir Edwin Montagu was appointed Secretary of State for India and he was therefore obliged to relinquish his roles with both the Reconstruction Committee and the Army Demobilization Committee. Brade took over the chairmanship of the Demobilization Committee. Shortly afterwards, Lloyd George decided that there should be a further reorganization of the Reconstruction Committee which was reconstituted as a ministry at Cabinet level. Lloyd George sent a message to all members of the Committee: 'with the appointment of a Minister responsible to the public and to Parliament for Reconstruction work, the relations of the Committee to their Vice-Chairman, the present Secretary of State for India, and to myself will come to an end'.[58] Dr Christopher Addison was transferred from the Ministry of Munitions to become the new Reconstruction Committee chairman and it was to Addison that Montagu, as out-going chairman, addressed the Second (Interim) Demobilization Report in October 1917. The War Cabinet approved 'the general principles laid down by the report' one month later.[59]

The new Ministry of Reconstruction was made up of a proliferation of committees. In September 1917 nine were listed of which the Army Demobilization was one and that itself was receiving input from committees of other government departments such as the War Office and the Ministry of Labour.[60] Such an inter-related web inevitably led to some confusion. An example concerned the definition of slip men. In May 1918 Addison wrote to Roberts of the Ministry of Labour drawing his attention:

> to the tendency which exists to express in varying terms the principles upon which the Government have decided that demobilisation is to be conducted. In view of the numerous committees which have been appointed … it is not unnatural that differences of wording should, from time to time, occur, but he feels sure that Mr Roberts will agree with him that it is desirable to present these principles so far as is possible, in the same terms.

Specifically concerning slip men, Addison pointed out that the principle embodied in the report was that the men to be given priority status were:

> those for whom immediate employment is known to be available, *and* who are required for restarting on a peace basis the more important industries of the country. This recommendation appears to have been incorrectly summarised at the conclusion of the Report by substituting the word 'or' for 'and' … This form of words is open to the interpretation that luxury and redundant industries will have as strong a claim for the early return of workmen as industries which are essential to the re-establishment of industrial activity … the intention is to bring home 'slip men' engaged in non-essential trades at a later stage than 'slip men' required for essential industries.[61]

It was an error that was later corrected.

In October 1918, when the end of the war was clearly in sight, General Smuts, a member of the War Cabinet, was appointed chairman of the Demobilization Committee. At this late stage, he found that certain important loose ends needed to be dealt with. While no specific pledge was made on behalf of employers that enlisted men could return to their former employment, the Committee agreed that they had 'a right to be employed by their old employer in preference to other people'.[62] Dominion troops would be repatriated in units as soon as the necessary shipping became available. The Foreign Office was urged to agree transportation facilities – rail and shipping – in France, Belgium and Italy, essential to the demobilization programme, 'without delay'.[63] Enemy aliens – the 30th and 31st (Infantry Works) Battalions of the Middlesex Regiment were made up of men who were either of enemy origin or who were of enemy origin but who had become naturalized British subjects – would not be demobilized on the same basis as British soldiers. It was considered that because of 'popular feeling … the longer they are kept in military service the better'.[64] The issue of unemployment insurance, referred to in November 1918 as 'Unemployment Donation', continued to be hotly debated. Sir Thomas Heath of the Treasury dissented from the Montagu Committee proposals since 'he was of the opinion that the scale of benefit … was too high, and he thought that the rates paid should be low enough to ensure that persons receiving the benefit would spare no effort to get employment'. Even as late as Armistice Day the final details of gratuity payments were still being discussed. In early December, following strong pressure from the Ministry of National Service and several medical bodies, the Demobilization Committee agreed the release of 1,400 RAMC doctors to help with the problems arising from the influenza epidemic then sweeping the country.[65]

By and large, however, the main arrangements for demobilization as set out in Montagu's First (1916) and Second (1917) 'Interim' Reports were maintained and followed when peace eventually arrived.

Having determined the principles of army demobilization and the details of its implementation, it was clear that an effective programme of publicity should take place. As Sir Reginald Brade had written in the Report of the War Office Demobilization Committee in April 1917: 'A great deal of the success of any scheme that is adopted will depend upon the manner in which it is announced and explained to the public and the Committee trust that when the time comes the Government will see that this is done'.[66] Addison, as Minister of Reconstruction, certainly made many speeches towards the end of 1918 outlining the work of his Ministry and these speeches were reproduced in a series of pamphlets under the general heading 'Reconstruction Problems'.[67] One of these pamphlets, Number 3, was devoted to 'The Demobilisation and Resettlement of the Army'. It was a curious document which started by referring to demobilization after the Old Testament campaigns of Moses and Joshua as well as to the dispersal of Wellington's troops after the Peninsular War. Nevertheless, it explained in thirty-three pages the principles behind the demobilization process and how individual soldiers would be treated. A Question and Answer section dealt with priority occupations, demobilizers, slip men, how a draft would be made up, Dispersal Stations, railway warrants to reach home, the length of furlough, what was to be done with the uniform, how to use the employment exchange, re-enlistment and so on. (See Appendix III.) A section 'Guide to Work and Benefits' covered in detail the amounts to be received in gratuity and unemployment pay. The information contained in the demobilization pamphlet came straight from the work of Llewellyn Smith, Brade, Montagu, Addison and hundreds of politicians and public servants. It was the result of countless hours of lobbying and committee work. The scene was set to start the demobilization of the British Army. Various trials of the dispersal system had taken place successfully – 500 men were processed at Purfleet on 7 February 1918 and a further trial took place at Wimbledon on 15/16 May – and the authorities were pleased with the outcome. As Addison wrote: 'In my opinion the Committee have produced a most useful scheme, clearly and carefully thought out and admirably explained, for dealing with this most difficult problem ...'.[68] At last, after four years of planning, and with soldiers impatient to return home, the smooth running and effectiveness of the demobilization system was to be tested.

Chapter 2

The Failure of the Demobilization Plans

The particular approach adopted by the British government to the demobilization of the British Army had evolved during the years of the war. It was firmly based on an assessment of the economic needs of the State and those needs determined the sequence in which the soldiers would return home. The decision to carry out demobilization in this way was to have profound consequences. How was this decision arrived at?

It was clear, as Sir Reginald Brade had pointed out in May 1916 during the first meeting of Montagu's Demobilization Committee, that it was 'in practice impossible to disband three to four million men all together, however desirable that might be from the point of view of the taxpayer'. At the same meeting, Sir Maurice Hankey had suggested that 'it seemed necessary to lay down certain principles or working hypotheses' which included the demobilization of men who had 'work waiting for them' and 'men from trades where there was insufficient labour'.[1] But nothing definite was decided about the sequence of demobilization and during the fourth meeting of the Demobilization Committee, in August 1916, Montagu felt it necessary to pose the question: 'How will the order of demobilisation be settled: (a) as regards troops at home when peace is declared; (b) as regards troops abroad; e.g. will it depend mainly on the geographical position of each unit when peace is declared whether it is demobilised early or late?' At that stage in the discussions Brade, representing the War Office, was only able to say that 'he would endeavour to obtain answers, but it would be difficult, as everyone in the War Office was very busy'.[2] In Montagu's First (Interim) Report of the Demobilization Committee (October 1916) both Llewellyn Smith and Brade referred to 'the order in which the various armies or their component parts can be returned to civilian life'.[3] The thinking here was that demobilization would take place in the sequence followed after previous wars – by army units such as battalions or divisions.

The whole question of the sequence of demobilization was placed in the hands of the War Office Demobilization Committee chaired by Sir Reginald Brade. The Report of this Committee, which was published in April 1917, stated the problem quite clearly: 'the choice appeared to be between, on the one hand, return by military formations in the order prescribed by military needs, and, on the other, return of individuals grouped according to civil occupations, the occupational groups being arranged in order, which would be determined by trade needs at the time of demobilisation'.[4] As a result of its deliberations the War Office Committee chose the second of these two options: 'The order in which various categories of men are selected for release from the Army must be settled for the most part in accordance with considerations other than military, in particular the economic needs of the country'. Demobilization by military formations and units was rejected because 'when complete with their transport and regimental equipment they could only be dealt with at a very limited rate; moreover, the men would then be returned to civil life indiscriminately, without regard to the fundamental trades required first'.[5] Both Montagu, in his Second (Interim) Report, and Addison, in a Memorandum to the War Cabinet dated 27 October 1917, supported the findings of the War Office Committee.[6]

There was some opposition to the proposed method of demobilization, but it was limited. During the meeting of Montagu's Committee in June 1917, Mr Bellamy tentatively 'raised the question of the early release of men who had joined the Army in the first stages of the war'. But this point was immediately squashed by Sir Reginald Brade who replied that 'the War Office would prefer that this should not be made a principle'.[7] Brade's response, and, indeed, the proposals of the War Office Committee regarding the sequence of demobilization are particularly interesting when compared with comments made during the meetings of Montagu's First Demobilization Committee in 1916. In May of that year Sir Clarendon Hyde asked 'whether individual men or a small number could be discharged apart from the rest of the battalion or other unit to which they belonged'. Brade replied that 'such a course would be very difficult. The War Office had always contemplated disbandment by complete units'. Colonel Strachey supported this view by adding that 'he did not think it would be possible to pick men out of a battalion'. At the June meeting General Auckland Geddes expressed the same opinion: 'he feared it was impossible to attempt to release individual men from a unit because they belonged to occupations in which there was a demand for labour'.[8]

However, between the Montagu Committee meetings of 1916 and the publication of the War Office Report in April 1917 Brade and his colleagues had undergone a significant change of view concerning the sequence of demobilization. There had clearly been some liaison between Brade and Montagu before the 1917 meetings of Montagu's Committee which began on 4 April. Montagu opened the meeting by 'proposing first of all to deal with the question as to how far it is possible and desirable to give priority of discharge to men of certain trades or professions' and the first part of that meeting was concerned with the 'early release' of such men. There was then some discussion about 'men for whom employers ask by name'; the 'priority of certain trades'; and the 'classification by trades' – all phrases that became familiar following the publication of the War Office Report some twelve days later. It is also significant that, while Montagu's Committee had not met since September 1916, all the members of the new Committee appeared, at their first meeting on 4 April 1917, to be well aware of the likely outcome of the discussions on demobilization priorities.[9] No evidence has been found to identify the source of the decision to use economic rather than military or personal factors to determine the method of demobilization. Did it arise from discussions between Montagu, Llewellyn Smith, Brade and Addison? The scheme was often referred to as 'the Derby Scheme', so was it a brainchild of Lord Derby, the then Secretary of State for War? Or was it an instruction from the Cabinet? However the proposal originated it received the full support of the Cabinet. A War Council note dated October 1917 read: 'the Council [were] instructed by the Cabinet to prepare detailed plans for demobilisation with the primary object of satisfying the industrial requirements of the nation at the time that the demobilisation takes place'.[10] Brade was a member of the War Council and all future discussions and decisions as to how the soldiers of the British Army would be discharged flowed from this instruction. The War Cabinet further confirmed its support of the principle that the order of demobilization 'should be governed by the needs of trade and industry' at its meeting on 15 November 1917.[11]

The origin of the decision to use economic factors as the basis for demobilization is further obscured because of evidence that the scheme actually implemented in December 1918 was being discussed outside the War Office and outside Montagu's Committee meetings even before Brade announced his proposals in April 1917. Some seven months earlier, in October 1916, the magazine the *Nineteenth Century and After* published an article by a Major General S.S. Long entitled 'Right and Wrong Methods of Demobilisation'.[12] This is a significant article in that it anticipates in some detail Brade's War Office proposal to give priority of release to skilled men for the purpose of the developing key industries and it also anticipates the concept of pivotal men, slip men, the classification of industries and the eventual discharge procedure. The *Nineteenth Century and After* was a widely read magazine and it can be assumed that Brade and his committee were fully aware of Long's article.

Long began his proposal by stating that demobilization must be in the hands of civilians: 'Demobilisation is, of course, to an extent a military problem, but it is one in which the social and industrial aspects and demands overwhelmingly predominate. When half our able-bodied manhood was needed for fighting, a soldier took command. When 5,000,000 men are to be returned to civilian life the soldier must give way to the statesman.' Long then developed his thoughts on the demobilization process: 'There is no secret that the War Office has already a scheme of demobilisation, and there need be no hesitation in saying what it is … The War Office proposes to demobilise either by whole formations – i.e. by brigades or divisions or else by units – in other words by regiment, battalion or battery'.

To Long this would be the wrong way to demobilize:

> If the War Office method of demobilisation were adopted and whole formations were sent home irrespective of the labour value of the individual unit, we should have few of the classes of workers whom we urgently need … In every regiment of the British Army there are numbers of men who should be restored to their work before their comrades. Industrial experts can tell us exactly who these men are and can describe the absolutely necessary functions which they and their class alone have been trained to discharge. Some of these classes of workers we shall need at the earliest possible moment in their full strength; trained workers on the land, for instance, cattle-rearers, skilled engineers … colliers, transport workers, and the like. Exactly what classes we shall want first, and how many in each class, only our experts will be able to determine … Certainly the War Office will not know, and probably will not care … As industry is re-established it will be able to absorb more and more workers, but even then care must be taken to return only men whose services are needed. [Having established] lists of essential or key industries … the employers will be able to say how many men they will be able to give work to and, roughly at what intervals they will be likely to be able to increase that number.

The method of releasing individual soldiers will depend on having 'lists of men in the first schedule of approved industries for whom immediate work is guaranteed'. These lists would be 'signed by the employer and also by a Trade Union official, counter-signed by the Ministry of Demobilisation and forwarded to the military authorities at the Front. Certain passes and pay warrants for each man on the list … will be ready and waiting for the day of discharge'.

Long also proposed that for men with jobs waiting for them 'the document of discharge might take the shape of a little book with perforated pages', copies of which would be given to various officials including the man's Commanding Officer. This little book would ensure that the man would not be impeded on his way home. In addition, he would receive a free railway pass, a warrant 'for a sovereign' to cover the cost of sustenance on his journey, further warrants for a sequence of sovereigns which would be paid at weekly intervals to cover the period before he enters work, and instructions for handing in his uniform and equipment. Long summed up his proposal for the 'Right Method' of demobilization: 'If demobilisation can be conducted on these lines in response to definitely ascertained industrial needs, the early stages, which, after all, will be the most critical, will be characterised by smooth working'.

In March 1917, again before the publication of Brade's War Office scheme, Lieutenant Colonel D. M'Ewen and Dr John Dallas, during their lecture to the Royal Philosophical Society of Glasgow, echoed much of Long's proposal: 'Essential and important industries must be recognised, and labour for these should first be drafted home … and men should only be withdrawn as it is known that there are openings and work ready for them'.[13] Whatever the sequence of thinking. it can be reasonably assumed that during the period between Montagu's First Demobilisation Report in October 1916 and Brade's War Office proposals in April 1917 the ground was well-prepared for the acceptance of a scheme firmly based on the needs of industry and commerce rather than the preferences of the military and the individual.

The author J.L. Hammond had reported 'on the mind of the soldier' following his lecture tour of army units in spring 1916. Several of his comments were relevant to the discussion on the sequence of demobilization: '[after the Armistice] there will be general reaction and depression and men left out will think the men already discharged are stealing a march on them'. Hammond's solution to this problem was to fill the time before discharge with 'definite instruction in agriculture and other industries … and teaching every man a trade'. This, thought Hammond, 'would prevent the waste of time and of six months of a man's life, and it would check the feeling that the men who stay longest in France are at a disadvantage from the point of view of employment openings'. Hammond went on: 'A soldier who served at the beginning of the War demanded that the Army should demobilise in the same order in which it had been recruited … The point was discussed by a group of soldiers … and several men mentioned that they had suffered by enlisting at the start and alleged that if the men who had taken their jobs and had been forced into the Army later were allowed to return before them it would be a crowning injustice'.[14] Hammond's Report was widely known in government circles, but it had no effect on the politicians and administrators who were deciding the order in which soldiers would return home.

On 18 October 1917, six months after Brade's War Office proposals, a note of caution was raised by Sir David Shackleton of the Ministry of Labour:

> It will be realised that any [job] preference given to individuals is likely to be strongly resented by the men who are not pivotal and who are consequently detained longer with the colours, unless that preference can be clearly shown to be based on purely national considerations, and that anything which may be regarded as personal favouritism will cause great dissatisfaction.

Again, this warning went unheeded.[15]

By far the greatest challenge to the proposed method of demobilization came from Field Marshal Sir Douglas Haig. Sir Reginald Brade, in his Demobilization Report of April 1917, had stated that the proposals of his Committee had been discussed with 'a similar Committee of the Staff in France' and that 'formal concurrence had been given by the Field-Marshal Commanding in Chief the British Armies in France'.[16] However, on 3 October 1917 Haig wrote to the Army Council saying that until recently he had given:

> the matter a comparatively perfunctory review, but now that details have been gone into and investigated it has been found that the procedure outlined in the War Office scheme of demobilisation (interim report) possesses certain serious difficulties, while the principle on which the scheme itself is based is open to grave objection if a well-regulated and disciplined departure from France is to be carried into effect.

Haig's first objection related to discipline:

> Immediately hostilities cease we must be prepared for a general relaxation of the bonds of discipline; men's minds, energies and thoughts will no longer be occupied by the task of defeating and destroying the enemy, but will trend naturally towards early return home … Hence as soon as demobilisation commences a feeling of jealousy will arise, men will keenly watch the dates of departures of others and will institute comparisons as to their respective claims, there will be generally an unsettled state … We have, therefore, to

> realise that the temper of the troops during this period will be a factor not to be lightly disregarded. In connection with the overseas Dominion troops it must not be overlooked that leave facilities to the Colonies have been practically nil, and that any delay in return – as compared with the despatch of troops to the United Kingdom – may cause a feeling of dissatisfaction and resentment ...

Haig's second objection concerned the relationships with France and Belgium. French and Belgian troops:

> will be returning to their families, to their homes and farms in which British troops have been and still are billeted ... the French and Belgian Governments will be directed to the early repatriation and reconstruction of the areas in occupation of the various armies ... Under these circumstances the presence of the British troops must be a hindrance and obstruction to the endeavours of both these nations ... Friction and jealousy, both national and individual, are likely to result if any delay in departure occurs ... under the most favourable circumstances, demobilisation is liable to lead to regrettable lapses from discipline.

Haig's third objection to the War Office scheme dealt with administration:

> The main obstacle lies in the proposal that all sorting, sifting and shuffling of personnel is to be undertaken in France. This proposal seems to me impracticable ... As many hundreds and thousands of men are concerned the cross country journeys involved preparatory to the actual homeward journey will be intricate and numerous. The railways could not guarantee to undertake these moves, while by road the length of time taken, coupled with the difficulties of supply and accommodation, render moves of any length by this manner practically impossible ... the facilities existing will not be adequate to deal with French needs as well as ours under the proposed demobilisation scheme.

Haig's letter then summarised his alternative method of demobilization:

> None of these difficulties would be apparent if demobilisation were to occur by complete units and formations; the latter would proceed to the various ports of departure direct from positions at conclusion of war, and embarkation would be supervised by the staffs and the officers known to the men ... If the departure of troops were based on length of service of a formation with an overseas force, the equity of this arrangement would appeal to all – civil and military alike ...[17]

Not all of Haig's arguments were watertight. For example, while a particular unit may have been in France since the beginning of the war, the turnover of troops because of casualties could well have meant that, by 1918, many soldiers in the unit had relatively short service. Every active service battalion of the Foot Guards had a casualty rate of around 100 per cent for 1914–18, as did, for example, the Northamptonshire Regiment and the Seaforth Highlanders. Also, it is likely that the logistics of rail and cross-Channel transportation would have been fraught whichever system of demobilization was applied. Nevertheless, the gist of Haig's letter, particularly as regards discipline and administration, made it clear that the army considered the War Office proposal to be ill-conceived.

Sir Reginald Brade was given the task of answering Haig's letter on behalf of the War Council. Brade's reply made it quite clear that the basics of the War Office proposal would not change:

> the Government has laid down that the requirements of the labour market to meet the reconstruction of the national industries must be made the priority consideration in any scheme for carrying out the demobilisation of His Majesty's Forces. Since the demobilisation at the end of the war will be a remobilisation of the industrial forces of the Empire rather than merely an Army demobilisation, it is considered that the requirements of reconstruction must have precedence.

Referring to Haig's concern about possible disciplinary problems, Brade commented:

> this has been fully recognised from the inception of the scheme put forward, and it is confidently anticipated that there will be considerably less difficulty in dealing with the men in France than if they were brought home and were then sorted on this side of the Channel, as there would be in this country so many more inducements and facilities for them to absent themselves.

A 'powerful aid' to the maintenance of discipline in France, wrote Brade, would be 'the knowledge that any active indiscipline [would] entail delay in the man's return to this country'. The reply to Haig also suggested that he and his Staff had 'to some extent misunderstood' the proposed system of demobilization and that the treatment of army units and the sorting out of individuals 'had not been adequately understood'. Finally, Brade relayed a message from the War Council: 'I am to add, further, that the War Cabinet, who were informed of your views, have now approved the principles of the original Scheme of Demobilisation'.[18] The War Cabinet had indeed been made aware of Haig's views at its meeting on 15 November 1917 through General Macready, the Adjutant General to the Forces, but no comments or discussion are recorded in the minutes.[19]

Thereafter, the mechanics of the Demobilization Scheme began to be implemented. At the War Cabinet meeting of 9 December 1918 a report by the War Office, under the heading of 'Progress', stated that 'arrangements for the collection of names of Pivotal Men' had been authorized in October; that the Prime Minister had endorsed the release of 150,000 miners; that the 'demobilisation of Demobilisers and Pivotal Men had been sanctioned on 22 November'; and that 'Six Dispersal Stations (capacity 12,000 per diem) were ordered to be opened for work'. It was further agreed by the Cabinet that men who had a job offer from their pre-war employer could be demobilized. This was a variant of the slip-man process and those involved became known as 'contract men' – a reference to the undertakings made by many employers at the beginning of the war.[20]

However, it was not long before the demobilization plan ran into trouble. By the end of 1918, some 7 weeks after the Armistice, only 261,000 men – around 7 per cent of the total – had returned home.[21] The press, especially those newspapers inclined to support the interests of the rank and file – the *Daily Mail*, the *Daily Express* and the *Daily Herald* – began a campaign criticizing the delays in demobilization. The *Daily Mail* of 29 November 1918 complained that: 'Demobilisation is proceeding with a leisured step. It ought to get into a quick march – not in dribbles but in a growing volume that will be evident to the man most concerned, the working man in the Army'. This was followed on 5 December by the claim that 'the demobilisation procedure was a maze of red-tape and official forms'.[22] And on 11 December: 'There is a stoppage in the pipes somewhere – the Machine must be speeded up'.

The *Daily Express* was equally critical. On 3 December 1918 it protested: 'Here sits a great army anxious to come back to work, waiting for the official to put his name to paper'. And on the following day: 'Men are urgently required out of the Army, just as urgently as they were required in it four years ago'. On 6 December it declared that: 'The whole of the demobilisation machinery is sticking, not from lack of goodwill, but from lack of organisation'. Throughout December the *Daily Express* attacked the government: 'will nothing bring home to the Government the seriousness of the immediate need for demobilisation ... The Daily Express does not believe that the Government realises the depth of hostile feeling that has been raised among all classes and particularly among fighting men, by all this deplorable delay' (28 December). On 30 December it asked: 'What is wrong with demobilisation? It may be sheer indifference on the part of those in power, or it may be the complicated red-tape bungle, or it may be a refusal by the military to release soldiers'. The *Daily Herald* asked on 7 December: 'Why in the world the delay? … Why not let them go home at once?'

Other newspapers, those inclined to support the government, were more tolerant of the delays in demobilization. On 9 December the *Morning Post* stated that: 'for many months as yet, at best, the bulk of our Armies abroad will have to remain on active service'. *The Times*, on 12 December, pointed out that general demobilization 'must wait until the political and military situation is sufficiently cleared up'. And this point was repeated in the *Daily Chronicle* of 1 January 1919: 'the slowness of demobilisation was inevitable until the government had formulated a clear plan for the future of British military policy'.

There was considerable substance in the various critical points made in the press and these points were reflected in the often terse exchanges between the various government offices and the military authorities. A War Office note dated 28 December complained that: 'Great difficulty has been met with in obtaining from France the names of those really required back … it is hoped that the names will now be forthcoming at once – officers to the War Office and other ranks to their Records Office'. The same note, under the heading 'Numbers Demobilised', stated that:

> Generally speaking, this has not been satisfactory owing to the fact that numbers allocated to Expeditionary Forces and Commands for dispersal daily have not been filled. It is most necessary that the daily allotments should be filled in order that the best use may be made of the limited facilities for transportation; and I would ask you to give special attention to this … It has been brought to notice by an Inspector of Infantry that many units are not organised for demobilisation, and that in consequence officers and soldiers who are eligible for release are not being sent to Dispersal Stations in accordance with the instructions issued[23]

On 19 December 1918 Sir Eric Geddes was appointed by Lloyd George to co-ordinate the work of the fourteen government departments involved in the demobilization process. At the turn of the year Geddes and the Minister of War, Lord Milner, clashed over the low rate of release. On 31 December Geddes wrote to Milner:

> I do not know whether you are seeing the figures of the men released from the Army regularly … I will be very glad to go into the figures with you any time you wish, but in the 48 hours ending at noon on 29th, only 4,729 Officers and men came out of the Army and of

> these roughly half were coal miners ... The present rate of discharge cannot, I am sure you will agree, be considered satisfactory, and it looks as if something pretty drastic will have to be done.

Geddes added a handwritten note: 'I am not blaming anyone or suggesting any fault. All I wish to suggest is that we must get more men out. How? is the question.'[24] The following day Geddes again wrote to Milner: 'In continuance of my note of yesterday, I understand that the Transportation capacity for men from France, exclusive of leave men, is 5700 per day, so that we are really utilising only about half the capacity'. Again there was a handwritten addition: 'Since writing I have got the figures for 24 hours 29/30 Dec – only 1542 men altogether ... from France'. Milner reacted to these comments: 'This correspondence is perfectly hopeless. From whom do you get your figures? They are totally different from those given to me.'

Other correspondence between Geddes and Milner indicates even more statistical confusion. Geddes admitted some errors in his figures, but added that he was still left 'in doubt on certain points'. He then requested more information about the number of pivotal men applied for, processed and released making the point that:

> The figures ... disclose a very small number of releases of Pivotal men, who, as you know, are being clamoured for by the business men of this country for the purposes of restarting their industries and affording employment to others. I am informed, however, that these figures do not disclose the whole position, and as it is impossible for me, in these circumstances, to form any idea of the real situation, I should like to be furnished with a statement which will disclose it.

Geddes asked for the same information relating to contract men. As regards coal miners, the Cabinet had authorized the release of 150,000 and Geddes pointed out to Milner that: 'Up till now only 61,000 miners ... have been released. The number in the Army must be very much greater than this figure; but I have no exact information, nor any estimate which is reliable. Accordingly I would like to know how many miners are still in the Army waiting release'.

On 7 January Geddes received the information he had asked for together with figures relating to demobilizers. It did not make satisfactory reading: 54,436 applications had been made for pivotal men and only 1,531 had been released by 4 January and that figure was 'not regarded as accurate'; there had been 31,971 applications for demobilizers and by 6 January 3,202 had been released; there was no information concerning contract men; the number of coal miners demobilized was 83,898 by 4 January and it was estimated that 'there are roughly 70,000 still to come'.[25] On 9 January Geddes acknowledged the information provided by Milner, commented on it unfavourably, and concluded his reply: 'even this preliminary consideration of the not very complete figures which we have got fully confirms what we agreed in my Office the other evening, namely, that the Army is not disgorging men at a rate which is reasonable to expect it to do'. Geddes added a handwritten note: 'I am sorry my job makes me such a bother. I like it less than you can imagine'. It was a human touch between two colleagues under great stress and it was also an indication of the general disarray surrounding the whole demobilization process. There was even a clerical error in communicating the total number of troops in the army. On 20 January the Adjutant General wrote to Winston Churchill, the then Secretary of State for War: 'As I have already told you the figures given in Sir Eric Geddes' paper are incorrect. The numbers of British troops i.e. the number of men to be demobilised is 3,350,000 not 6 million, and the total number of officers to be demobilised or to be kept being regulars only 170,000 instead of 550,000'. It was a symptom of over-work and confusion.[26]

There was also an issue concerning the demobilization rate of officers as compared with that of other ranks. It was intended that these two groups should be demobilized on a pro rata basis, but on 18 January 1919 a memo from the War Office to Sir Auckland Geddes, then the Minister of Reconstruction, read: '6,200 officers have been demobilised out of 558,000. This means that whereas 1 man in every 13 or 14 is being demobilised, only 1 officer in 95 has been released ... Obviously your system absolutely choked up and not working ... You cannot possibly face figures like this'.[27]

There was pressure on the government from all sides to increase the rate of demobilization. On 5 January Lloyd George received a letter from C.A. Henderson, the Secretary of the National Union of Railwaymen. The letter quoted a resolution 'which was unanimously agreed upon at a well-attended meeting ... and we trust that an effective action will be taken to give effect to the men's decision thereon'. The resolution read:

> That this meeting of the Railwaymen in considering the relief of Railwaymen from H M Forces, are of the decided opinion, that every effort should be made to release Railwaymen at once, as after working four years of lengthy hours, which we have done, intend at an early date to take decided action, to work no further overtime, and that the Secretary be desired to call a Mass Meeting on Jan. the 12/19 at 6 pm to see how and what effect we can give to this decision.

Henderson added: 'I would deem it an extreme favour if you could let me have a reply at an early date, and would you mind me saying not a stereotyped reply, please, as the men are in no humour to look kindly on this situation now'.

On 7 January Geddes received a letter with much the same content from Charles E. Musgrave of the London Chamber of Commerce:

> As one of the bodies authorised by the Ministry of Labour to make recommendations for the immediate release of 'pivotal' men, the London Chamber of Commerce has already made recommendations to the Demobilisation and Re-Settlement Committee, numbering nearly one thousand (dating from December 10), and while we are learning of the release in a few isolated cases, we are receiving each day verbal and written communications from firms, whose names were on our lists, to the effect that the men concerned have received no intimation concerning their release.

The letter went on: 'In certain circumstances the position has become more difficult as the result of the release of certain "slip" men, who have been demobilised while on leave from overseas, and many firms having undertaken to receive these men back, are without their "pivotal" men to manage them or organise their work'. The letter ended with an acknowledgement of 'the complexity of the whole problem and the difficulties which confront various departments' and with a plea for the urgent release of pivotal men.[28]

The demobilization plans, so carefully prepared over so long a period, were unravelling. Soldiers were not being released at anything like the rate anticipated (up to 40,000 per day); relationships between the State departments concerned and between them and the army were deteriorating – each was blaming the other; frustration was mounting in both commerce and industry as the promised men failed to appear; and the government was being attacked in the press for the generally perceived lethargic progress. How did this come about?

A document dated 14 January gave the army's view of the matter. It was headed 'Demobilisation' and a pencilled note addressed to the Secretary of State for War, Churchill, and initialled by the CIGS, Sir Henry Wilson, read: 'This paper was drawn up by GHQ France and was given to me on the boat coming over this morning'. The document made it clear that the central problem for the army was that, although an armistice was in force, the war was not over. If the peace negotiations failed, hostilities could be resumed and the German Army was still essentially intact. Moreover, apart from having to organize an army of occupation in Germany, Britain had military obligations around the world. The extent of its involvement in Russia was still uncertain. It also had to maintain in France large numbers of men to control stores and equipment. And yet, it was being pressed daily from London to release soldiers and from the soldiers themselves who were anxious to get home. As the opening paragraph of the document stated:

> Although general demobilisation has in theory not yet been ordered, it has, in fact, not only begun, but is being allowed to 'take charge'. This false start is the basis for all our difficulties. We are not ready for general demobilisation yet, either from the point of view of the military situation, or from that of our readiness to begin the process.

The document went on to list the reasons why the army was unprepared for demobilization. The Army Demobilization Regulations, i.e. the details of the internal army procedures, 'had not been issued. Indeed they had not been finished'. Particularly troublesome were the 'improvisations that have been resorted to', which included the 'contract' scheme, the accelerated release of miners, the demobilization of men on leave, and men over 41. This meant that 'much of the voluminous Regulations is already out of date, or inapplicable'. Moreover, the transportation facilities necessary for the sorting out of the drafts in France were not available. Referring to Haig's memorandum of October 1917, 'this contingency was foreseen and pointed out by GHQ'. In addition, the paperwork for demobilizers and pivotal men was not available. No guidance had been given as regards the size and disposition of the post-war army and, finally, the document complained that demobilization had become 'an Election cry' and that the press had 'run wild on the subject'.

The problems facing the army were summed up as: 'The meticulous complexity of the process of demobilisation as laid down, the volume of clerical work involved by it, the mass of instructions to be studied and followed, and the number of exceptions, and alternatives, already made'. And even if the laid down process of demobilization could be followed, the army would be left with 'a medley of all Arms, and not a properly balanced force' as required by an army of occupation – it would cease 'to have any fighting value …'.[29]

The points made in the army document were valid. The central proposal of Brade's War Office scheme was that soldiers should be demobilized only as required by key industries and in a strict order of demobilizers, pivotal men and slip men. According to Sir Reginald Brade, 'nothing but adherence' to the principles of this approach was 'likely to allay private dissatisfaction'.[30] But this advice had been disregarded by the government in its anxiety to speed up the process, hence the reference in the army document to 'improvisations' – the insertion into the demobilization priority list of miners, contract men, men over 41 and men on leave. The inclusion of contract men in particular, even though sanctioned by the Cabinet 'as a temporary measure', had the effect of favouring both those on leave and those on home service – a measure certain to antagonize the majority of soldiers.[31]

Nor did it help that the system was open to abuse. Private Frank Richards, of the Royal Welsh Fusiliers and an ex-miner, noted in his memoirs:

> Miners were sent home first, so I was lucky ... One man admitted to me before he left the Battalion that he had never been on top of a coal pit in his life. I gave him a few particulars and he passed the mining officers' [questions] all right. No doubt he had saved himself another six or twelve months' soldiering. I expect many more did the same'.[32]

Private Fred Lloyd, serving with the Veterinary Corps, made the point: 'I got home quicker than most because I had a job to go to. People waited a long time to get home and they were telling lies about who they were going to work for, when they had nobody'.[33]

The documentation and procedures in the army had become chaotic. As Lord Cavan, the Commander of British Forces in Italy, wrote to the CIGS, Sir Henry Wilson, on 14 December 1918: 'Demobilisation people are not quite fair to us. They wire for our A7.Z8 [release documents] Urgent – on which all depends – but they have never sent us any but a couple of specimen copies! Consequence is that at this moment only six men have left Italy!'[34]

By the beginning of 1919 whatever chance the proposed War Office demobilization scheme had of success had disappeared. It was not only that the process was slow and cumbersome, it was, in the minds of the generality of soldiers, simply unfair. How could men with relatively short service, many of whom had not left the shores of Britain, be given priority over men with home responsibilities and who had seen years of active service abroad? As Captain Bundy wrote when in Salonika: 'I am longing to get home. It seems so hard that I, a married man with children, should be retained while younger men without responsibilities have been demobilised'.[35] In the correspondence section of the *Manchester Guardian* of 13 January a writer, 'Perplexed' from Eccles, made the point that 'The men at the dispersal camps are objecting to having to demobilise men younger than themselves and in non-combatant groups. Their objection is shared by the parents of those boys who went out in 1915 and 1916, and who appear likely to stay out for a long time yet'. In the same correspondence column the suffragette Sylvia Pankhurst, of the Workers'

Socialist Federation, summarized the dissatisfaction of many soldiers: 'These [demobilization] schemes appeared, even from the Government's statements, to be designed mainly in the interests of the employers, without regard of the needs and desires of the men and their families … '.

The frustration of the soldiers was further increased as a result of Lloyd George's decision to call a General Election immediately following the Armistice. The process of electioneering lasted through December with a leisurely fourteen-day gap between polling day and the declaration of the results. The politicians were more focused on winning parliamentary seats than about the concerns of the soldier whose main preoccupation was to return home. With all the delays in demobilization Lloyd George's election pledge to release soldiers as quickly as possible was perceived as a cruel irony. On 7 January 1919 Sir Henry Wilson wrote to Lord Derby: 'The heart of our present troubles … lies in the reckless speeches and promises made during the recent elections and in constant civilian and therefore ignorant and dangerous interference in our demobilisation scheme … Exactly where we are drifting to – for we are drifting – I don't know'.[36] Sir Thomas Munro, of the Ministry of Labour, sought to explain the difficulties caused by the General Election 'which took away prominent men for practically six weeks', adding that 'the Ministers of Labour, Munitions and Pensions were all new to their posts'.[37] As Sir Henry Wilson wrote to Sir Douglas Haig: 'With all these games of musical chairs going on you can imagine that there is not much real business being done'.[38] The government pamphlets on *The Aims of Reconstruction* and *The Demobilisation and Resettlement of the Army* were published in December 1918, but, as a consequence of the election activities, insufficient time was spent on the necessary careful and detailed explanation of the thinking behind them. This important opportunity to win the minds of the soldiers and convince the military of the anticipated economic and social advantages of the proposed scheme was lost.

Demobilization was by no means the only problem facing the government in January 1919. Industrial disputes, both official and unofficial, were widespread and were aimed mainly at improving pay and working conditions and protecting jobs. A summary of disputes prepared by the Ministry of Labour for the Cabinet covering the week ending 29 January showed an alarming situation. In Scotland demands for a 40-hour week 'in all trades without any reduction in wages' resulted in stoppages involving 'many thousands of workpeople … principally shipyard workers and engineers on the Clyde, the Firth of Forth and in Edinburgh'. In Belfast a strike of shipyard workers and engineers for a 44-hour week spread to municipal employees working in the gas, electricity and the tramways sectors. Shipyard workers and engineers in the North East and Humberside had been on strike for most of the month. Between 12,000 and 15,000 ship repairers on the Thames were in dispute over a claim for a 15*s.* a week increase in pay. Similar disputes among ship repairers were taking place in Bristol, Barrow and Southampton. A claim to extend the length of mealtimes affected the whole of the Yorkshire coalfields. Spasmodic outbreaks of industrial unrest involving thousands of workers occurred in the Fifeshire, West Lothian and South Wales coalfields aimed at reducing the working week. Skilled engineers at the firm of J. Sagger in Halifax walked out because the company refused to dismiss the women who were employed as turners.[39]

Several strikes involved the employment of demobilized soldiers. In Mansfield there was:

> a huge concentration of miners … following the laying-off of 25 miners at Mansfield Colliery earlier in the week to make way for returned soldiers. Each day saw fresh collieries strike in sympathy … At a consequent huge demonstration in Chesterfield of local miners estimated at 600–700 men a march began to Sutton in Ashfield and Mansfield … It was eventually agreed that the miners would return to work with conditions on both sides.[40]

As disturbing to the government as industrial disputes were the race riots that took place in nine seaports beginning in January 1919.[41] The cause of these riots was mainly a fear that job opportunities were being lost to foreign workers especially at a time when soldiers and merchant seamen were returning home. This fear was fuelled by a shortage of housing and poor living conditions. The riots took place in Glasgow, South Shields, Salford, Hull, London, Liverpool, Newport, Cardiff and Barry between January and June 1919. Thousands of white men in these ports targeted ethnic groups including Africans, Caribbeans, 'Arabs', South Asians and Chinese. The events in Glasgow in January were typical. On 23 January the British Seafarers Union organized a meeting protesting against the use of cheap overseas labour in the port. The branch secretary, Emmanuel Shinwell, urged the government to tackle unemployment in the area and particularly spoke against the use of Chinese labour. Shortly afterwards a riot began in James Watt Street – the place where both white and foreign sailors gathered for the opportunity to be signed on to vessels. Insults were exchanged, the windows of the shipping office were smashed and what amounted to a pitched battle began. Some thirty black sailors were attacked by a crowd of hundreds of white sailors and local people. One group of black sailors fled to the nearby Glasgow Sailors' Home for safety.

Windows were broken and only after the arrival of fifty police officers was the home cleared. Another group of black sailors ran from the crowd and barricaded themselves into their boarding houses in the Broomieland area. Shots were fired into the crowd and two white men, Duncan Cowan and Michael Carlin, were seriously injured. One black sailor, Tom Jackson, was stabbed. Eventually the police arrived and took a number of black sailors, all from Sierra Leone, into 'protective custody'. None of the white rioters was arrested and at the court hearing a number of black sailors, including Tom Jackson who had a 'gaping wound', were charged with shooting offences.

The riots in the nine ports, with those in Liverpool being the most ferocious, were generally white inspired, often involved soldiers and were against what was described as 'trouble-making' black and Asian sailors. The local feelings about these alarming events were summed up in the *Liverpool Courier* of 11 June: 'There is an unemployment grievance – the fact that a large number of demobilised soldiers are unable to find work while West Indian Negroes brought over to supply a labour shortage during the war are able to swank about in smart clothes on the proceeds of their industry'.

Unemployment in the weeks immediately following the Armistice was indeed rising, particularly in areas around sea ports. The Cabinet was informed on 14 January of the latest overall figures: 6 December – 2.5 per cent; 20 December – 4.5 per cent; and 3 January – 6.7 per cent.[42] The War Office Weekly Appreciation to the Cabinet of 21 January confirmed that unemployment was continuing to rise and that the Out of Work Donation Policies numbered 449,252 on 10 January which was 70,000 more than the previous week.[43] The government saw the race riots, along with the strikes in industry and mining, as signs of potentially serious civil unrest, possibly led by communists, that might spread out of control. Lloyd George, using his customary dramatic language, expressed his personal concern about the domestic situation: 'Here we had a great inflammable industrial population'.[44] While much reliance was placed on the police to maintain order, the government could hardly forget that in August 1918 around 12,000 members of the Metropolitan Police had themselves taken strike action for improved pay and union recognition.

The insidious threat of Bolshevism seemed an increasing danger that might percolate into both civilian and military life. In mid-October 1918 the head office of the British Socialist Party was raided and police seized thousands of copies of Lenin's 'Lessons of the Revolution'. In the same month Sylvia Pankhurst, who edited the *Socialist Workers Dreadnought*, was prosecuted for sedition. Sir Henry Wilson wrote on 8 November 1918:

'Our real danger now is not the Boche, but Bolshevism'.[45] Even before the Armistice was signed Churchill was considering the possibility of rebuilding the German Army as a buffer against the spread of Bolshevism.[46] With this background of social, political and economic unrest it was understandable that the British government desperately wanted to avoid dissent, disturbance and serious disorder in the army. However, even before the end of 1918, that grim prospect became a reality. At the centre of the unrest was the now thoroughly discredited demobilization policy.

Chapter 3

Disobedience, Unrest and Mutiny

It was not unusual, during the First World War, for the British Army to have its authority challenged. Senior officers were obliged to deal with breaches of discipline ranging from mild disobedience to outright mutiny. At an individual level, over 300 soldiers were executed during the war for disobeying orders – mainly connected with desertion at the front.[1] There were other, lesser, penalties for recalcitrant individuals – loss of pay, confined to barracks and, for more serious misdemeanours, there was Field Punishment No. 1 and Field Punishment No. 2. Field Punishment No. 1 called for the soldier to be tied to an upright post or a gun wheel for up to 2 hours per day, a limit of three days out of four, and for no more than twenty-one days in a sentence. Sometimes the arms of the individual were outstretched in the 'crucifixion' position. He would forfeit his pay and could be made to carry out hard labour. During the war there were over 60,000 Field Punishment No. 1 sentences and it has been estimated that such a sentence was received by 1 out of every 50 soldiers serving in France.[2] Field Punishment No. 2 involved the use of handcuffs and fetters but not the attachment to a fixed object.

Evidence suggests that penalties for less serious breaches of discipline were administered by COs and company commanders in a reasonably impartial and consistent way, though practice varied from one battalion to another and from one location to another. The 14th Royal Irish Rifles, for example, had a relatively small number of courts martial during their period of training in Ireland simply because the battalion adjutant refused to refer absence without leave cases to courts martial.[3] Battalions serving in Britain had higher crime rates than those at the front probably because being nearer home resulted in increased absence and desertion.[4] The British Army in Italy had no capital convictions and this has been attributed to a more lenient approach to discipline because of poor local conditions and the incidence of illness.[5]

It was not unusual for groups of soldiers to take matters into their own hands. During the first winter of the war there were several outbreaks of indiscipline. At the Halton Camp in Buckinghamshire over fifty members of the 21st Division deserted complaining of poor food and unacceptable living arrangements. A group of Canadian soldiers based on Salisbury Plain reacted to the harsh winter conditions and poor accommodation by creating disturbances both in the camp and in the city of Salisbury.

In May 1915 a battalion of young miners in the Welsh Regiment reacted against what they considered to be unreasonably callous behaviour by their training instructors drawn from the Metropolitan Police and from the Brigade of Guards. The soldiers refused to attend parades for four days and demanded that the instructors should be replaced. New instructors were brought in and normal training was resumed.

A particularly serious outbreak of disruptive behaviour took place in Étaples, the location of the despised parade ground known as the Bull Ring. On 9 September 1917 an altercation between a group of New Zealand troops and the military police developed into a full-scale mutiny involving thousands of soldiers. One man, who was not directly involved in the proceedings, was accidentally shot by a military policeman and later died. Tempers became even more inflamed when a corporal in a Northumberland regiment made threats to kill an officer who was attempting to control the demonstrators. The corporal was later court-martialled and sentenced to death. The base commander called in reinforcements and eventually, after six days of disturbances, Étaples returned to a reasonable state of military control.

The Commander in Chief of the British Expeditionary Force, Sir Douglas Haig, was inclined to lay the blame for the disturbances at Étaples on trouble-makers among the conscripted soldiers. Haig was of the opinion that conscripted soldiers, forced into the army because of the 1916 Military Service Act, lacked both loyalty and a real wish to serve their country. Haig made clear his views in a letter to Lord Derby dated 3 October 1917: 'Men of this stamp are not satisfied with remaining quiet, they come from a class which like to air real or fancied grievances, and their teaching in this respect is a regrettable antidote to the spirit of devotion and duty of earlier troops.'[6] This analysis by Haig, however, hardly fitted the situation at Étaples. Australian troops had played a significant part in the disturbances and they were all volunteer soldiers. Moreover, the corporal who was court-martialled and shot as a result of his activities on 9 September was a regular soldier who had served two years in France.

The disturbances and rioting that took place in the British Army at Étaples in 1917 were regarded as serious by the military authorities. An investigation into the morale of the BEF was ordered and the letters of soldiers writing home were examined by the Military Censor. The Censor's report concluded that the morale of the army was sound and that the soldiers were convinced that they could defeat the enemy. The Censor concluded that although 'war- weariness was evident ... there is a strong current of feeling that only one kind of peace was possible, and that the time has not yet come'.[7]

A second example of serious disruption occurred on Sunday, 21 July 1918 at Beaumarais near Calais. The occasion was a Belgian national holiday which was being celebrated in various parts of northern France. British troops in the area decided to take part in the holiday festivities and, contrary to orders, entered Calais. During the afternoon trouble broke out and a demonstration was organized against the military police. More demonstrations, involving hundreds of soldiers, took place during the Monday and Tuesday and it was only when the 1st Battalion East Lancashire Regiment was called in that order was restored. Minor disturbances recurred at Étaples, in August 1918, and, again at Beaumarais, in September 1918, but in both cases a show of force prevented serious disruption.

The disturbances of 1917 and 1918 had no common underlying cause. They were the result of specific local situations. At Étaples in September 1917 the rioting arose because of a general hatred of the unnecessarily harsh discipline and insensitive conditions of the Bull Ring together with a loathing of the instructors and the military police whose aim was to control the camp by a regime of repression and fear. Soldiers who had already served at the front resented having to follow the same heavy training schedule that was applied to new recruits. It did not help that since the camp was essentially a transit location, with both officers and men moving in and out as individuals or in small groups, the normal regimental disciplinary ties between officers and men were practically non-existent. At Calais in July 1918 the frustration brought about by irksome restrictions was again vented mainly on the military police, the obvious representatives of military authority.

The 1917/18 disturbances at Étaples and Calais were resolved partly by a show of force and partly by judicious concessions. At Étaples, the appearance of a detachment of the Honourable Artillery Company served to calm the situation. Training in the Bull Ring was virtually abandoned within two weeks of the September rioting and the base commander and his adjutant were replaced. At Calais, the arrival of fresh troops sent to control the situation was also a critical factor in restoring discipline. Speeches by the base commander advising the troops to present their grievances in an orderly manner did much to restore normality in the camp.

The troops dispatched to Étaples and Calais to restore order were not required to fire on the rioters, mainly British and Dominion troops, though they were prepared to do so. This was in stark contrast to the treatment of several Egyptian Labour companies stationed at Boulogne. In September 1917, a few days before the riots in Étaples, these labourers, dispirited by the cold weather and frightened by a recent German air attack, refused to work and broke out of camp. The guard was called out and, before order was restored, a total of twenty-seven labourers had been killed and thirty-nine wounded. In October and December 1917 groups of Chinese labourers went on strike. They returned to work, but only after several of their number had been shot. The authorities had clearly calculated that while concessions and official courts martial were appropriate for British and Dominion troops, more direct action could be taken against the Egyptians and the Chinese. In December 1918 the same approach was taken by the military authorities in Taranto, Italy. The 9th and 10th Battalions of the British West Indies Regiment mutinied in protest against differences in pay between white and black soldiers. Units of the Worcester Regiment and a machine-gun company were brought in to restore order. The ringleaders were arrested. One of the mutineers was executed by firing squad and sixty received prison sentences varying from three to twenty years.

Indiscipline, mainly in its minor forms, can be said to have been endemic in the British Army. However, compared to that of other armies, its general morale was remarkably good. The British Army, alone among its major allies, showed no sign of collapse, even during the German near-breakthrough of March 1918. In 1917 the armies of France following the disastrous Nivelle offensive, of Russia after the October Revolution, and of Italy at Caporetto, all succumbed to mutiny or flight on the field of battle. Indiscipline in the British Army was controlled at an acceptable level mainly because of loyalty to comrades, the fostering of regimental pride, the great emphasis placed on good working relationships between officers and men and the essentially fair method of dispensing justice.

The situation changed dramatically in the weeks following the Armistice. In December 1918, and through much of 1919, unrest, disturbances, riots and strikes were prevalent in the British Army. Appendix I lists over sixty examples of disturbances, riots and mutinies that took place after the November 1918 Armistice.[8] This list can be considered as far from exhaustive, but it illustrates what FM Haig called 'a general relaxation of the bonds of discipline'. Several demonstrations and riots are described in some detail to illustrate what was an exceedingly unstable period in the history of the British Army. The disturbances arose mainly out of the civilian-soldiers' frustration at being retained in the army when they considered that, having carried out their duty to the country, they should be allowed to return home. The lack of purposeful activity in the camps gave rise to boredom, indiscipline and extreme irritation at army rules and regulations. Lieutenant James Worthington of the Lancashire Fusiliers noted in his memoirs: 'discipline worsened. My own CSM was arrested very drunk and put on a charge for telling the 2nd in command to perform a physical impossibility upon himself. I sat on the Court Martial as a prisoner's friend. What could we do with him? He had a splendid record MM and DCM.'[9] Captain A.E. Bundy, of the Royal Engineers, was stationed in Salonika at the end of the war. He noted, somewhat laconically: 'Men coming and going. Nothing exciting except reports of murder, robbery and rioting. Armed guard around camp strengthened. If this is peace, war is better.'[10]

Many of the men involved in the army disturbances, particularly those in the RASC and the RAOC, had a trade-union background and were familiar with industrial disruption. Grievances, real or imaginary, were rife.[11] There were complaints about poor food, excessive drill, long hours, low pay, lack of leave and a growing conviction that the system of demobilization was inefficient and basically unfair. As Prime Minister Lloyd George made clear to his War Cabinet colleagues on 8 January 1919:

> They had to recognise that the position was inevitably one of great difficulty. Between four and five millions of men had been undergoing for years the severe strain of war, with death confronting them. That stress had suddenly ceased and a violent reaction was natural especially as nine out of ten of the men knew that they would not serve as soldiers again.[12]

On that same occasion, Lloyd George called his colleagues' attention to a situation that would inevitably lead to discontent within certain military units – when skilled soldiers 'saw around them civilians drawing very high rates of pay'. It was that issue, together with the length of the working week, that led to a series of strikes by members of the Royal Army Ordnance Corps in France. On 18 December men in the ordnance shops in Le Havre stopped work. Their usual working week was made up of over 9 hours per day for six days and their demands now included a shorter working week, an increased amount of time outside camp, longer holidays at Christmas and New Year and an improved bread ration. On 21 December men in the nearby ordnance workshops of the Tank Corps refused to take on any additional work. While the men at Le Havre were treated in a conciliatory manner, the Tank Corps ordnance workers were immediately put under arrest. Nevertheless, the Director of Ordnance Services, Major General Sir Charles Mathew, had some sympathy with their claims and in a report to the Quartermaster General made his view clear that men compelled to stay in France 'should not be at any disadvantage as regards pay, etc., as compared with their fellow workers who are fortunate enough to be sent home early'.[13] The Quartermaster General accepted this argument and wrote to the Army Council advising that soldiers in France should be paid civilian rates.[14]

On 3 January 1919 there were rumours of pending strike action at the RASC Motor Transport Depots near Calais and Boulogne and it was agreed by the Deputy Director of Transport that concessions should be made. On 9 January it was announced that working hours would be 7 per day (from 8½) with Sundays off.[15] This new 42-hour week was extended to RASC repair shops further south – around Rouen and Le Havre. It was while this news was being communicated that a new issue became prominent – that of demobilization. The problem was that the men of the RASC were required to remain in France as part of the force responsible for clearing up the debris and stores left over from the war. The men of the RAOC were subject to the same ruling and on 3 January soldiers at the ordnance depot at Le Havre approached their CO. The record of the meeting noted that while the delegation was respectful, 'they represented the very strong feeling which exists regarding the restrictions placed on the ROAC in connection with the Demobilisation Scheme and urged the possibility of its ultimately serious handicapping their future prospects in civil life'.[16] This issue was discussed at a meeting at GHQ and on 12 January the restrictions on men of the RAOC were amended so that a quota of tradesmen could be demobilized each week. Initially, this easing of the scheme rules was not applied to warehouse men and clerks, but the threat of a strike ensured that groups of these men would also be discharged. Before the end of January the same relaxed provisions were applied to the RASC, though only in batches of fifty per week. The authorities hoped that 'the raising of the embargo of the RASC as regards demobilisation and the fixing of a number to be demobilised weekly, small as it is, will go a considerable way towards allaying the discontent which has existed amongst a portion of transport personnel who did not consider themselves being fairly treated as regards demobilisation'.[17]

On 21 January a particularly serious incident occurred at the RAOC workshops in Calais. A deputation approached the Chief Ordnance Officer at the base and raised questions of demobilization, hours of work, food and time allowed when outside the camp.[18] A member of the deputation, Private John Pantling, had previously been charged on some minor offence and his colleagues considered, probably erroneously, that Pantling had been singled out for punishment because he was considered to be an agitator. The Chief Ordnance Officer for the Calais area denied this but decided to cancel Pantling's charge. However, on 26 January Pantling led a further protest meeting and was arrested. His fellow workers again considered this to be victimization and on 27 January stopped work and picketed the camp. They refused to take part in any discussions until Pantling was freed.

On the same day, a second group of Ordnance soldiers from a depot at nearby Vendroux had arranged to meet the Chief Ordnance Officer with complaints about hours of work and camp conditions, but, in support of the Calais ordnance men, they also refused to have discussions until Pantling was released. In the afternoon of 27 January the soldiers from both camps, now numbering several thousand, marched into Calais. The strike grew larger and was joined by soldiers in Dunkirk, a Motor Transport Depot in Calais and a number of Royal Engineer railway units. French railway workers, supporting the protesters, refused to take over the rail system and before long trains ceased to operate.[19]

It was an extremely difficult situation for the British Army. Transport and maintenance work had come to a stop in the key areas around the Channel ports and this affected food supplies, repairs, equipment replacement and, ironically, the leave and demobilization arrangements of thousands of troops in France. The Ordnance headquarters in Calais was surrounded by the protesters and, under the circumstances, it is not surprising that Brigadier Wroughton, of the Adjutant General's staff at GHQ, took the decision to authorize Pantling's release.

On 28 January Pantling returned to his unit and the main cause of the disturbances was removed.[20] The railway engineers returned to work as did the men of the Army Service Corps and by the morning of the 29 January only the Ordnance Corps protesters remained on strike. A decision was made at GHQ to bring the strikers under control by sending to Calais the 105th Brigade, 35th Division, from General Sir Julian Byng's Fifth Army. The 1st, 2nd and 3rd Guards Machine Gun Battalions were also despatched and concentrated near Calais.[21]

However, at this point, the situation became even more complicated and threatening for the army authorities. The disruption to rail and communications systems on 27 and 28 January meant that thousands of soldiers on their way to and from Britain were stranded in the camps around Calais.[22] They knew little about the protests of the ROAC and RASC men, but the delay to their movement schedule caused considerable frustration. Men from No. 6 Leave Camp, on the outskirts of Calais, had just returned from Britain, but they refused to move to their destinations in France and demanded that they should be given a further ten days' leave to look for employment. Representatives met the Calais base camp commandant and General Wroughton on the afternoon of 28 January. The representatives were told that, while their demobilization complaints would be looked into, they would not be given additional leave. In the meantime, men of the 104th and 105th Brigades of the 35th Division had moved to picket the perimeter of No. 6 Leave Camp and GHQ had brought up a second division, the 31st, to stabilize the situation. General Byng was placed in command.[23] Attempts by the Camp 6 delegates to persuade the men of the two brigades of the 35th Division to join the strike failed. On the morning of 30 January the 35th Division carried out their orders which were to occupy No. 6 Base Camp 'with such force as was necessary'.[24] Men who wished to break off the strike and return to their units in France could do so with the assurance, from General Byng, that there would be no reprisals. The soldiers' committee, which attempted, unsuccessfully, to persuade their colleagues to stand firm, was immediately arrested. Lieutenant James Worthington, Lancashire Fusiliers, recorded the events:

> Company Commanders were told by the CO that there was a riot in Camp 6, where several thousand leave men had imprisoned their Officers and locked the Guard in their own Guard room. We had to sort them out, one depleted but armed Brigade versus 6,000 mutineers, unarmed thank Goodness. A nasty situation indeed. The prospect of having to fire on our own troops was not alluring. Meantime all three Battalions marched into the compound in single file and occupied two sides, facing the milling crowd. Ostentatiously we loaded. Guarded by the Military Police, the Brigadier invited the ringleaders to submit their grievances. The principal moan was that, by reason of the Railway strike in England the previous batch of leave men had had an extra week. They wanted the same. Moreover they meant to have it. Unfortunately for their hopes they did not notice the Redcaps' cautious approach. By the time their pals had let out a warning it was too late: they were in handcuffs.[25]

FM Haig was of the opinion that the ringleaders should be shot, but Winston Churchill, the Secretary of State for War, persuaded him otherwise.

Dramatic activity was simultaneously taking place at the Calais base camp. On 30 January the base camp commandant, General Wroughton, and officers from GHQ convened a meeting with representatives of the ROAC, who were still on strike, and also delegates from the RASC and the Queen Mary's Army Auxiliary Corps. The representatives opened the meeting with a startling demand. They claimed that since Private Pantling had secured his release when the army authorities were under duress, the authorities could claim, under military law, that Pantling could be re-arrested and tried again – possibly revoking his acquittal. The representatives therefore wanted a retrial of Pantling to take place before any other business was discussed. The officers present eventually agreed to this. Pantling was brought in and was duly acquitted for a second time.[26]

The demands of the strikers were then tabled. The ROAC and RASC delegates wanted a shorter working week, though they did not agree with each other on the number of hours to be worked. The RAOC wanted a 36-hour week while the RASC pressed for a working week less than 45 hours. There were also demands for speedier demobilization, higher rates of pay, longer opening hours for the cafe and the recognition of a soldiers' council. The meeting went on for 5 hours, but no agreement was reached. The officers were in no mood for compromise and ordered the strikers to return to work the following morning. Surprisingly, given the potential strength of the ROAC and RASC units to disrupt the lines of communication around Calais, the strike ended.[27] Shortly afterwards, hours of work were reduced and rates of pay were increased. As a footnote to the strikes in the Calais area in January 1919 it should be mentioned that Private John Pantling, a key figure in these disturbances, died on 13 February 1919, a victim of the influenza epidemic. He is buried in Les Baraques Military Cemetery, Sangatte.

While the serious events at Calais were taking place, a bizarre strike occurred at the Crystal Palace demobilization centre near London. The soldier/clerks there were in the habit of receiving bribes 'to grease the machinery of demobilisation'. On 23 January this practice was prohibited and the clerks promptly went on strike. Their claim was that they were paid less than civilian clerks and the bribes, amounting to around 5*s.* each per day, supplemented their income. They returned to work when they were assured that their grievance would be sent to higher authorities.[28]

The post-Armistice malaise that affected the British Army spread to Egypt. As in France, the frustration of soldiers no longer facing war-like conditions and concerned primarily with getting home, focused on the poor standard of food, unacceptable living conditions, over-strict discipline, rates of pay and, particularly, the slow procedure for demobilization. The large camp at Kantara held some 3,400 ex-miners and 605 demobilizers and pivotal men, all of whom had expected a quick return home, but by the end of December not a single soldier had been shipped to Britain.

Several serious incidents had taken place in Egypt in December 1918. On four occasions New Zealand and British troops had looted shops and damaged property in Ismailia. In Port Said Australian soldiers had assaulted a group of Italians. The first organized strike took place in the Kantara base on 13 February when men working in the Ordnance depot refused to carry out their normal duties. The GOC of the Kantara area gave the RAOC men an undertaking to present their grievances on demobilization and leave to GHQ and work was resumed the following day.

To some extent the soldiers in Egypt accepted that they had serious military obligations. Territories annexed from the Turks required forces of occupation. In March 1919 anti-British nationalists, hoping to strengthen their case for Egyptian independence at the Versailles peace talks, rioted in the cities and damaged railway lines and roads. Communications with Cairo and Alexandria were cut.[29] Moreover, the ratio of British troops to local and Indian soldiers was critically low. Only a third of RASC personnel were British. Rather than reduce the number of soldiers in Egypt, the British military authorities were desperate to have reinforcements. At Kantara nearly 8,000 troops were awaiting embarkation, but they were not allowed to leave. Soldiers already on troop ships were ordered to disembark and be ready for active service and a number were sent south to deal with an uprising in the Sudan. The camp commandant addressed the troops and announced that, under the circumstances, demobilization was on hold.[30]

There was no mutiny in Egypt on the scale of Calais, but resentment grew among men who considered that they deserved to be sent home. Their method of showing their disaffection was to organize themselves into groups, elect delegates and inform the authorities just what they were prepared to do. Over the Easter period 1919, for example, the troops in the demobilization camp refused to carry out any duties other than those that were essential. They were addressed by the GOC who failed to persuade the men to resume normal duties. On 21 April General Allenby wrote to the CIGS, Sir Henry Wilson:

> I'm sorry to say that some 3,000 men at the Demobilisation Camp at Kantara have refused to allow men to come on as helpers on the railways ... I can't shoot them all for mutiny, so I must carry on as best I can, & I must resume demobilisation ... Demobilisation must go on, or my troops will mutiny.[31]

The contingent that had been sent to the Sudan had carried out their task and demanded to be sent back to Kantara. There was a delay in receiving a response and the soldiers announced that they would no longer carry out guard duties. The incidence of strike action spread throughout the area of the Egyptian Expeditionary Force and disruption was reported in Port Said, Haifa and Beirut. Acts of arson took place at the Kantara camp including the burning of the office of the Deputy Assistant Director, Ordnance Services. Following a mass meeting of troops in Kantara on 11 May, General Allenby reported to the War Office that:

> There is great unrest and discontent throughout my Army; and, in the case of the Administrative service, unrest verges on mutiny ... I have as you know a very large proportion of '14 and '15 men. These men would, most of them, have been dead by now – no doubt – if their service had been in France – but they take no comfort in that consideration ... it is no use my trying to hide from you the gravity of the situation here.[32]

The authorities were obliged to concede and, exactly six months after the Armistice, demobilization began in earnest.

The greatest number of strikes and the largest demonstrations of frustration and anger at the slow pace of demobilization took place in England during January 1919. In terms of the number of soldiers involved, the single biggest outbreak of serious indiscipline began on 3 January in Folkestone. On that day thousands of British troops were stationed in camps around Folkestone returning from home leave. Their transportation back to France was scheduled to begin at 8.15am when the first 1,000 were to embark. The second 1,000 were due to sail at 8.25am. However, instead of parading on the quayside, men from No. 1 Rest Camp marched across Folkestone to No. 3 Rest Camp gathering additional soldiers on the way. Soldiers from both of these camps, numbering around 10,000, then marched down the Sandgate Road shouting slogans against a return to France and indicating their firm intention to be demobilized and go home.

The soldiers gathered around the town hall and met the mayor who unsuccessfully attempted to get them to return to their camps. The town commander, Lieutenant Colonel Mill, promised that their complaints would be listened to and a procession, preceded by a large drum, made its way back to the rest camps. Having arrived at the camps, the demonstrators were told that pivotal and slip men, who had work to go to, could be demobilized at once and those who wished to return to France could do so.

The following morning, 4 January, there was more disruption by groups alleging that men were being forced to return to France. The demonstrators posted pickets at the harbour and the railway station and soldiers arriving from leave were persuaded to join the strike. It was reported in the national press that an official military guard, which had been posted at the harbour to control the demonstration, fell back when approached by the strikers, unwilling to apply force. The *Herald* newspaper reported that the strikers were shouting that the war was over and that they meant to go home.

Later in the day it was announced that a 'Soldiers' Union' had been formed and that nine representatives were to discuss the situation with a general and the town commandant at No. 3 Rest Camp. A massive crowd of around 10,000 men waited outside the camp and, after several hours, their delegates announced that the undertakings given the previous day would stand. During the evening, clerks from the Ministry of Labour arrived at the Camp and the required paperwork and formalities began. So ended the largest mutiny experienced by the British Army. There was no bloodshed and, in speeding up the demobilization process, the strikers achieved what they wanted.

On 4 January a demonstration in Dover, no doubt fuelled by the activities at Folkestone, demanded that their spokesmen should meet civic and military representatives. As trains arrived at Dover, new troops, bound for France, joined the demonstrators and a crowd of some 2,000 marched to the town hall where they were received by the mayor. Following discussions with General Dallas, GOC Canterbury and General Woolcombe of Eastern Command, the demonstrators were assured that they would receive the same undertakings that had been given at Folkestone. Immediately, the soldiers were provided with facilities to contact potential employers.

There was a certain amount of press censorship of the events at Folkestone and Dover and *The Times* of 8 January, in support of the government, condemned the strikes and commented that 'these demonstrations have gone far enough'. But word of the mutinies had already spread and, in Kent, copycat demonstrations had begun in camps at Shortlands, near Bromley (6 January), Maidstone (7 January), Biggin Hill (7 January) and Richborough (8 January). Press censorship might have been possible for a short period in London, but the provincial press continued to publish accounts of the various strikes. On 7 January the *Manchester Guardian* reported that 'Camps were broken yesterday at Shoreham-on Sea, Grove Park, Sydenham and Shortlands by soldiers who hold that they have a grievance in respect of their demobilisation'. And on 10 January the same newspaper carried an article on 'RAMC Demonstrations at Blackpool' in which it listed the lengthy demands of the medical staff. Apart from the main issue of slow and unfair demobilization, the list of demands included: 'breakfast at 8.30am each day and first parade 9.30; no afternoon parades; only voluntary church parades on Sunday; abolition of gas and gymnasium classes and better meals'. It was a list that might be regarded as inconsequential, but it illustrated a deep frustration.

The *Manchester Evening Chronicle* of 9 January gave a detailed account of 'sensational happenings' at Heaton Park with the headline: 'Disgruntled Troops: Protest To-Day'. The article read:

> Some 600 soldiers belonging to a Labour company at the camp went 'on strike' as a protest against certain grievances, particularly in regard to demobilisation. Most of these are men who have been wounded and disabled, long service men who have been in the thick of the fighting on the various fronts. Many joined up in 1914 and a good number are Mons men.

On the same day a contingent of Royal Engineers at Kilnsea stopped work 'owing to the water-logged state of trenches'. They repeated the strike on 20 January, this time because of 'insufficiency of food'. Both incidents ended with appropriate concessions.[33]

A demonstration that received much press coverage and caught the attention of the public took place on 6 January at a RASC depot in Osterley, West London. The men, most of whom had served in France, had recently aired their complaints about demobilization to their CO, but had received no reply. The *Manchester Guardian* reported:

> At Osterley Park several hundred men refused to do duty and, commandeering a number of army motor-lurries [*sic*] drove to London. Arriving at Whitehall they wished to see the Premier, but on finding that he was not at home, they went to the demobilisation offices of the Ministry of Labour, where a deputation stated their case. An undertaking was given that their grievances should be at once enquired into, and the men returned to camp, insisting, however, on taking with them the Staff Major appointed to look into their case.

On 7 January the Osterley men were told that demobilization would take place at the rate of 200 per day. The War Office followed this by saying that the Army Council had decided to put the RASC on the same footing for demobilization as other units and that none of them would be sent overseas.

Two days after the Osterley Park incident some 4,000 RASC men from Park Royal in North-West London approached their CO with ten demands including speedier demobilization, shorter working hours and no drafts for Russia. The CO agreed most of these, but, on 8 January, 1,500 men decided to take their grievances directly to Whitehall with the intention of confronting the Prime Minister. The strikers were met by General Fielding, the commander of the London District, and by General Sir William Robertson, the former Chief of the Imperial General

Staff, who promised to send a general to Park Royal to investigate their complaints. In addition, the men were told that the Service Corps men would be demobilized at the same rate as other units and they would not be posted to Russia. These undertakings satisfied the Park Royal men who returned to their camp.

It so happened that a meeting of the War Cabinet took place on 8 January and the minutes of that meeting give an insight into the thinking of the Cabinet ministers on the military disturbances:

> The Prime Minister informed the War Cabinet that he had just learnt that that some 1,500 soldiers belonging to the Army Service Corps at Park Royal had arrived in Downing Street and were asking for an interview with him ... Sir William Robertson was prepared to believe that some of their grievances were genuine ... He had asked that the delegates should be sent to see him.

The Prime Minister then said that he:

> was quite prepared to see the delegates of the soldiers in a body if the War Cabinet thought that would be the right course ... Lord Milner said he doubted the wisdom of the Prime Minister seeing the soldiers or their representatives, as it would form a bad precedent, and similar processions would attempt to march to London from other parts of the country. It was important to make perfectly plain to the soldiers that such processions would not be allowed.

Sir William Robertson agreed with Milner. He 'strongly disliked the suggestion that the Prime Minister should confer with the soldiers' delegates who had disregarded their officers. The soldiers' delegates bore a dangerous resemblance to a Soviet. If such a practice were to spread, the consequences would be disastrous'. Sir Eric Geddes suggested that 'the men might be drawn up in the Horse Guards' Parade in military formation, under their officers, and that they might be addressed by the Prime Minister'. General Fielding then joined the meeting and 'in reply to a question from the Prime Minister said that at present only a small minority of troops were disaffected, but the agitation would spread if demonstrations were not prohibited'. The Prime Minister responded: 'They [the Cabinet] must be quite sure that any steps they decided on with a view to suppressing the demonstrations that were taking place were certain to be successful'. The meeting ended with the resolution that:

> General Sir William Robertson would meet the delegates of the soldiers in the Horse Guards' Parade and inform them that officers would be sent to Park Royal to investigate their alleged grievances … and that the Prime Minister in consultation with the Secretary of State for War, was preparing a statement on demobilisation, which would appear in the press on the following morning.[34]

It was clearly a critical time for the members of the War Cabinet and fears of riots, military demonstrations and possible Bolshevik activity were uppermost in their minds. In particular, there was a realization that the demobilization plans were flawed and some alternative process was urgently required.

The promise of a statement on demobilization, made by the Prime Minister at the meeting of the War Cabinet on 8 January, was welcomed by Sir Henry Wilson. In a letter to Lord Derby, Wilson wrote: 'At the present moment there are rows of lorries outside [the War Office] … one thing is certain that unless the PM buckles to and makes it quite clear that he and the Govt. are solidly behind the W[ar] O[ffice] and the Officers of the Army then we shall lose the Army, and then the Navy and then the Air Force'.[35] It was a sentiment echoed by Haig who considered that 'the state of the army is deplorable'.[36]

On 8 January Philip Kerr, Lloyd George's secretary, sent a copy of the Prime Minister's statement to Wilson. It contained what Wilson wanted to see – the Prime Minister:

> considers that his first duty is to make sure that the fruits of victory … are not jeopardised by any apparent weakness on the part of Britain during the critical months of the Peace negotiations. For this purpose it is imperative that we should maintain a strong army on the Rhine and of course the necessary services behind the front both in France and at home. Although the fighting has stopped the war is not over … Demobilisation cannot be carried out in any way that would undermine the military strength of Britain until final peace is secure … One thing is certain, the work of demobilisation is not going to be quickened, on the contrary, it is bound to be delayed by the men trying to take the law into their own hands …[37]

A short paragraph in Lloyd George's statement read: 'Furthermore, fair and even treatment must be noted as between men bearing the hardships of the field and those whose duty is discharged at home'. This was a clear reference to the problematic 'contracts' system that allowed soldiers in

Britain, including those on leave, to contact a previous employer and gain their demobilisation ahead of soldiers abroad.

On 8 January the Secretary of State for War, Lord Milner, announced that:

> no officer or soldier will be permitted to proceed to England on leave from France except on the distinct understanding that he returns to his unit on the expiration of his leave, and that he will not be demobilised on any pretext whatever during his period of leave … It has been found that, in a high proportion of cases, leave drafts from France now consists of men who have been overseas for six or nine months only, and the demobilisation of all men on leave would thus be unfair to long-service men still overseas.

This was certainly a step in the direction of righting a situation that was causing considerable unrest. The announcement, however, still confirmed the basis of the government's demobilization plan – 'the release of men most urgently required in the national interest'.[38] In other words, the main grievance of the soldiers, that short-service men were being demobilized before long-service men including those who had been wounded and had families, was not addressed. Lord Milner's statement only touched the edge of the problem and did little to reduce the injustice felt by many serving soldiers.

In a post-election Cabinet re-shuffle in early January, Lord Milner was replaced by Winston Churchill as Secretary of State for War. Churchill took up his duties on 10 January and immediately grasped the demobilization nettle. As he wrote some years later:

> I was immediately confronted with conditions of critical emergency … the fighting man has a grim sense of justice, which it is dangerous to affront … the discipline of the whole Army in all theatres of war was swiftly and simultaneously rotted and undermined. For nearly two months this process had continued, and it had become intolerable to the fighting troops.[39]

The underlying reason, said Churchill, was that 'soldiers did not think that the [procedure] was fair and by the time I went to the War Office a convulsion of indiscipline shook the whole of our splendid Army …'.[40]

Even before the end of 1918 Sir Eric Geddes and other members of his Demobilization Coordination Committee had reached the conclusion that the scheme was inoperable. On 30 December Geddes gave his opinion that the system was unsatisfactory 'on account of its slowness and also because the selection method [was causing] dissatisfaction among the troops not demobilized'. Sir Philip Nash, who served on the Geddes Committee, pointed out a weakness in the use of pivotal men: 'although pivotal men are only of value in their own particular industry, no connection can be established between the pivotal man and the group sequence; so that a pivotal man released first may only be pivotal on a group which will be released last'.[41]

On 11 January Churchill telegraphed Haig asking him to come to a meeting in London along with Wilson, Geddes, Horne, Robertson and Macdonough. The eventual outcome, which was reached on 17 January, dealt with the two main issues – demobilization and the need for a standing army. The basic plan was that all men who had enlisted in 1914 and 1915 would be demobilized as soon as transport was available – thus establishing the principle of first out, first back. The remainder would be retained, compulsorily, on improved pay and extra leave. In terms of numbers it was estimated that around 2.2 million men would be demobilized and some 1.2 million held back.

The discussions leading to the revised arrangements were not without heated debate. Sir Eric Geddes wrote to Churchill on 15 January: 'I have been studying the existing machinery for demobilising the army and have formed the opinion that it is based on wrong principles and that if it is allowed to continue to operate it will produce results deplorable alike in civil life and the forces'.[42] On the other hand, Christopher Addison, the Minister of Reconstruction, wrote to the War Cabinet stressing that it would be 'a grave mistake to alter the principles' of the existing scheme and warned that any significant change would 'throw the country into hopeless confusion'.[43] Addison was supported by Sir Richard Horne who considered that there would be a strong adverse reaction from chambers of commerce and trade unions if the existing demobilization scheme was scrapped. Haig believed that 'the existing system had produced a very bad effect on the troops' and Wilson's view was that 'there was much to be said for this [new] arrangement – we must do something drastic to stop the present stampede'. In response to Sir Richard Horne's concerns, Churchill said that he was prepared to facc any opposition 'in ordcr to gain a lasting Peace'.

Churchill now had to convince Lloyd George, at that time embroiled in the peace negotiations at Versailles, that the new proposals should be adopted. Lloyd George, however, felt that he had not been consulted on the issue and was not inclined to make a quick response. In frustration Churchill telegraphed Lloyd George on 19 January saying that if there was delay in settling the demobilization question there would be nothing left of the army but 'a demoralised and angry mob'. In order to gain Lloyd George's attention, Churchill summarized his proposal: 'Briefly the scheme consists of releasing two men of three and paying the third man double to finish the job'. At a lunch in Paris on 24 January Lloyd George met Churchill, Haig, Wilson and Macdonough and agreed the new arrangements and a reduction of divisions in France.[44] The revised demobilization scheme was detailed in the Army Orders 54 and 55 of 29 January. *The Times* of 7 February published the details of the revised system of demobilization:

> The men who will be kept – men serving under pre-war conditions of service who have not completed their term of Colour service and those who joined the Colours on or after 1 January 1916, except men who are over 37 years of age and men who have more than two wound stripes. The men to be demobilised – men who have completed their term of Colour service, men who joined the Colours before 1 January 1916, men who are over 37 years of age, and men who have more than two wound stripes.

It was a scheme not dissimilar to the one operated by the French which was based on age, length of service and combat experience.

The Times article also detailed 'the weekly bonuses over and above their present pay' that would apply to 'officers and men retained in the Armies of Occupation'. The bonuses ranged from 10*s*. 6*d*. per week for a private to 38*s*. 6*d*. for a lieutenant colonel. *The Times* backed the proposals: 'First Out, First Home – that is the just principle at the foot of the demobilisation plan ... The members of the Armies that must be maintained to back our demands at the Peace Conference will have their compensation in bonus pay'. The article ended: 'Patience, Co-operation and an intelligent appreciation of the Nation's needs will win us the Peace'.

When Churchill, some twenty-five years later, recalled the events of early 1919 he wrote: 'I persuaded the Cabinet to remove the foolish and inequitable plan and substitute the single rule "First Out, First Home", and the process of demobilisation went forward in a smooth and orderly fashion'.[45] Although Churchill chose to emphasize 'the single rule', elements of the 'inequitable plan' continued. As *The Times* article of 7 February made clear: 'Civil demobilisers and pivotal men duly certified by the Ministry of Labour whose names have been received by the War Office before 1 February 1919 will still have prior claim. Contract men, slip men, compassionate and One Man Business cases will all be released in their turn provided they are otherwise demobilisable'. An article in the *Ashbourne Telegraph* of 14 February quoted a statement by Churchill: 'When men are marked for release they obviously ought to go home in the order which will most quickly restart our industries … For otherwise they would leave their means of livelihood in the Army and relinquish their rations and their separation allowance only to become unemployed in great numbers'. Churchill's plan was, in practice, a mixture of both the old and the new arrangements.

The emphasis on the 'First Out, First Home' principle certainly satisfied the general feeling among the soldiers that a much fairer system was necessary. In early 1919 Major H.J.C. Marshall, who was successively in charge of the 466th and 468th RE Field Companies, had disregarded the then existing system and demobilized men by length of service abroad 'which the men themselves considered the fairer way'.[46] And various striking soldiers had made similar proposals. At Kantara in Egypt the number one demand of the strikers was that 'those serving longer abroad without home leave be the first to be demobilised'. At Shortlands, Beckenham, a group of RASC soldiers, together with men from Grove Park and Sydenham, drew up a 'points' system to determine the priority of men for demobilization. The longer the service, the higher the score and the greater entitlement to an early discharge.[47]

But Churchill's claim, following the introduction of the new rules in February 1919, that demobilization proceeded in a 'smooth and orderly fashion' was far from the truth. Entries in Hansard provide evidence of continued frustration and unrest. On 8 April Churchill was asked in Parliament 'whether his attention had been drawn to the discontent which exists among the military personnel of the Machine Gun Corps Record Office in reference to their demobilisation – the majority of them are soldiers of three and four years' service'. On the same day, Churchill was questioned by MPs: 'If I bring before you a certain number of cases of officers who have absolutely nothing to do, will you hasten their demobilisation?' And, 'Has the Right Hon. Gentleman made personal enquiry into the number of men who are simply fooling about at the present time in France?' Numerous individual circumstances were brought to Churchill's attention: 'Why is Private FJ Briggs, No. 36793, 9th Field Ambulance, Guards Division, still retained in the Army, considering that this man joined in September 1914?' 'Will the Secretary of State for War cause enquiries to be made as to the reason for the non-release of Corporal R Grundy, No. 6121, Military Mounted Police, who, as a member of the Yeomanry prior to August 1914, has served throughout the War, in addition to being a tenant farmer?' One soldier, J.W. Burford, who had a wife and seven children, told his local newspaper that he could not gain release from the army, even though he had a job waiting for him. 'Mr Burford stated that all he and another man had to do in the army was to look after 70 pigeons'.[48]

Criticisms of the demobilization arrangements were put forward in Parliament on 5 June 1919 by the Member for West Derbyshire, Mr C.F. White:

> We have been told a good many times in this House that there is no discontent in the Army today ... There is the greatest discontent existing today, and a large part is due to the miserable methods of demobilisation. It is not too much to say that demobilisation has broken down ... Hundreds of thousands of men have been sent back to join the ranks of the unemployed ... while men who joined in 1914 and 1915 are still being kept in the Army although they have essential industries to go back to with places being kept open for them ... One case is typical of hundreds of others. It was that of an engineer who joined up in 1914 and who has for months been employed washing up pots and pans in a canteen ... I have a letter here from the War Office stating that the man is eligible for demobilisation, but explaining that the officer commanding the regiment says he is indispensable although he is only engaged in washing pots and pans.

Mr White cited several other cases.[49]

An example of how soldiers involved in demobilization disturbances were dealt with and how perceived injustices festered well into 1919 concerns Sergeant S. Smith of South Shields.[50] This soldier took part, peripherally, in a rowdy disturbance on 8 February near Victoria Station, London. A large group of soldiers, who were returning from leave, objected to being sent back to France. They marched by Horse Guards' Parade and on to Whitehall to air their grievances. The noisy and ill-disciplined demonstration was only brought under control when a detachment of cavalry and infantry arrived and escorted the rioters to Wellington Barracks. Here, their names were taken and subsequently passed to the War Office and the BEF in France with the suggestion that those involved should have their demobilization delayed and their leave allowance withdrawn.

In March 1919 Sergeant Smith, now in France, wrote to his wife, Lily Smith, claiming that the demonstration was orderly and that he was 'simply dragged into it'. He went on:

> You will be surprised and sorry to know that the victimisation has begun. I have been placed at the bottom of the Demobilisation list ... I'm afraid that it is going to be first out, last home. They are not doing fair at all. There are hundreds of men here 1914 and 1915. Men with no prospect of demobilisation. I wonder what they take men for? ... Employers are not going to keep our jobs open. It is the unskilled men that are being released.

Smith had been a merchant seaman before the war and his case was taken up by Mr Havelock Wilson, the Secretary of the Merchant Seamen's League. Havelock Wilson, who questioned the legality of Smith's treatment, sent all the details to Churchill at the War Office who 'refused to argue the question in detail with Mr Havelock Wilson'. On 7 June Havelock Wilson was informed by the War Office that 'No further action can be taken'.

One of the most disturbing riots of 1919, fuelled by poor discipline and boredom, took place in Epsom on 17 June.[51] Two Canadian ASC soldiers from Woodcote Park Camp were arrested at 10pm for disorderly conduct. The CO of the camp was informed and he promised to send an escort for them. However, at about 11pm some 400 Canadian soldiers marched to the police station 'with a bugler at their head'. On their way they pulled down fences and broke windows. When they reached the police station they attempted to occupy it, demanding the release of the two prisoners. The local police, headed by Inspector Pawley, attempted to calm the soldiers, but a major riot developed. The police called in off-duty reinforcements, one of whom was Sergeant Green.

As the riot was clearly getting out of hand, Inspector Pawley offered to release the prisoners. Stones were thrown at the police officers and, when the rioters broke into the station, the officers were attacked with metal bars and wooden staves. During the melee Inspector Pawley was hit on the head and fell dazed. Sergeant Green was also struck on the head 'with a piece of railing or heavy piece of wood' and collapsed to the ground. Green was eventually taken to the Epsom Infirmary where he died without regaining consciousness. Thirteen other police officers were injured.

The two prisoners were now freed and the riot petered out. The following day an investigation took place at the camp. Despite 'the marked reluctance shown by nearly every member of Woodcote Park Camp' seven men were identified as taking part in the riot and were arrested. Their trial took place at Guildford Assizes on 22/23 July and five men were found guilty of riot and sentenced to twelve months' imprisonment. In passing sentence the judge informed the prisoners that he was 'pleased the Jury had not returned a verdict of manslaughter against them and he was exceedingly sorry to see men, who had served the country as soldiers, and were not in the ordinary sense of the word criminals, in such a serious position'. On 9 June 1920 a memorial was erected in Epsom to commemorate the incident. A local resident, Mr J. van Maurik, donated a hundred cigars 'to the men who so bravely defended the station against great odds'.

Ten years later one of the convicted Canadians, A.J. McMaster, voluntarily gave the following statement to the police in Winnipeg, Ontario:

> On the night of 17 June 1919, I remember that it was the night of the first Derby after the war, I was in company with a number of comrades who went to the Police Station in Epsom to effect the release of some comrades who had been arrested by the Civil authority. There were about 800 of us and we smashed in the Police Station. Police Sergeant Green was in charge of the Police at the station … I struck the Sergt. on the head with an iron bar … I saw him falling backwards, he was bareheaded at the time … The reason I make this statement is because I feel a burden on my conscience and know that I would have to confess it sometime.

The Winnipeg police contacted Scotland Yard who responded on 3 August 1929: 'Allan McMaster, with four other men, was sentenced at the Guildford Assizes to 12 months' imprisonment for riot that resulted in the death of Station Sergeant Green … They were also charged with manslaughter, but were found not guilty of this offence. In these circumstances McMaster is not wanted here'.

There is much evidence to show that the process of demobilization, even following Churchill's change of procedure in February 1919, was by no means trouble-free. In July 1919, six months after the new scheme was introduced and when most men had returned home, a soldiers' riot took place in Luton and the town hall was burnt down. And in August a group of 200 soldiers at Southampton protested against the demobilization system and refused to board a ship for 'distant parts'. At that stage, however, with the passage of time and as the size of the army reduced, protests and disturbances were rare events.

By August 1919 over 3 million men and women (including Dominion troops) had been demobilized. It was a process that took place with many difficulties, not least the disruption and misery caused by the influenza outbreak in the first three months of 1919. Its peak was reached at the end of March when 3,889 deaths from influenza were recorded in a week in London and the other '96 great towns'.[52] Soldiers as well as civilians suffered. Among these was Major C.J. Phipps of the 1st King's (Liverpool) Regiment who had served throughout the war and been wounded twice. He had been awarded the DSO and the MC and had been mentioned in despatches three times. He died of the 'flu' in February 1919 in Duren, Germany. Such circumstances, far from unique, were particularly ironic and sad.

Chart I on the page opposite shows the rate of demobilization (four-weekly averages) between 11 November 1918 and 9 August 1919.[53] November/December 1918, complicated by the election and the Christmas break, had a low rate at 17,436. January was high at 619,554 and

February showed a peak of 785,644. Thereafter the four-weekly averages reduced quite markedly. The changes in the demobilization procedure are likely to have affected the February figure only partially. Indeed, the first week of February saw the highest weekly number of demobilizations at 235,000, i.e. before the new scheme was fully operational. There is therefore an argument to suggest that demobilization would have been largely completed by August 1919 whichever system had been in place. Overall, the daily rate of demobilization averaged around 12,500 per day which was significantly lower than the average figure of 40,000 per day promised by the War Office in April 1917. Small contingents of troops due to return home were retained in service after August 1919, and it was not until 17 October that Churchill was able to report to the Finance Committee of the Cabinet that demobilization had been completed.[54]

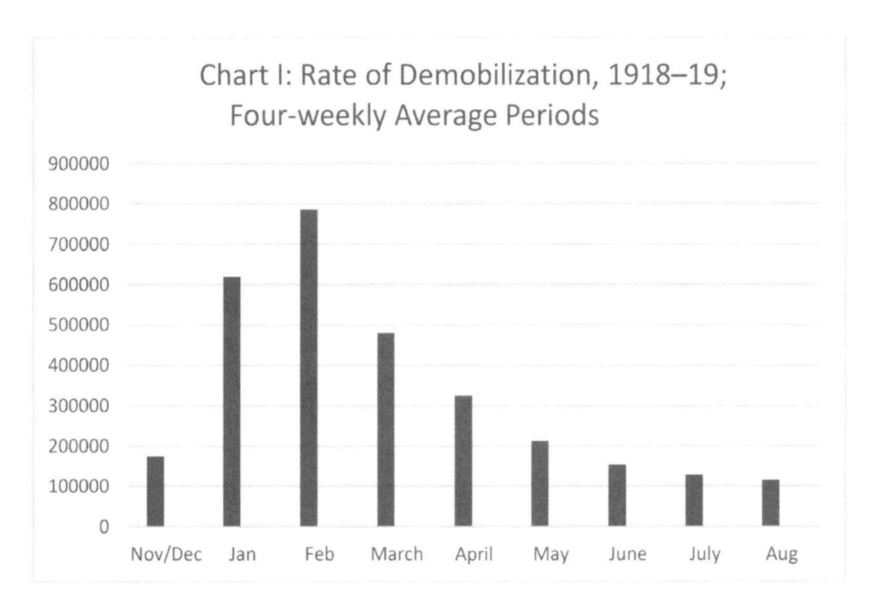

Nevertheless, taking everything into account, the demobilization of 3 million soldiers over a period of 9 months was no mean achievement. Two-thirds of the army had returned home within five months of the Armistice. The merit of Churchill's new procedure in February 1919 was that it removed the soldiers' main grievance by establishing the 'First Out, First Home' principle. It provided the all-important element, even if illusory, of perceived 'fairness'.

Chapter 4

Demobilizing

Apart from the problems associated with the demobilization of British troops, the British government, together with the governments of the constituent parts of the British Empire, had to deal with issues connected with the return of Dominion soldiers to their home countries. In November 1918 the numbers of Dominion troops in France totalled some 300,000, made up mainly of Canadians (154,000), Australians (94,000) and New Zealanders (25,000).[1] In addition, there were over 100,000 Dominion troops and women and children in Britain.[2] Of these, 15,386 wives and other dependants wished to return to Australia with the AIF in 1919.[3]

The basis of repatriation was agreed at a conference of Dominion heads in London in March 1917. Sir Robert Borden, the Prime Minister of Canada, summarized the proposal: 'It was agreed that all Dominion contingents in France should start as soon as possible with their equipment from a French or Belgium port, but arrangements will be made to give individual soldiers desiring to visit this country [Britain] furlough for that purpose'. It was a proposal that appeared straightforward but which gave rise to considerable debate and complication. The initial interpretation of this resolution was endorsed at a meeting of the Empire Military Demobilization Committee: 'on demobilisation those troops who desire to come to England for furlough and who have not done so previously should be afforded the opportunity'.[4] This interpretation took account of 'the fact that practically the whole of the Australian Forces in France have already had leave in this country' and therefore the great majority of Australian troops could embark for home from ports in France and from Taranto in southern Italy. At that point the Canadian government had made no request for their troops to visit Britain on demobilization.

Sir Reginald Brade of the War Office had put forward a memorandum to the Imperial Conference of 1917 acknowledging 'the Imperial and other advantages that might accrue from the visit of Dominion contingents to this country at the end of the War' but which, nevertheless, made it quite clear that that considerable problems would result.[5] There would be difficulties accommodating troops from France, especially as there would be over 100,000 Dominion soldiers already in England. It would be necessary to ship out these soldiers before other troops arrived from France thus causing lengthy delays. Transportation would be a problem: 'during the first few months of demobilisation it will be necessary to utilize fully all the ports and shipping facilities that can be allotted for the repatriation of the British troops and for foreign garrison reliefs for India and Imperial Stations'. Also, there would be considerable strain on the rail networks in Britain and France which would be operating at full capacity moving British troops to their dispersal stations. Bringing Dominion troops to England instead of sending them home direct from France would increase the overall cost because of maintenance, accommodation and transport expenses. Brade stressed the potential disciplinary problems:

> Discipline may be difficult to maintain with troops who have completed their active service and are compelled to remain in camp ... Under the relaxation of discipline which may arise upon the declaration of peace there might be an undue amount of absence, insubordination, and other disorders'. Brade summed up: 'The [Army] Council therefore consider that the advantages of a visit to this country for the men in the Dominion Expeditionary Forces will be adequately secured by each man having the opportunity of visiting England on furlough. All the men of the Canadian contingent have already visited this country, and can therefore be sent back to Canada direct when peace is declared. This is in conformity with the desire of the Canadian Government. The bulk of the Australian and New Zealand forces have also visited this country already, and, as leave is granted in rotation, within the next two or three months every one of the men serving in Dominion contingents in France will have been to the United Kingdom. Should all not have had an opportunity of seeing England by the end of the War it is suggested that the men should come over in parties on leave to England from the Continent and should then rejoin their division in France.

It was later pointed out that transporting men from France to Britain and then shipping them from Britain to their home would delay their eventual demobilization by around four weeks.[6]

All in all, the idea of Dominion soldiers coming from France to England en masse was clearly most unwelcome to the British authorities. The War Council therefore 'urged that the Dominion troops should return to the Dominions in which they were raised, without first being concentrated in England'. Brade added that the governments of Canada, Australia, New

Zealand, the Union of South Africa and New Foundland had all been consulted on this matter and 'with the exception of the Government of New Zealand each has replied that their contingent may be returned direct and as rapidly as possible to the Dominion'.

Despite Brade's arguments to the contrary, the representatives of the various Dominions who had taken part in the 1917 Imperial Conference finally decided that they did want their troops to visit England before embarking for home. Their general view was expressed by the representatives from New Zealand, led by their Prime Minister William Massey: 'it would be disastrous from the point of view of Imperial interests if any man from Australasia were in a position to say on his return to his Dominion that, after travelling several thousand miles from his home to fight the Empire's battles, he had come back without being given an opportunity of seeing the old country'. This was later followed by a statement from the Director General of Repatriation and Demobilization, Australian Imperial Forces: 'practically all the members of the Australian Imperial Force in France should obtain from 10 to 14 days' leave in England prior to embarkation'. To this was added the recommendation that 'Australian troops in France be finally embarked from ports in the United Kingdom'.

Discussions on this issue dragged on into January 1919 by which time Canada, which had initially been prepared to ship its troops back to Canada direct from French ports, now requested that 'repatriation of all Canadian troops from France should [take place] via this country'. The then Secretary of State for War, Winston Churchill, persuaded by representations from the Canadian military leaders General Currie and Colonel Gibson, and from the Prime Minister of Australia, William ('Billy') Hughes, finally agreed to these proposals on 3 February 1919. Hughes followed up this decision with a note to Churchill: 'Many thanks for your letter of the 6th instant, intimating that you will be glad to arrange for our men to visit England before returning to their own country. My Government will greatly appreciate your kindness in this connection.' Hughes then took the opportunity to press a further point: 'Could you, at your convenience, let me know whether arrangements can be made for 362 Australians in Mesopotamia and 48 in India to be returned to Australia in an Imperial transport taking troops from Egypt to India and proceeding thence to Australia for cargo to Europe?'[7] Churchill agreed to this request on 17 March. At least there was no requirement for these men to have leave in England.

In retrospect, it can be seen that the problems resulting from the well-intentioned policy of allowing all Dominion troops to transfer from France to Britain and take leave in Britain before their repatriation were exactly as

Brade had predicted. Appendix I gives examples of disturbances and riots that occurred because of alleged poor accommodation (at Witley involving Canadians); because of indiscipline arising from sheer boredom (Canadians at Epsom); and because of delays in transportation (at Kinmel and Victoria Station involving Australians and Canadians). What with transportation and shipping delays in France and in England, the remaining Dominion soldiers were repatriated some twelve months after the Armistice.[8]

The shipping problems were exacerbated by the need to repatriate troops spread in more distant theatres of war. On 13 January 1919 it was estimated that in India there were 20,000 British soldiers; in Mesopotamia there were 80,000 British and 200,000 Indians; in Salonika 70,000 British; and in Egypt 110,000 British and 60,000 Indians, all waiting to be demobilized. Transportation and the need to provide replacement troops were the bottlenecks and, in January 1919 the estimated dates of repatriation varied from February 1919 from Egypt to June 1919 from India and Mesopotamia.[9] The 80,000 Chinese coolies in France had even longer to wait. Again, their repatriation depended on available shipping and they returned home at the rate of about 6,000 per month.[10]

In the weeks following the Armistice the Canadian government had problems of its own to solve. In April 1917 the Ministry of the Overseas Military Forces of Canada decided to follow the then British approach to demobilization which emphasized economic factors rather than the psychology of the soldier. To avoid unemployment problems the Canadian authorities laid plans to demobilize first those men who had the skills to regenerate industry and commerce. The Canadians were to have their own version of 'demobilizers' and 'pivotal men'. Major General P.E. Thaker, the Canadian Adjutant General, summarized the approach by saying: 'There is only one Canadian army overseas'. It was a sentiment that echoed that of the British War Office in April 1917: 'the army will be considered as a mass of individuals'. In other words there would be no distinction between those soldiers who had enlisted early in the war and those who had joined much later. Long-term servers would, as in the original British plan, be disadvantaged.

The reaction of Canadian soldiers to this approach was just the same as that of the British soldiers when they became aware of the government proposals. They made it clear that their main concern was to get home as quickly as possible and the only system that was acceptable to them was: first over, first back. Sir Arthur Currie, the Commander of the Canadian Corps, put forward a compromise proposal; units of the Corps should return home intact. Currie claimed that 'he had yet to hear of a single instance in which the men do not express not only a preference but an intense desire to return to Canada in units'.

The Canadian Prime Minister, Borden, and the Canadian Cabinet eventually accepted Currie's proposal, persuaded by the arguments that discipline would be best maintained if soldiers were brought home accompanied by their own officers and that other Dominion countries were following the same policy. Dispersal units, prior to embarkation, were established in England at Bramshott, Witley, Kinmel, Buxton, Ripon and Seaford but the process of repatriation was frustrated by the shortage of shipping and even more so by rail restrictions in Canada. Given the circumstances – dreary and uncomfortable camps, bad weather during the 1918–19 winter, boredom and the slowness of demobilization – it is little wonder that Canadian troops were frequently at the centre of disturbances and riots. It was a situation made worse as the flaw in Currie's plan became clear – that returning home by units often meant that short-service soldiers were released before those with longer service. The demobilization process dragged on and it was not until January 1920 that the last group of Canadian soldiers left Britain.[11]

Arrangements were made for the British wives of Dominion troops to accompany their husbands home. An article in the *Manchester Evening News* of 6 June 1919 noted that: 'New Zealand is claiming a number of our girls, but in this respect, Canada is leading the way, with Australia a good second. Americans, too, are marrying our girls'. Generally, these war brides were 'welcomed with cheers for all', though there was at least one case in New Zealand when 'quite a display of feeling was shown by the young ladies of the town who openly resented the action of their menfolk in bringing back English wives'.

Along with the Canadian soldiers who were repatriated were 'many thousands of British women who will be returning … with the troops as wives and mothers'. It is worth noting that, during a period of general disruption and uncertainty, serious consideration was given to these women who were about to live in a completely new environment: 'Conditions in the new country are, in many instances, similar to the old, but, on the other hand, there are many points where they differ'. The Canadian immigration authorities worked with the London County Council and the YMCA to form a Department of Home Economics 'which will be of enormous advantage to those availing themselves of the opportunities it offers. The aim of the work is to acquaint women with conditions in Canada, and to provide instruction with a view to meeting these conditions and thus bring about a speedy assimilation of the English and Canadian people'. Evening courses were organized covering dressmaking, home upholstery, first aid, home nursing, dairying, bee-keeping, infant care, boot repairing and citizenship. It was also publicized that 'an experienced Canadian lady shall travel with all large parties of soldiers' dependants to advise them *en route*'.[12]

There is little indication that a similar level of thought was given to the future of the British women who had joined the Queen Mary's Army Auxiliary Corps or who had served as nurses, drivers or administrative staff with organizations such as the RAMC, the VAD, the British Red Cross, the St John Ambulance Brigade, the Friends' Ambulance Unit or the First Aid Nursing Yeomanry. In total some 80,000 women had joined these various units and of these around 10,000 were serving in France when the war ended.[13] A proportion of these women were from well-to-do backgrounds and, on demobilization, had little need for paid work. Many, however, had grown accustomed to a regular income and a measure of independence and, with the coming of peace, wished to enter the labour market. It soon became apparent that they were in competition with returning soldiers as well as the 1.5 million women demobilized from the munitions industry who were also looking for jobs. In general, women, especially married women, were expected to leave the way clear for returning soldiers to find work. The main refuge of women was therefore in domestic occupations as it had been before the war. Labour exchanges reported that placements in domestic work increased by 40 per cent during 1919.[14]

As regards demobilization, the Women's War Workers Resettlement Committee recommended that: 'Women who have worked continuously in an organisation under the control of any of the War Departments should be released as far as possible within the organisations with which they are serving in order of priority determined by length of service'. Women 'in combatant Departments, and are mobile and whose term of contract is for the duration of the war' were granted twenty-eight days' furlough on full pay. They were also granted an 'unemployment donation' of 20*s*. per week (men received 24*s*.). Those who were 'in immobile organisations for the duration of the war' were given fourteen days' furlough on full pay and all others were given their contractual notice, but of not less than fourteen days. They received no unemployment pay.[15]

Little help was offered to women to find employment other than that 'women under the control of the War Departments should be brought in touch with the Ministry of Labour machinery by means of Civil Employment Forms' and the tentative suggestion that 'Booklets of Instructions should be prepared for officials and members of the Women's Corps analogous to those for officers and men of His Majesty's Forces'. The Women's War Workers Resettlement Committee suggested that those seeking employment might become prison wardresses or, failing that, consider emigrating.[16] The official attitude was clearly that the pre-war working situation should be resumed and that any woman who wanted work would have to find it herself.

British military units returning from abroad were given enthusiastic receptions particularly when they reached their home towns. An example of this, which also gives an indication of the effects of demobilisation on the size of some units, was recorded in the *Derby Mercury* on 23 May 1919:

> Derby townspeople turned out in their thousands on Sunday morning to welcome home the cadre of the 1st Battalion Sherwood Foresters (Notts and Derby Regiment) … the cadre had been the guests of the City of Nottingham the previous day. The Deputy Mayor, who was accompanied on the platform by members of the Corporation, extended Derby's cordial welcome … Lieut-Colonel Mitchell, DSO, replied on behalf of the cadre of the battalion (5 officers and 36 men) and on behalf of the whole battalion now practically demobilised.

Individual soldiers, having left the army, were frequently welcomed home by local organizations. The Derwent Foundry in Derby held a dinner on 19 May 1919 in The Royal Hotel in honour of its employees who had recently been demobilized. 'The Chairman pledged the health of the Soldier Boys and gave them a hearty welcome back to Derby and to the firm'.[17] Corporal Holmes VC, of the King's Own Yorkshire Light Infantry, received, understandably, a hero's welcome when he returned to his home in Bermondsey in January 1919. The *Manchester Guardian* reported that Corporal Holmes 'turned his smiling face towards the little low-browed house … Here was the welcome he wanted most. His mother, a large matron, was standing in the doorway, and on chairs against the wall was a grand stand of his relations'.[18]

While most soldiers received a similar warm welcome, formally at some official function or informally within the family circle, there were, inevitably, instances of domestic discord. Arthur Page was demobilized in February 1919 and, for a time, lived with his wife in the home of his mother-in-law. He was receiving 29*s*. per week out of work pay, 16*s*. 6*d*. per week pension, and 6*s*. per week for one child. He had also received his gratuity payment. His wife, whom he had married in April 1918, alleged that Page had not given her any money and she summoned him for desertion. Page claimed that he could not live with his mother-in-law and had taken rooms elsewhere. At the trial, the judge encouraged some amicable arrangement between Page and his wife, suggesting that they should live together away from the mother-in-law, but Mrs Page refused to live with her husband. The outcome was that Page was ordered to pay £1 per week to his wife who was to have custody of the child. The judge's concluding remark was that: 'When a man marries a wife he should marry her and not the rest of the family'.[19] After serving four years in France, Salonika, Serbia, Palestine and Egypt, Henry Delahaye experienced a particularly grim homecoming. The *Observer* reported that Delahaye 'found his wife away in the public house – she had given way to drink – he learned that two of his children were dead and there was an illegitimate child'. The report ended: 'I fear there will be many men come home to find that things have not gone as they ought to have done'.[20]

A pressing issue for the British government was the plight of British prisoners of war. By the end of the war 168,000 British troops were held as prisoners (around 5 per cent of the army).[21] To this number should be added 20,000 prisoners from the Dominions. It is estimated that many hundreds of prisoners, counted among the British 'missing', were also in captivity but were not registered by the Germans. One estimate gives an 'unregistered' figure of 2,000.[22] Of the total number of prisoners, 165,000 were captured on the Western Front mainly during the 2 periods of mobile warfare in August–November 1914 and March–June 1918.

Those who were captured on the Western Front were spread about in over 300 camps in France, Belgium and Germany with officers (placed in Offizierslager) separated from Other Ranks (in Mannschlaftslager). Conditions were variable, but generally they were poor. The Hague Conventions of 1899 and 1907 set out how prisoners of war should be treated. Chapter II, Article 4 stipulated that prisoners should be dealt with in a humane manner. Article 6 allowed prisoners to be used as labourers 'but tasks should not be excessive and shall have no connection with the operations of war'. And Article 7 stated that 'prisoners of war shall be treated as regards board, lodging and clothing on the same footing as the troops of the Government who captured them'. These international rules of conduct were often ignored by the Germans. Brigadier General J.H. Morgan, who was on the Adjutant General's staff in France in 1915, later wrote that he had seen an army order from Prince Rupprecht, the commander of the Bavarian troops, instructing his soldiers to treat British prisoners with 'particular ferocity' – a reaction to the naval blockade imposed by the British.[23] Sir James Edmonds, the British Official Historian, concluded that while the treatment of British prisoners varied from camp to camp:

> there is no doubt that in the majority of them gross cruelty and brutality were either deliberately practised or allowed to obtain though indifference ... At one camp there was only one medical officer for 13,000 prisoners; at another, where about a thousand men were working, there was no medical officer at all ... During the

> reburial of prisoners who had died in captivity, a number were found with their skulls battered in.[24]

The feelings of Private Herbert Gutteridge, who was captured in April 1918 while serving with the 16th Battalion, Kings Royal Rifle Corps near Bailleul, were no doubt similar to those of many prisoners: 'For me the next eight months [in captivity] were the most unhappy, miserable, horrible months of my life'.[25]

As the war progressed the effects of the British naval blockade meant that the rations of German soldiers gradually worsened both in quantity and quality. It was therefore inevitable that prisoners of war suffered accordingly with food that was meagre and of limited nutritional value. Many British prisoners survived only because of the food parcels sent by organizations such as the International Red Cross, the Order of St John and from local groups in England. When Private W. Holland, of the Sherwood Foresters, returned home to Dove Holes in Derbyshire in January 1919 he stressed that: 'The hardships of a prisoner's life were considerably mitigated by the supply of parcels which he had received from his depot in Lichfield'.[26] Private Dawe of Chapel-en-le-Frith praised 'the grand work of the British Red Cross Society. I am grateful for their goodness to us; the parcels have been the saving of our lives'.[27] The Wendover Red Cross Working Party adopted a POW in Germany – Private Glynn of the 17th Battalion the Middlesex Regiment – and sent two parcels each month. A Mrs Walter Stevens, a member of that working party, ensured that the monthly administration fee of 2 guineas was sent to the Central Red Cross organization.[28] The efforts of countless individuals to send food parcels was regularized from November 1916 when Regimental Care Committees were set up. One such Committee, that of the Royal Scots, regularly sent three parcels per fortnight to each prisoner connected to the regiment.[29] The Care Committee of the Queen's Own Royal West Kent Regiment sent 52,203 food parcels to prisoners in Germany and 95 parcels to Turkey.[30]

The lack of food, together with harsh treatment, forced labour, poor hygiene and disease, resulted in an official total (thought to be considerably under-stated) of 16,402 deaths among British and Empire prisoners in France and Germany.[31] Since the chances of being killed as a British soldier on the Western Front during the war was around 1 in 8 and the death rate among prisoners of war was around 1 in 10, there was clearly little difference, from the point of view of survival, between active service and life in a prison camp.

The repatriation of British prisoners of war from France, considering the rail and shipping problems of the time, was carried out with reasonable speed and the first group was transported from Dunkirk to Dover on 15 November. By 23 January 1919, 7,176 officers and 150,847 other ranks had reached England. Among these were 12,546 men 'in medical charge'.[32] The last repatriations took place in March 1919. The returning prisoners had mixed emotions. They were naturally relieved and thankful to be on their way home and to be shortly reunited with their families and friends. But they were also aware that, as prisoners of war, they had surrendered to the enemy and their reception might be, at best, muted. As Private William Tucker wrote: 'All prisoners, or all those with normal reactions, suffer a sense of humiliation for having been captured and, if only for that reason we did not look for or expect any tumultuous reception on our return home'.[33]

Prisoners of war were, however, welcomed home no less enthusiastically than troops returning from active service. Prisoners Reception Committees were ready with tea, sandwiches and bags of cakes at Dover, Leith and Hull, the main ports of arrival. Bands played and crowds waved. The ex-prisoners were given a good meal and then sent off to the dispersal centres. Here they were disinfected and given a complete set of new clothes including a uniform or an overcoat. They received identity cards, travel vouchers and back pay, and completed forms about their treatment in the camps. Officers were obliged to write about the circumstances of their capture.

When they returned home, ex-prisoners, many of them withdrawn and bemused by the situation, continued to receive a hero's welcome. On 6 December 1918 the *Ashbourne Telegraph* reported:

> Enthusiastic scenes have again been witnessed in Ashbourne and Clifton during the week end on the return of several more local prisoners of war ... On Friday evening Private Pegge of Clifton arrived and was met by a bugle band and a large assembly of parishioners and friends. The general feeling of welcome was appropriately expressed in short speeches by the Rev. SH Cubitt (Vicar), and Mr GM Bond, JP, and rousing cheers were given for Pte. Pegge who briefly acknowledged the cordial welcome.

Over the following few days Ashbourne gave similar welcomes to Sergeant R. Taylor of the Pals Manchester Regiment, Private Bertram Plant of the North Staffs Regiment and to Private F. Edge and Private James Renshaw. At Ashton the Mayor gave £5 to each of 183 local ex-prisoners.[34]

Occasionally the information in local newspapers gave some insight into an ex-prisoner's experience. The *High Peak News* of 11 January 1919 reported:

> All are pleased to welcome home Pte W Holland, of the Sherwood Foresters, who has been a prisoner of war in Germany. It is now nearly four years since he joined the Army and on one occasion was severely wounded in several places. He has been in Germany for eighteen months, and although his experiences have been quite bad enough, our friend has been fortunate in several ways ... Pte Holland brings back with him a piece of black bread which was given him as a ration on Christmas Day. This is now as hard as a piece of brick, and totally unfit for food. For some time Pte Holland acted as a stretcher bearer in one of the German prison camps, after which he was a valet to a doctor.

At Chapel-en-le-Frith, there was a welcome home gathering on 18 January 1919 for ex-prisoners Corporal Robert Jowle and Private J.F. Allen. Company Quarter Master Sergeant J. Ford, himself a recently returned prisoner, spoke, as recorded in the *High Peak News*, 25 January 1919:

> I feel it is up to me to thank you all for our reception. I can't help but remark on the welcome that the people of England have extended to us. As we approached Hull, scores of ships were lined up, and three sirens sounded out 'Welcome'. As we landed a message from the King was read to us, and the welcome continued with us as our train passed through the country. We have indeed had a great welcome.

The 'great welcome' was continued when every ex-prisoner received a signed letter from the King:

> The Queen joins me in welcoming you on your release from the miseries & hardships, which you have endured with so much patience. During these many months of trial, the early rescue of our gallant Officers & Men from the cruelty of their captivity has been uppermost in our thoughts. We are thankful that this longed for day has arrived, & that back in the old Country you will be able once more to enjoy the happiness of a home & to see good days among those who anxiously look for your return.[35]

Unfortunately not every ex-prisoner was to experience 'happiness' and 'good days'. For some, disillusion began immediately after returning to England when, at the dispersal centres, ex-prisoners were offered a choice of either applying for a pension, which entailed a medical and a delay of several days before returning home, or a gratuity of £2. The gratuity could only be received if a form was completed disclaiming any war-related injury. Many took the £2 just to avoid form-filling and to speed their return to their families. Corporal Alfred Schofield, took the £2 option and later regretted his decision. Schofield returned home to his wife and children suffering from acute depression and memory loss. He was killed when he walked in front of a train near London on 23 February 1922. Mrs Schofield applied for a pension for herself and her two children but her application, and a later appeal, was turned down because her husband had taken the £2 gratuity and had completed the form saying that he was not suffering as a result of the war.[36] There were many ex-prisoners who received the same treatment as Schofield.

Because of their suffering and malnutrition in the prison camps many men were ill-prepared for the English winter of 1918–19, especially with the re-emergence of the influenza epidemic. A notable example was Captain Leefe Robinson VC who had received brutal treatment in the Holzminden Camp and who had returned home in extremely poor health. On 31 December 1918 Robinson contracted the 'flu' and died. In the 1920s and 1930s the mortality rate of ex-prisoners was five times higher than that of other veterans.[37]

Perhaps those prisoners of war who survived and were able to return home from their ordeal could have gained some satisfaction if the camp commandants and guards who had treated them so badly had been brought to justice and punished for their conduct. This was not to be.[38] Indeed, the German authorities were inclined to give little help in providing information about the precise number of Allied prisoners and their whereabouts. A review dated 9 January 1919 estimated that there was a discrepancy of 22,000 between the British account of prisoners of war and the figures given by the Germans. There is no record of this discrepancy ever being resolved.[39] The Versailles Peace Treaty, Article 228, sanctioned the 'right of the Allied and Associated Powers to bring before military tribunal persons accused of having committed acts in violation of the laws and customs of war'. There was an original list of 853 Germans with the rank of general and below, who were wanted for extradition to face trial for war crimes, in many cases against prisoners of war. But a policy of appeasement developed. It was brought about by the fear that an extensive persecution of war crimes would act to destabilize Germany even more than it already was and encourage the spread of Bolshevism. The Allied governments allowed the trials, which eventually took place in Leipzig, to be conducted by German officials. The outcome of the trials was, predictably under the prevailing political climate, a failure of justice. The number of Allied cases was heavily reduced with Britain pursuing only seven and these resulted in token sentences. A motion in the House of Commons for a debate on the trials was defeated. The British Official Historian, Edmonds, was politically constrained when compiling his volume on 1918–29 and sections of his work were criticized for presenting Germany in a bad light. Publication was delayed until 1945 and then in a limited edition of 100.[40] In 1947 the type of the volume was destroyed and it was not until 1987 that a copy in the hands of the Imperial War Museum was reprinted for public use.[41] British prisoners who had been held in Germany were not well-served.

POWs in the African theatre of war were reasonably well treated. There were around 2,000 British and Belgian prisoners in East Africa, mainly held at Tabora. The Germans allowed them to walk outside the prison area and no roll call was taken. At the end of the war the prisoners made their way by foot and train to Mombasa and thence to England. On their journey to Mombasa they flew a large Union Jack made up of a blue sheet, a red tablecloth and a white apron. An African was hired to carry it. In the South African camp at Tsumeb the British prisoners were well-cared for with adequate food and clothing and even the occasional beer. The main complaint came from a prisoner who was indignant that 'white men should be guarded by Hottentots'.[42] There were some 13,500 POWs held by the Turks in the Mesopotamian theatre. Life was hard and many died. Immediately after the Armistice the prisoners were gathered in Constantinople and shipped home.

A particular demobilization problem for the government concerned conscientious objectors. The introduction of the Military Service Act of January 1916 meant that every eligible man was liable to be drafted into war service. However, there was provision within the Act to exempt those with a conscientious objection to combatant service. Local tribunals examined those who claimed exemption in an effort to sift genuine conscientious objectors from those who just wanted to dodge the war. It soon became clear that the issue was fraught with difficulties. Was acceptable objection to be based on moral, political or religious grounds? How was the genuine objector to be identified? What was being objected to – directly taking another man's life or taking part in the process of war? And what should be done with the objectors? The whole process was carried out against a background of widespread hostility against the objectors who were often labelled cowards and shirkers.

A total of 16,600 conscientious objectors were registered during the war – a minute proportion, a third of 1 per cent, of those who enlisted. Some took on work on farms or in factories. Others joined the Non-Combatants Corps or the RAMC and, although refusing to bear arms, carried out dangerous work near the front line. Among this group was the Friends' Ambulance Unit. The 'absolutists' were the hardcore who refused to accept conscription, the tribunals, military orders or work of any kind that might contribute to the war effort. During the war there were some 1,350 of these and they were often subjected to great hardship and repeated imprisonment with hard labour. In March 1919 the then Home Secretary, Edward Short, announced that there were 947 'absolutist' conscientious objectors currently serving sentences and, of that total, '732 have served in the aggregate more than 12 months' imprisonment with hard labour'.[43]

When demobilization came, conscientious objectors were an inconvenience to the government. Hansard records that on 3 April 1919 the Marquess of Landsdowne made the point in the House of Lords: 'at a moment when demobilisation is not yet completed it might have a very unfortunate effect upon men serving in the Army if these people were released from prison ... they might occupy a number of attractive posts to the exclusion of meritorious soldiers'. Sir William Whitla, speaking in the House of Commons on 26 February, was particularly bitter and suggested that the services of conscientious objectors 'may be utilised for the cleansing of latrines in different camps at home and abroad, a duty presently imposed on fighting men'. On the same day Churchill commented that he was not inclined 'to consider general issues involved in these questions until demobilisation had made further progress'. The Post Office took the same line and the Post Master General stated in February 1919 that 'there is no intention of reinstating' conscientious objectors and that 'their position will be considered later when demobilisation is further advanced'.[44] As far as the government was concerned, there was no hurry in dealing with what had become an embarrassment. It was not until the end of July 1919, nine months after the Armistice, that the final group of conscientious objectors were released into civilian life. The absolutists were disenfranchised for years after the war had ended.

In January 1919 there were 122,120 German prisoners in Britain captured mainly in 1917 and 1918. While the terms of the Armistice demanded the immediate release of Allied prisoners, this was to be done 'without reciprosity'. German prisoners were useful on the land and for general labouring work and by May 1919 only 30,000 had been sent home. Repatriation was accelerated after the Versailles Treaty and on 21 August Churchill ordered that 'repatriation should begin immediately. Their work is done, they are costing us more than £30,000 a day ... The operation will begin at the earliest possible moment and at latest by September 1.'[45] By December 1919 only 3,621 Germans were still in Britain and these had all been shipped home by the end of January 1920.[46]

Among the millions of demobilized soldiers was a group requiring special attention – the disabled. It is estimated that of those who returned from the war around a quarter suffered from some form of disability;

41,000 men had lost at least one limb.[47] Sir Douglas Haig was a forceful advocate for the disabled. On 21 November 1918 he wrote to the CIGS, General Wilson: 'I feel very strongly regarding the way the disabled, the widows and the children have been neglected up to date. And I consider that it would be very wrong of me to accept any reward until the government gives a definite assurance that they will receive adequate help in a practical way'.[48] On 27 November Haig noted in his Diary: 'On the way to Montreuil, the King said to me that he had told the PM to offer me a peerage. I replied that I had been offered a Viscountcy, but had requested leave to decline accepting any reward until adequate grants for our disabled had been voted.'[49]

Haig had a particular concern for disabled officers. The government had made the assumption that officers in general would be able to cope with their infirmity from private means and were content to leave cases of hardship to charity. A year before the end of the war Haig had written to the War Office recommending that disabled officers should receive a pension which, for the totally disabled, should be at a level that would be 'sufficient to maintain them in reasonable comfort'. Haig also proposed that the disabled should receive suitable remunerative employment and appropriate medical benefits. The letter ended: 'I strongly urge that there should be no delay in dealing with this matter, which, if allowed to continue, will constitute a scandal of great magnitude'.[50]

It was on this same issue that, on 26 November 1918, Haig wrote to the War Office:

> the problem presented by large numbers of officers unable through their injuries to support themselves in circumstances appropriate to their standing in the Army is thought to be one which has not yet received the attention that it deserves … The present assistance available for officers who have been disabled, it is understood, is limited to a wound gratuity and a wound pension in addition to the war bounty given under the Royal Warrant to those who were not in the Permanent Forces. Though the scale on which those grants are made is relatively generous they do not yet meet the problem of the officer who, without private means, is called to face life handicapped by total or partial disablement. Even the maximum wound pension given to the totally disabled would not permit a retired officer to live in a manner befitting the position he has filled in the Army. It would be most undesirable that the form in which assistance is given should be in the nature of charity, as being both distasteful and humiliating to natural feelings of personal respect, pride and independence.[51]

Haig was a tireless advocate for the disabled officer and brought to the attention of General Wilson many examples of apparently heartless decisions made by the pensions authorities. One such, wrote Haig, was 'a dentist [who] gave up everything and took a commission. Two and a half years in France having an awful time, never sick or sorry for a day. He was sent to Italy where he was gassed. A gratuity was refused, as before he joined the army he had double pneumonia and went for a short time to a sanatorium'.[52]

The government first approached the problem of the disabled in May 1916 by forming the War Injury Pensions Committee. In December 1918 this Committee published pension levels for NCOs and Other Ranks according to a scale of severity and the rank of the recipient. There were seven degrees of severity from 100 per cent to 20 per cent disability. A fully (100 per cent) disabled private, for example, would receive 27*s*. 6*d*. per week while a WO I would receive 42*s*. 6*d*. For the private it was a sum little different from the wage of an unskilled labourer. A private who had lost an entire right arm (90 per cent disability) would get 24*s*. 9*d*. while a WO I would receive 38*s*. 3*d*. A private who had lost his left arm above the elbow (60 per cent disability) was compensated at the rate of 16*s*. 6*d*. per week. If the same man had lost an arm below the elbow he would receive 13*s*. 9*d*. The left arm was valued less generously than the right arm, though a footnote to the pension schedule thoughtfully noted: 'In the case of left-handed men, certified as such, the compensation in respect of the left arm, hand etc. will be the same as the right arm, etc.'. The same mechanistic logic was applied to other parts of the body.[53] This approach almost certainly disadvantaged the private as against more senior ranks in that the private was far more likely to have been a manual worker and would therefore find it more difficult to get work.

It was not until November 1919 that the Ministry of Pensions produced 'A Disabled Officer's Handbook on Gratuity, Retired Pay, Etc., On Discharge From Service'. (See Appendix IV.) It summarized the allowances as: 'A War service gratuity from the War Office paid to an Officer whether disabled or not; A Wound Gratuity or pension from the War Office; Retired pay or gratuity (corresponding to the disablement pension or gratuity awarded to non-commissioned ranks) from the Ministry of Pensions'. The Handbook set out a highly complicated series of disability payments according to rank, degree of disablement and whether the individual held a Permanent or Temporary Commission. The highest pension for a Temporary Commissioned Officer was set at £350 per year for a major general with 100 per cent disability down to £35 for a second lieutenant with a 20 per cent disability.[54] The government's approach to compensation for the disabled could be criticized for lacking both logic and the human touch. The problem was that the number of disabled was vast and the authorities found it impossible to devise what would inevitably be a more complicated system focused on an individual's specific needs.

In December 1919 the Minister of Pensions, Sir L. Worthington-Evans, informed the House of Commons that: 'The number of persons receiving pensions was 2,621,313. These included 33,876 Officers and Nurses; 1,025,460 Men of other ranks; 9,775 Widows of Officers; 179,712 Widows of other ranks; 5,680 Other dependents of officers; 327,820 Other dependents of other ranks; 9,112 Children of officers and officers' widows; and, 1,029,878 Children of other ranks'.[55] These startling numbers can only be regarded as under-stating the problem in that illnesses associated with war service often took years to develop. The Pensions Act stated that claims had to be made within seven years of the date of discharge from the army thus excluding ex-servicemen whose disability became apparent after that time.[56]

This ruling excluded many cases of 'shell shock', or what would later be called post-traumatic stress, on the grounds that the symptoms were not registered during the war.[57] Both public and official attitudes to those suffering from shell shock were confused. The thought had developed that shell shock was equivalent to lunacy. Although a report to the House of Lords in 1915 had stated that the War Office 'had no intention of treating these unfortunate men as ordinary lunatics', the number of ex-servicemen in public asylums increased by more than 40 per cent between early 1920 and October 1921. A charity, the Ex-Services Welfare Society, was set up specifically to support psychological casualties and their families. It reported in November 1924 that 5,000 ex-servicemen were in pauper lunatic asylums.[58] In 1922, some 50,000 men were in receipt of pensions as mental cases.[59]

The national administration of pensions was cumbersome and slow-moving – the result of a centralized and bureaucratic system that was made up of some 2,200 Local War Pensions Committees. These Committees had little discretion and were obliged to make constant references to the headquarters in London. Various veterans' associations such as NADSS, NFDDSS, CGW and the Soldiers, Sailors and Airmen's Union (SSAU) put pressure on the government to improve both the administration and the level of pensions. These associations were instrumental in bringing about the government pension changes of August 1919.

When Sir L. Worthington-Evans visited Manchester on 7 August 1919 he outlined proposed improvements: 'the new scheme was framed in the interests of the disabled man, his widow, dependents, and children. In the course of the last week the scale of pensions had been considerably increased and what was required now was to secure good and speedy administration and the removal of any grounds of mistrust'. The future organization was to be based on regions. Manchester would be the headquarters of the north-western region with fifty-four Local War Pensions Committees:

> which in future would make their references to the headquarters in Manchester instead of London. Roughly, the men pensioners in this area would be just over 100,000, the widows about 27,000 and the dependents about 40,000… … the Chief Medical Officer would be primarily responsible for seeing that there was sufficient hospital accommodation and enough clinics attached to hospitals to take the treatment as near as possible to the homes of the men.

The meeting agreed that 'these were steps in the right direction'.[60]

There were other efforts to help the disabled. The King's National Roll scheme encouraged employers to take on disabled servicemen to a minimum of 5 per cent of their workforce. Government departments and local authorities, when awarding contracts, gave preference to firms on the King's Roll. By 1926, 365,000 disabled men were employed in 28,000 firms.[61] Various training programmes were introduced. The Board of Agriculture was responsible for the training of men in horticulture. At the Carrington Nursey, near Manchester, the Board supplied 'huts, bedding and cooking utensils … These men are to be paid their full pension during the time of training'.[62] After a period of training at St Dunstan's Hostel, Private W.G. Parker, blinded in August 1916, became a 'proficient telephone operator. He memorises many numbers, and he has also formed a self-made directory in Braille'.[63] Lord Reith staffed the 'Addressing Department' of the *Radio Times* with facially disfigured veterans

A number of organizations were founded during the war to help disabled soldiers. Among these was the Star and Garter Home in Richmond which opened in January 1916 under the auspices of the British Red Cross Society. Soldiers received nursing and therapeutic care and training in various skills. In 1917 the New Zealand surgeon Harold Gillies established the first plastic surgery unit for disfigured soldiers at the Queen's Hospital in Sidcup. The Lord Roberts Workshops gave disabled soldiers the opportunity to learn craft skills such as basket- and furniture-making. By 1920 there were twenty such workshops. St Mary's Hospital in Roehampton, founded by Mrs Gwynne Holford in 1915, became a leading centre for limb fitting and the rehabilitation of amputees. From 25 beds in 1915 it grew to 900 beds in 1918. That there was a waiting list of 4,000 for St Mary's in 1918 gives some indication of size of the problem faced by the country in caring for the seriously disabled.

At a meeting in Glasgow on 21 August 1919, Sir Robert Horne, the Minister of Labour, announced that: 'Facilities for training men whose injuries had disabled them from following their previous occupations ... were being greatly increased. He had succeeded in making arrangements whereby partially disabled men who were undergoing training would receive the full pension allowance given to entirely disabled men'.[64]

It was inevitable, however, that the more seriously disabled found it difficult to find any kind of work and this problem was discussed in a joint memorandum to the Cabinet from the Minister of Pensions and the Minister of Labour dated 4 December 1918: 'We see very little prospect that the whole number of men who are fit only for light work can be absorbed into industrial and commercial employment through the ordinary operation of the demand for labour'.[65] Their proposal was to give more seriously disabled men a measure of priority when competing for jobs in certain occupations. Examples of the occupations included are: lift attendant, watchmaker, gatekeeper, timekeeper, caretaker and billiard marker. However, the implementation of this proposal was 'to rely on the voluntary action of employers ... avoiding any measure of compulsion'. When unemployment increased later in the 1920s, the disabled were frequently among the first to lose their jobs. It was estimated that in March 1924, 38,000 disabled men were unemployed. Nevertheless, in a relative sense there is evidence to suggest that the wide-ranging efforts to find work for the disabled was not without success. In mid-1924, of the total number of men, able-bodied and disabled, who were covered by unemployment insurance, 1 in 10 were unemployed. The figure for disabled men alone was 1 in 20.[66]

Since Haig strongly believed that charitable giving should not be relied on to support the disabled it was somewhat ironic that the British Legion, formed with Haig's support in June 1921 and with Haig as president, introduced the annual Poppy Day. The red Flanders poppy became the symbol of the Legion and of remembrance and the proceeds from the sale of poppies has contributed significant sums of money annually for the benefit of disabled soldiers. The first Poppy Day in 1921 was a great success and, because of the profusion of poppies, London was described as a 'scarlet city'. A total of £106,000 was raised on that occasion and it was generally thought fitting that each poppy bore the inscription 'Haig Fund'.[67]

Once he had been demobilized the prime task of the ex-serviceman was to find work. Many complications arose. In Salford, the Council had promised to reinstate all servants on their return from war, but the application of a demobilized ex-policeman to resume duty was turned down by the Watch Committee because the man had 'committed an offence in the Army'. The Salford Council discussed the case and, on the grounds that the man had already been punished by the army, recommended to the Watch Committee that the man should be reinstated.[68]

The issue of reinstatement was far from straightforward. Employees who had joined an organization during the war and replaced individuals who had enlisted in 1914 may themselves have later joined the forces and been replaced. Employers were often obliged to choose between several ex-employees who were claiming reinstatement to the same job. Salford Gas Corporation dealt with the problem by announcing: 'Men who were in the service of the department before 8 August 1914 are to be reinstated … under the same conditions as would be obtained had there been no war … those who entered the department after 8 August 1914 will not be reinstated if there are no vacancies'.[69]

The issue of women 'keeping ex-servicemen out of their old jobs' was highly sensitive. On 31 May 1919 a leading article in a Manchester newspaper was headed 'Women Workers in Soldiers' Jobs'. It asked the question 'Are we on the eve of a new sex war?' The article pointed out that 'while there were 17,000 ex-soldiers drawing unemployment pay in the Manchester area last week, there were 18,000 women in the same position … the required readjustment of male and female labour is far from simple'.[70] In June 1919 the Manchester Corporation Parks Committee was criticized for employing women. 'Demobilised heroes who have gone to the Whitworth Institute in order to obtain their out-of-work dole have witnessed the spectacle on the last three mornings of three women engaged in the task of mowing the grass. This has caused some of the demobbed furiously to think and to speak'. However, the Parks Committee was able to point out 'that these women have taken the place of men who have not yet returned to the service of the Corporation. These women will have to go as soon as the men come back'.[71] One commentator observed:

> The flapper of 1914 [is now] a woman of 22 or 23 at the present time and it is not much use saying she ought to give up work because she did not work before the war. What is to become of her? Some people tell us she ought to be married, but there is a shortage of husbands. At the same time it is the nation's duty to restore ex-soldiers to civil employment. If it fails, the results will be serious.[72]

Many women were obliged to return to domestic work and *The Times* regularly carried half a dozen columns of advertisements for female servants.[73]

Minimal government support was given to soldiers' widows and their children. It was not until 16 August 1914, twelve days after the declaration of war, that the government, through the War Council, announced that separation allowances and widows' pensions would be available for all wives. For a private's wife the separation allowance was set at 11*s*. 6*d*. per week, the widow's pension at 5*s*. per week with 1*s*. 6*d*. per week for each child. If a war widow were to re-marry she would receive a one-off gratuity of £13.

In October 1914 these payments were reviewed and the pension level for the widow of a private became 7*s*. 6*d*. per week. The rates of payment were graded according to rank with the widow of a colonel eligible for £200 per year. Following a report from a Select Committee in 1915 the payments were again increased. Separation allowances began at 12*s*. 6*d*. plus additional amounts for children. Pensions were increased to a minimum of 10*s*. per week and re-marriage gratuity went up to £39 or a two years' sum. In 1917 an alternative pension system was introduced. If it could be shown that the dead soldier's civilian earnings were greater than the level of a total disability pension then the widow could receive a pension at the rate of half the disability amount.

The problem for the government, ever attempting to keep expenditure at a minimum, was the unexpectedly high number of claimants. At the beginning of the war Kitchener had estimated that the total number of war widows would be about 50,000. It was an estimate that proved far from accurate. In 1919 there were 200,000 war widows in receipt of pensions. This number rose to 235,200 in 1921. It was indicative of the rapid increase in the number of war widows that the staff of the Pensions Issue Office increased from 20 in January 1915 to 4,262 in March 1920.

The level of a widow's pension was miserly. The *Daily Express*, in September 1914, described it as 'a paltry allowance' and 'contemptible in the extreme'. Subsequent increases did not alter that situation. The wage of a labourer at that time was 27*s*. per week and of a skilled worker around 35*s*. per week. Even though additional financial help was often provided by charities, notably the Prince of Wales National Relief Fund and the Soldiers and Sailors Families Association, the war widow had great difficulty in making ends meet. Matters were not helped by the heavy bureaucracy that surrounded the system. The widow had the task of completing an application form and having it counter-signed by a responsible person. Pensions could be stopped if the widow was thought to be 'misbehaving'. Pensions could be claimed only if the soldier's death was proved to be due to military service and death had to be within seven years of the original war injury. When queries arose the burden of proof rested with the widow. All in all, the government's arrangements for war widows were neither generous nor administered in a way that could be described as particularly sympathetic.[74]

Fortunately for the returning soldiers, and for the government who feared unemployment and its potentially dire consequences, the economy experienced a mini-post-war boom. Available unemployment figures show that unemployment for the period 1910–14 averaged some 4 per cent.[75] During the war years unemployment was, understandably, very low averaging around 0.8 per cent. Then, in 1919, as industry and commerce adjusted themselves to post-war conditions and soldiers returned home, the figure rose to 6 per cent falling to 3.9 per cent in 1920. After 1920 serious levels of unemployment occurred moving to 16.9 per cent in 1921 and 14.3 per cent in 1922. The remainder of the 1920s averaged around 10 per cent with 1927 at 9.7 per cent and 1926 at 12.5 per cent. These figures therefore show that unemployment for 1919–20 was relatively low and differed little from pre-war levels. From the point of view of many demobilized soldiers, these years provided a short period of employment opportunities.[76] Sir Douglas Haig was able to write, on the first anniversary of the Armistice, 11 November 1919: 'It is satisfactory to learn that 90 per cent of those who have been demobilised during the past year have already been absorbed into civil life'.[77]

The generally low unemployment rates immediately after the war masked significant differences from one industry to another. At the end of 1918, for example, there was low unemployment in the chemical industry at 2.9 per cent, in clocks and jewellery 1.1 per cent and in iron and steel 1.1 per cent. However, in metal work the rate was 6.3 per cent and in engineering 5.9 per cent.[78] At the end of January 1919 most of the industries for which figures are available showed an increase in numbers employed as compared with the beginning of November 1918. Employment in the building industry was up by 4 per cent, clothing by 5.5 per cent, paper and printing by 7.2 per cent and food, drink and tobacco by 5.1 per cent. On the other hand jobs affected by the cessation of war, arsenals, dockyards and national factories, fell by 26.9 per cent.[79]

There were, then, signs in the wider economy that job prospects were improving in 1919 though those prospects often depended on the ex-soldier's level of skill. By mid-1919 it was not unusual for local newspapers to advertise several columns of job vacancies each week. In June, for example, there were opportunities in the Manchester area for slaters, tilers, piano repairers, sheet metal workers, platers, experienced motor mechanics and fitters. British Westinghouse in Trafford Park advertised for a wide range of skilled men including a blacksmith, a grinder, a joiner, a moulder and a tinsmith. There was an opportunity for 'a young man … as Night Chargehand, preferably a discharged soldier now able to follow ordinary employment'. And Pemberton's of Deansgate, Manchester, placed an advertisement: 'Fed Up, Out of Work? Take that Demobbed Course of Motoring ... A Trade in Your Fingers in a Week'.[80] There was even the opportunity to transfer from one industry to another. In West Lancashire there was a shortage of skilled farm workers: 'thousands of acres had not been touched by the plough [because] discharged soldiers who had previously been farm workers preferred better paid employment'.[81] Skilled manual workers were generally able to find a job, but those without such a skill, no matter how personable, often struggled. An article in the *Manchester Evening Chronicle*, also in June 1919, read:

> While there seems to be a shortage of skilled mechanics the market is glutted with men who have 'brains and business ability' to sell. A businessman who had recently advertised for an outdoor salesman showed a pile of letters he had received. There were something like 300 in all and most of the applicants were Army officers ... all keenly anxious for the job, which was only worth £5 a week.

Similarly, an entry in the 'Jobs Wanted' section of the 1 February 1919 *Manchester Guardian* read: 'Gentlemanly man, demobilised, good appearance and address, well-educated, thoroughly reliable, brains, has had business experience, wishes position at nominal salary with object of securing Traveller or Salesman's position'.

Some government schemes to provide employment for returning troops were still-born. Much had been said during the war about the benefits of providing parcels of land for ex-soldiers. Christopher Addison, the ex-Minister of Reconstruction, later noted that a scheme was developed 'by practical men ... which lacked nothing in comprehensiveness and contained some very drastic provisions'. Tracts of land were to be bought by county councils, if necessary by compulsory purchase, which could become 'gardens, allotments, small-holdings, housing and otherwise'. Special training was to be given to suitable individuals who would pay a rent for their holding. But, because of the country's 'straightened financial position' the necessary money to buy land was not forthcoming. 'Thousands of men who had been passed, after a rigid scrutiny, as approved applicants were left unprovided for'. Addison bitterly commented: 'In the end [the scheme] was as completely and effectively torpedoed as any set of projects prepared for the post-war period'.[82] By 1921 only 9,000 men had been allotted smallholdings. The failure of the land settlement programme was a major factor in the government's encouragement of ex-servicemen to emigrate to parts of the Empire. In April 1919 it was announced that free passage to the Dominions would be available, for a limited period, for ex-soldiers and their dependants and a total of around 86,000 men, women and children took up this offer.[83]

While the employment situation improved through most of 1920 the year ended with disappointment. An article in The *Times* on 20 December 1920 was headed 'The Debt of Honour: Barometer Still Going Down'. The article gave the numbers of the unemployed at the beginning of December under the categories Disabled Men, Ex-Servicemen, and Officers. In each case the figures, compared with those of November, had increased. 'The progress made month by month up till September was continuous and steady … Since then the barometer began to fall and the downwards tendency still continues. Many of the men already settled in industry are being thrown back on the unemployment registers, and this applies not only to the fit ex-servicemen, but to the disabled and ex-officers'. In London the number and frequency of street collections for the unemployed had increased to such an extent that the Commissioner of Police introduced new regulations to ensure that bona fide organizations 'may be helped, while the public will be protected from annoyance and imposition by doubtful or unscrupulous collectors'. The mini-boom of 1919–20 had arrived suddenly and unexpectedly. It disappeared with equal speed and with desperate consequences for the British workforce.

Chapter 5

Dismantling

The dismantling of the infra-structure that supported the British Army presented a series of difficult problems. After the Armistice, the massive amounts of supplies and equipment necessary for the prosecution of the war became redundant – at any rate in relation to its original purpose. In some way or other all the surplus equipment had to be accounted for and disposed of. At least, stores and equipment were inanimate and some time could be spent in deciding what to do with them. More pressing was the problem of dealing with the livestock that had played such an important part in the war effort – particularly the vast numbers of horses and mules. Horses had provided a reliable means of transport for officers and the cavalry and, together with mules, had pulled and carried supplies, ammunition and guns to the front line – generally in highly dangerous and inhospitable conditions. The use of vehicles, even tracked vehicles with an internal combustion engine, was limited because of the nature of the terrain and the condition of the ground. In the First World War, an army could not function without the horse and the mule.

In August 1914 the BEF had 25,000 horses with a further 25,000 in reserve under the care of farmers and landowners. However, it was estimated that a total of 165,000 horses would be required immediately and the balance of 115,000 was obtained by means of impressment over a period of 12 days. Impressment was far from popular. As John Grout of the village of Akenfield said: 'A lot of farmers hid their horses ... when the officers came round. The officers always gave good money for a horse, but sometimes the horses were like brothers and the men couldn't let them go so they hid them'.[1] An example of the 'good money' referred to was itemized in a 'Daily Account (6 August 1914) – Purchase of Horses on Mobilisation' in the Mansfield area. A Mr Kirby of Southwell received £360 for eight horses and Messrs Lewin (Halam), Brocklebank (Upton) and James (Bleasby) each had one horse impressed and received £38, £52 and £47 respectively.[2] A Mr Keevil of Melksham in Wiltshire sold thirty-one horses for £1,238 and ten for £466.[3]

It was soon clear that a continuous supply of horses and mules was required and agents were despatched to North America, South America, India and Spain. The number of animals bought in this way, and landed in the UK by the end of the war, was impressive: 617,935 from Canada and the US; 6,148 from South America, mainly Argentina and Uruguay; 331 from India; and 2,889 from Spain. Among these was a total of 209,618 mules. Because of German submarine attacks the transportation of animals across the oceans was not without risk. Of the horses and mules shipped from North America 13,724 were lost at sea.[4]

A report from the Quarter Master General's Office in 1918 throws some light on the various breeds of horse and their suitability for military purposes. It states that:

> Among the heavy draught horses those found the most useful were Clydesdale, Suffolk and the Welch cart horse, but it was not possible to supply the requirements of a large army from these breeds. The next best horse available was the clean-legged American pure bred and half bred Percheron horse. The Shire horse was suitable for heavy traction work in docks. Of light draught horses by far the best was the British or Irish Artillery Horse, and the half-bred American Percheron did very useful work when of the compact type. The Hackney breed generally proved lacking in staying qualities. Among riding horses the British or Irish Cavalry Charger and Troop Horse of the smaller type, and the British Cob were second to none for toughness and ability to maintain their condition in adverse circumstances.[5]

In 1912, in preparation for possible requisition, detailed information was circulated as to the needs of the Army:

> The Household Cavalry need black horses of 4 years, 15.3 hands or at 6 years 16 hands. Cavalry of the Line – the horse needs deep, short legs, short back, good barrel (of the hunter stamp), light, active, and moved easily without brushing of joints. Well ribbed and plenty of bone. Need 1,000 horses. Royal Artillery – need weight carrying hunter. Able to take its place in a gun team in an emergency. At 4 years, 15.2 to 16 hands. Royal Engineers and ASC – draught horses known as 'parcel vanners', able to trot with a good load behind. At 4 years, 15.2 to 15.3 hands. Need 1,300 horses. ASC horses – at 4 years, 15.2 to 15.3 hands.[6]

By November 1918 the British Army, in the various theatres of the war, had 735,409 horses and mules, referred to as remounts. As an indication of its importance, the number of personnel in the Remounts Department (which reported to the War Office) increased from 351 in August 1914 to 18,766 at the end of 1918.[7] On the Western Front, 256,000 horses died in service. Of these, 58,000 were killed by enemy fire. The remainder died mainly from exposure to terrible weather and ground conditions and from digestive and lung problems.[8] Horses and mules suffered particularly badly during the period of the Battle of the Somme. Between 1 July and 31 December 1916, 3,974 animals were killed and 6,415 were wounded.[9] In 1913 a professional Veterinary Corps was formed and during the war, for the first time in history, sick and wounded horses were evacuated to field and base hospitals for treatment. Veterinary hospitals in France treated 2,562,549 animals over the course of the war and the great majority of them were able to return to duty.[10] The RSPCA supported the Army Veterinary Corps by providing funds, trained inspectors, horse ambulances and hospitals and convalescent depots in France capable of accommodating around 20,000 horses.

Horses not only made a tremendous contribution to the war effort, they had, in countless cases, become close companions of the men who worked with them. As Driver Kibblewhite of the Royal Horse Artillery (RHA) wrote about two of his horses: 'At feed time I would only have to undo their head rope and say, "Go on, water" and both would back out of the stall, go to the water trough, take a drink and return to me for their feed … they were to me like a pet dog or cat'.[11] Private Fred Lloyd, serving with the Veterinary Corps, noted: 'The Veterinary Corps was always very kind to their horses – they thought a lot of them … They had some lovely horses and I often used to scrounge bits of sugar for them. I remember a lot of them coming back in relays from Passchendaele and we used to look after them when they'd come in. Horses understand'.[12]

After the Armistice the British authorities took a less sentimental view of animal welfare. Their main preoccupation was to dispose of the thousands of army horses and other animals (referred to as 'casting') and convert them into cash as quickly as possible and in any possible way. Some fortunate horses were bought by the soldiers who rode them. Captain J.C. Dunn's history of the Second Battalion of the Royal Welsh Fusiliers noted for 30 January 1920: 'officers were offered the option of purchasing their chargers, subject to veterinary inspection as to fitness for importation. Yates got Girlie. James Ormond kept her for him pending his eventual settlement. She was ridden with the Wynnstay Hounds, and reared a foal, which was ridden with the Winnstay; she lived until 1934'.[13] David, a wheelhorse of 107 Battery, RHA, was a veteran of the Boer War and served through the First World War with only one slight wound. He was bought by four officers of the Battery and ended his days peacefully on a Hertfordshire estate in 1926.[14] Other horses were retained for work and breeding in England. Some 94,000 were repatriated from France, Flanders and the Rhine area for the post-war army and for sale in Britain.[15]

But these horses were the exception. The fate of horses and mules was determined by how fit they were and how far they were from England. The RAVC was given the responsibility for the disposal of animals which were categorized as for: 'sale for work in France; sale to horse butchers in France and Italy; slaughter for human food in France and England; fats, fertilizers and animal foods from carcases of animals unfit for human consumption'.[16] The income from these various forms of disposal was significant.[17] From the Armistice until 31 March 1920 the sale of animals for human food realized £1,009,243. Horses sold for work brought £6,064,329 and the bi-products from carcasses earned £33,573. Horses that were fit for work were sold at an average price of £37 3*s*. 3*d*.; a mule brought £36 10*s*. 8*d*.; and a donkey £9 1*s*. 6*d*. In Palestine and Egypt a camel sold for £22 0*s*. 2*d*. and an ox for £1 17*s*. 4*d*.

A variety of regimental histories describe the fate of their animals. The historian of the 8th Battalion Royal West Kent Regiment recorded: 'On 2 March 1919 five riding horses were transferred to 9th East Surreys, who are going to the Rhine Army, fifteen other animals went off by train for demobilisation, and a further five left to be sold locally'.[18] On 19 February 1919 the animals of the 1/8 Battalion Sherwood Foresters were at Bettencourt in France: 'From here we sent back most of our horses and mules, with others from the Brigade, to an auction sale at Prisches where they were sold ... at good prices to the local inhabitants'.[19]

In October 1918 the total number of horses and mules in Mesopotamia was 84,190; in Egypt and Palestine 118,580; and in Salonika 63,891. As was anticipated before the end of the war, 'few ships, if any, will be available to transfer [these] animals to other countries', and, following the Armistice, there was no prospect of returning them to England. They presented a special problem. In October 1916 there had been discussions in Parliament concerning the 'cruelty of selling cast horses to be maltreated by Eastern peoples'. Lloyd George, who was then Secretary of State for War, responded to these concerns:

> As far as the East is concerned ... the case is completely established. I do not think that under any circumstances we ought to sell our old War horses to the Easterners to be dealt with in their usual way ... where you have not got the same assurances with regard to the treatment of animals as you have here.[20]

As the war came to an end, the disposal of animals in the Eastern theatres became a live issue. Attached to a War Office memorandum on this matter was a note that was typical of feelings among certain horse-lovers: 'The Serbs are to be trusted with animals, but not the Greeks ... not a single animal should be sold to Greeks, Jews, or in fact anyone in Macedonia'.[21] To this 'untrustworthy' list could be added Egypt, Palestine and Mesopotamia.

When the Armistice arrived, Lloyd George's 1916 pledge became an embarrassment to the government especially since it had been immediately followed by instructions to the 'General Officers Commanding in Chief in Egypt, Salonika and Mesopotamia prohibiting the sale of animals cast from the Service'. In a note to the Cabinet, dated 3 October 1918, Lord Milner, the Secretary of State for War, attempted to find a way around the problem. Lloyd George had referred to 'our old War horses' and Milner pointed out that this could be taken as referring only to English horses: 'The mules are of Australian, Indian, and Chinese origin; the bulk of the horses are Australian, Indian and American'. Milner had to concede, however, that there were also 'some few thousands of English animals' and that the RSPCA were 'watching this question'. It was a problem that no one wanted to deal with and it was passed from one body to another: 'This situation was placed by the War Office before the Ministry of Reconstruction who in turn referred it to the Surplus Government Property Advisory Council'. In his turn, Milner passed the issue to the Cabinet.

The outcome was finally determined by what Milner described as the 'altered circumstances of demobilisation'. Economic factors took over. It was estimated that, at £25 per head, it would cost around £6,250,000 to have these animals destroyed. Selling them locally would bring in a sizeable income. In any event, the Ministry of Agriculture and Fisheries were opposed to the repatriation of any animals from the East because of the potential spread of disease. The Surplus Government Property Advisory Council had recommended that 'animals no longer required by the Armies in the Eastern theatres of War should be disposed of to the best advantage', and that is what happened.[22]

The decision to sell animals for work in the Eastern theatres was considered by many as a protracted death sentence carried out under terrible conditions. The GOC of the Yeomanry Division, Major General Sir George Barrow, protested against this situation, but without success. Barrow turned a blind eye when officers of the Desert Mounted Corps took their favourite chargers out into the desert and shot them rather than let them be sold for work. As a postscript to these events, Mrs Dorothy Brooke, the wife of the Cavalry Brigade commander in Egypt, who was appointed in 1930, set herself the task of finding possible survivors among the animals sold in 1918–19. She managed to find several, emaciated and suffering but recognizable as British cavalry horses. She bought them and had them put down. Following an appeal for funds, Dorothy Brooke raised £40,000 from subscribers worldwide and during the next four years she rescued some 5,000 ex-army horses and set up the Old War Horse Memorial Hospital in Cairo.

The official numbers of animals sold for work or for meat in the period 11 November 1918–31 March 1920 is shown in Table 1, below:[23]

Table 1: The Sale of Animals, 1918–20

Area of Disposal	Nos Sold for Work	Nos Sold for Meat
Britain	132,649	6,247
France and Flanders	197,181	40,638
All Other Areas	169,331	14,347

Dealing with the inanimate hardware of war was also a considerable problem. The historian of RAOC noted the situation at the end of 1918: 'Our national assets of war material were obviously far in excess of what could possibly be wanted to maintain our small peacetime army for many years to come – in many cases they could not have been exhausted in a hundred years of peace'.[24] The matter was further complicated with the continued manufacture of certain war equipment even when hostilities had ceased. An example of this was discussed at a meeting of the War Cabinet on 9 July 1919: 'The Chancellor of the Exchequer said that at the date of the Armistice the Ministry of Munitions appeared to have on order for the Army 2,500 of the new 18-pr. guns and it had been maintained that it was necessary to continue the contracts for these guns in order to employ labour'. The Chancellor then made it clear that, although he had sympathized with that view at the time he 'must now press for a reconsideration of the artillery position with a view to effecting all possible economy'. The Secretary of State for War justified the actions of the Ministry of Munitions by pointing out that at the time of the Armistice the War Office was half way through re-arming the artillery 'which, when completed, would have the effect of making it the finest artillery in the world'. After considerable discussion the matter was closed by Bonar Law:

> As he saw the situation, the Ministry of Munitions had to make more guns in order to employ labour, and they had also continued the contracts as a means of cutting down the compensation … He thought, however, that no fresh money should be spent on the arming of Forces in the future, but that we should live on the armament which had been left over from the War.[25]

Bonar Law's decision summed up the approach of the government to the dismantling of the army – it was intent on making economies and making money.

Much surplus military equipment was sold off. The total number of mechanical transport vehicles of all descriptions and in all theatres at the end of the war was 119,372 and by April 1920 the number had been reduced to 8,040. Among those transport vehicles, lorries made up the largest group and their number fell from 46,565 in 1918 to 3,187 in 1920. 893,195 proof gallons of rum were 'sold to trade' at a profit of £190,000 and 12 million pounds of tea, valued at £353,202, were transferred to the Ministry of Food. The disposal of surplus army boots made an interesting case. Although reserves of boots had been built up, they were reduced by transferring them to the American and White Russian armies.

Where possible, contracts with supplying organizations were liquidated. The contracts for army clothing, normally on four weeks' notice, were allowed to run down progressively until the products could be converted to clothing for discharged soldiers. A harsher line was taken with biscuit suppliers. All contracts were stopped on 20 November 1918 thus saving £54,000 per week. Undelivered quantities, valued at £60,000, were cancelled.

The scrap that littered the front-line areas potentially represented much-needed income for the British Treasury. The salvaging of items that could be re-used or recycled from former battle zones was a process that had been followed throughout the war. As the size of the army increased and the duration of the war lengthened, the importance of salvage increased. By autumn 1918 each division had a Labour Corps Salvage Section made up of one officer and forty other ranks who were responsible for sorting and listing the scrap gathered by infantry units. The Salvage Section was augmented mainly by French female workers, prisoners of war, Indians and Chinese. The 'Notes on Salvage' for Labour Corps officers contained a helpful warning: 'The selection of white supervisors should be carefully made. It should be remembered that the Native is a good judge of character and that the best choice of supervision is therefore necessary in order to obtain satisfactory results.'[26] The impact of their work was significant. A report dated 28 September 1918 valued the articles salvaged in the previous four weeks at over £2.2 million. The items included, clothing, boots, carts, horseshoes, tools, metal, rifles and ammunition.[27] The historian of the Ministry of Munitions pointed out that: 'An 18pdr cartridge case can be re-formed six or eight times and as each weighed 3lbs the possible net savings in metal was large … during 1916 about 59 per cent of the 18pdr cartridge cases fired and about 41 per cent of 4.5 inch howitzer cases were returned'.[28]

Fight INFLUENZA with BRAND'S ESSENCE of BEEF

Evening Standard

No. 29,428. LONDON, MONDAY, NOVEMBER 11, 1918. ONE PENNY.

Sell your Waste Paper to Lendrum's

END OF THE WAR

GERMANY SIGNS OUR TERMS & FIGHTING STOPPED AT 11 O'CLOCK TO-DAY.

ALLIES TRIUMPHANT.

FOCH AND LLOYD GEORGE TELL NEWS THAT SENT THE WORLD REJOICING.

BRITISH BACK AT MONS!

The following historic announcement, which means that the world war has come to an end at last, was issued by Mr. Lloyd George to the nation at 10.20 this morning:—

"THE ARMISTICE WAS SIGNED AT 5 a.m. THIS MORNING, AND HOSTILITIES ARE TO CEASE ON ALL FRONTS AT 11 a.m. TO-DAY."

The following message was sent out to-day through the wireless stations of the French Government.

"Marshal Foch to Commanders-in-Chief.

"Hostilities will cease on the whole front as from November 11th at 11 o'clock (French time).

"The Allied troops will not, until a further order, go beyond the line reached on that date and at that hour.

(Signed) MARSHAL FOCH.

The armistice negotiations opened on Friday morning, when the Germans were given until 11 a.m. to-day to accept or reject the Allied terms.

The signing of the terms of course means the end of the war, as the safeguards are such that it will be impossible for Germany to renew the struggle.

AT THE PALACE.

TERRIFIC OVATION FOR THE KING AND QUEEN.

"With you I rejoice and thank God for the victories which the Allied armies have won and brought hostilities to an end and peace within sight."

PEACE IN BRIEF.

BRITISH RECAPTURED MONS BEFORE THE FIGHTING STOPPED!

Armistice signed 5 a.m. to-day.

Hostilities ceased at 11 a.m.

British recaptured Mons this morning, and thus ended the war where our "Old Contemptibles" began it for us.

Erzberger evidently signed the armistice at Foch's G.H.Q. for the Germans.

German armies must evacuate to the east bank of the Rhine in 31 days.

London's lights are to go up to-night (full details on another page).

BACK TO THE RHINE.

One of the armistice terms is the withdrawal of the German armies to the east bank of the Rhine. The following table of distances will be of interest therefore:—

Town.	Front.	Miles.
Ghent	Belgian	140
Mons	British	148
Maubeuge	British	155
Mezieres	French	162
Stenay	American	150
Alsace	American	20

ENVOYS RETURNING.

The German Plenipotentiaries are returning to Spa to-day.

THE ORDER OF GOING.

Armistices have been signed as follows:

Bulgaria	Sept. 29, 1918
Turkey	Oct. 30, 1918
Austria-Hungary	Nov. 3, 1918

FULL ARMISTICE TERMS

EVACUATION TO THE RHINE AND BRIDGEHEADS FOR ALLIES.

U-BOATS TO SURRENDER.

GUNS HANDED OVER AND BATTLE SHIPS DISARMED.

REPATRIATING PRISONERS.

The terms of the armistice signed by the German plenipotentiaries were read in the House of Commons this afternoon by Mr. Lloyd George.

The armistice terms include evacuation of invaded territories, Belgium, France, Alsace-Lorraine, Luxembourg, to be completed within 14 days. Railways of Alsace-Lorraine to be handed over.

German troops who have not left these territories within 14 days to be treated as prisoners of war. The occupation by the Allied and United States forces will keep pace with the evacuation.

The evacuation by the enemy of Rhine lands must be completed within 16 days.

Immediate repatriation without reciprocity of Allied and United States prisoners.

All German troops in Russia, Rumania, and elsewhere to be withdrawn. Complete abandonment of the treaties of Bukharest and Brest-Litovsk.

Immediate cessation of all hostilities at sea. Handing over to Allies and United States of all submarines.

The surrender by the German Government of the following equipment:—5000 guns, of which 2500 will be heavy and 2500 field guns, 30,000 machine-guns, and a large number of trench-mortars.

Six battle cruisers, ten battleships, eight light cruisers, 50 destroyers, and other services are to be disarmed, and the Allies reserve the right to occupy Heligoland to enable them to enforce the terms of the armistice.

BREST-LITOVSK TREATY ABANDONED.

By Our Parliamentary Representatives.

HOUSE OF COMMONS, Monday.

morning, and the war ceased at 11 o'clock this morning.

Immediate evacuation of invaded territories,

CLAUSES RELATING TO THE WESTERN FRONT.

Cessation of hostilities by land and in the air six hours after the signature of the armistice.

(Continued on Page 3.)

The Evening Standard *announces the end of the war.*

Victory celebration in front of Buckingham Palace.

Sir Edward Llewellyn Smith, Secretary to the Board of Trade.

Sir Reginald Brade, Secretary to the War Office.

Sir Edwin Montagu, Chairman of the Demobilization Committee.

Herbert Asquith, Prime Minister, 1908–16, who set up the First Reconstruction Committee in March 1916.

David Lloyd George, Prime Minister, 1916–22, who set up the Second Reconstruction Committee in March 1917.

Dr Christopher Addison, Chairman of the Reconstruction Committee, 1917–19.

Winston Churchill, Secretary of State for War, 1919–21. He brought in the revised demobilization plan in February 1919.

Andrew Bonar Law, Chancellor of the Exchequer, 1916–19.

General Jan Smuts, member of the Imperial War Cabinet, 1917–19, and chairman of the Demobilization Committee in 1918.

The Big Four Lloyd George (Britain), Orlando (Italy), Clemenceau (France) and Wilson (USA) at the Versailles peace negotiations in 1919.

General Sir Henry Wilson, CIGS, 1918–22.

General Sir William Robertson, CIGS, 1915–18, Commander in Chief British Army of the Rhine, 1919–20.

Field Marshal Sir Douglas Haig, Commander in Chief the BEF, 1915–19. He opposed the original demobilization plan.

Field Marshal Haig and General Plumer at Cologne when Plumer was appointed commander of the British Army of the Rhine, December 1918.

A nursing sister tends the wounded in France. There were 10,000 women serving in France when the war ended.

Horses and mules were essential to the war effort. By November 1918 there were over 700,000 in the British Army.

Police Sergeant Thomas Green (second from right, second row up) was killed during the Epsom riot, 17 June 1919.

Cortège at Sergeant Green's funeral, 23 June 1919.

A tank in post-war Aberdeen. Tanks were presented to those towns who did well in selling war loans.

'Your Country Needs You. Nobody Wants You'. In early 1919 many soldiers found it difficult to find work. Things improved later in 1919 and through 1920, but unemployment increased towards the end of that year.

The Lee War Memorial, Buckinghamshire. Thirty men from this small village were killed in the war.

Memorial at Stoke Hammond, Buckinghamshire – A Thankful Village. No men were killed during the war from this village.

The Tomb of the Unknown Soldier, interred in Westminster Abbey, 11 November 1920.

Following the Armistice the whole character of salvage changed: 'Vast quantities of serviceable stores in dumps and depots were becoming surplus to military requirements and had to be concentrated and disposed of … nearly everything had become salvage, or, to look at it another way, salvage material had become merely one of many forms of surplus Government property'.[29] Examples of 'unserviceable' stores reported between 11 November 1918 and 1 September 1919 show the extent of the disposal problem: ferrous metals 59,066 tons; non-ferrous metals 4,767 tons; miscellaneous 12,286 tons; boots, 607,092 pairs.[30] In March 1919 the gathering and control of materials became part of the QMG Department and in July the function was taken over by the Ministry of Munitions.

Storage dumps proliferated to contain the military materials. The armies, now relieved of their combat duties, turned 'their chief energies to the intensive collection of stores and material'.[31] These old armies gradually diminished as demobilization progressed and a new army was formed to take over the 'custody and care of the goods and the animals in the old theatre of war'. It became known as the 'Clearing Up Army'.[32] General Wilson had an ambivalent view of this new army. On the one hand it was doing a worthwhile job in France, but on the other it was a source of men urgently required for active service elsewhere. By April 1919 six battalions had already been sent to Egypt and Italy:

> It is considered that no further numbers can be drawn from this source without dislocating the whole organisation for the recovery of the vast amounts of stores and equipment now scattered throughout this area, at the mercy of the climate and open to the depredations of the civilian inhabitants. It must be pointed out, however, that the 120,000 troops now locked up on these duties are fulfilling no military functions, but are being so employed with a purely financial object, and it is for consideration whether the ultimate financial return will be commensurate with the enormous cost of maintaining this large number of fighting troops, in addition to German prisoners, Chinese coolies, etc.[33]

The various technical corps were responsible for dumps dealing with items appropriate to them. Hence, The Royal Engineers (RE) stored timber, railway materials and other engineering supplies. As examples of the amount of stock in France at the end of the war, the RE stores included 131,862,080 sandbags; 16,678,518 pickets; 5,115,315 screwposts; and 2,123,078 shovels and picks.[34] The Signal Services dealt with the salvage of signal line and equipment. The Tank Field battalion of the Tank Corps salvaged derelict tanks. The RASC gathered mechanical transport vehicles and containers of all kinds including jars, drums, bottles, sacks and boxes. The RAOC was particularly concerned with ammunition of all kinds and built up vast quantities of shells and Small Arms Ammunition (SAA), including German ordnance.

What happened to this mass of equipment? The collection and storage of the immense quantities of materiel was the responsibility of the War Office which initially was also responsible for the disposal of surplus stores. Inevitably problems arose. An Allied conference in March 1919 ruled that any property seized by the Germans and subsequently recaptured was not a prize of war, but should be returned to its original owner. Similarly, the Germans, during their retreat, had sold confiscated animals and equipment to locals and these had now to be returned to the real owners. Both of these situations were not only time-consuming, but called for considerable tact.[35] A further problem was caused by the insistence of the French authorities that British motor vehicles, if sold in France, should be subject to a 70 per cent duty. The outcome of this imposition was to close down the sale of surplus vehicles. Brigadier General R.D. Legge of the Administration Liaison Bureau in Paris received hundreds of requests from French individuals and organizations for British cars and lorries, including one from a M. Henri Vincent wishing to buy a car – 'du préferénce Daimler'. Legge's reply to Vincent was, as to many other potential buyers: 'The British authorities up to the present are not selling motor cars in this country'.[36] In consequence of the large duty, the great majority of British cars and lorries were shipped back to England and dumped in depots in Shortlands, Kempton Park and Slough for public auction.

As from July 1919, the task of selling surplus equipment was taken on by the Surplus Government Property Disposals Board of the Ministry of Munitions. Such a Board, which had been proposed as early as May 1917, was to have 'full powers to sell, or give away or destroy all property… no longer required for military purposes'.[37] By February 1919 the War Office had decided what ordnance and equipment it needed for the Army of the Rhine and also what was required in England as a base store for the post-war army.

Surplus live ammunition was disposed of in a variety of directions. Canada took 60,000 tons of ammunition, Australia 80,000 tons and New Zealand 10,000 tons. The White Russians, who were fighting the Bolsheviks, received 1,962,200 18pdr shells, 521,000 4.5in howitzers, 896,172 grenades, 811,499,236 SAA, 379,727 rifles, 10,989 machine guns and 13,089 swords. The total value of this equipment assigned to Russia was £25,445,000. Despite the disposal of these large quantities of ammunition, there still remained some 350,000 tons of shells in France which were finally sold to contractors who extracted nitrates for fertilizers and metals for recycling.

The favoured method of disposal was by 'mass deals'. The United States took ½ million knives, forks and spoons for use by its troops in the process of demobilization.[38] The South African government bought 300 miles of railway track for £500,000. The French government wished to buy vast quantities of British materiel including railway rolling stock, port equipment, tugs, barges and road-making plant. This matter was of such importance that it was discussed, in January 1919, at Cabinet level. The necessity of revitalizing the worn-out infra-structure in Britain was a key factor. It was decided that the French could have light railway stock, workshop and engineering equipment only. The French took over all the available German ammunition in France.[39] Much German ordnance was dumped into the sea. A memorandum from the Disposal Board to the QMG dated 6 March 1919 requested authority to dump in the sea 'all gas shells, gas bombs, gas grenades (156,000) and all stick hand grenades (198,500) and rifle grenades (174,000)'.

The Official History of the Great War lists a vast amount of surplus materiel collected in 1919 by the army in France. Among these items were: 'Tanks: 1,350, with large workshops, and 13,000 tons of tank stores'.[40] Tanks were generally broken up and sold for scrap, but some were awarded to cities and towns for their performance selling War Savings Certificates.[41] During the 1920s and 1930s most of these presentation tanks were sold off as scrap. In August 1923 Goole removed its tank which had been displayed on the local children's playground. In August 1927, Lincoln sold its tank, together with some German field guns, for the benefit of ex-servicemen's dependents. Some of these tanks had a reprieve: 'As a result of public protest [October 1928], the Peterborough Town Council has rescinded the resolution passed at its last meeting to scrap war trophies consisting of guns and a tank.' The Aylesbury Council sold its tank for £22 10*s*. in June 1929 'to make room for an omnibus park'. The tank was broken up using oxy-acetyline torches which caused petrol, still in the tank after ten years, to explode. Two men were severely burnt. Yarmouth sold its tank for £12 10*s*. and High Wycombe founded a university scholarship on the proceeds of its tank. When, in June 1923, Guildford disposed of its tank at £3 per ton, the local newspaper said farewell: 'Poor old tank ... we raise our hat to you and what you stood for'.[42]

War Office materiel in England was sold off piecemeal. In May 1920, for example, the 150 huts and buildings that made up Clipstone Camp in Nottinghamshire were disposed of in 2 days. A Mr Frank Blythman bought Hut No. 86 for £52.[43] Other less formal 'sell-offs' took place. When the 34th

Division Motor Transport Section was disbanded at Grove Park the occasion was marked by 'Raffling the Games Club property among members of the company who were serving on Armistice Day … Staff Sergeant Routledge won the piano; Corporal Reading the cricket bat and CQMS Hilton won the stage effects'. The proceeds from the Raffle went to the Poor Boys' Camp Association.[44]

In such diverse ways the materiel left over from the war was disposed of. Stores and equipment in distant theatres of war were sold off at the best prices possible, but the bulk of material was in France and Flanders. A report of September 1920 by Brigadier General Gibb valued the stores and animals sold on the Continent at £152,820,920 and those shipped to Britain at £141,730,000.[45] They were significant and much-welcome contributions to the depleted British Treasury.

Chapter 6

The Army of 1919

Throughout the war the British government had been unwilling to answer questions about the size and role of the army once hostilities had ended. The various Reconstruction and Demobilization Committees were well aware that the numbers to be demobilized would clearly be affected by the size of the post-war army. In September 1916, when the Battle of the Somme was at its most intense, Sir Reginald Brade of the War Office had pressed the government to give a forecast of the possible number of soldiers that might be required when hostilities ceased. The government's response to Brade, that the army might be between 200,000 and 750,000, was so broad as to be of no practical use. In the same year, W.H. Beveridge of the Board of Trade estimated that 500,000 soldiers would be needed after the war. In both the First and the Second Demobilization Reports of 1916 and 1917 Edwin Montagu had requested from the government 'the number of the Standing Army to be maintained for the first few years after the war'. Montagu also asked for information as to 'the manner in which the requisite number of men is to be obtained on the conclusion of peace'. The government refused to commit itself on either of these two questions. This was hardly surprising. There was no definite sign that the war was nearing its end until well into the second half of 1918. Moreover, it was impossible to know just what the future role of the army might be – either at home or abroad.

While the Cabinet had, for good reasons, avoided being specific about the size and disposition of a post-war army, the signing of the Armistice meant that the issue could no longer be put off. In April 1919 the government set up a Committee on the Organization of the After War Army under Lieutenant General Sir Alexander Hamilton Gordon. Within three months the Committee arrived at its recommendation that the army should consist of twenty divisions each capable of generating a second division plus a Guards division – therefore an army of potentially forty-one divisions supported, if required, by compulsory service. The government considered the proposal to be both unnecessary and financially unwelcome and the recommendation was ignored.

Nevertheless, the circumstances in 1919 presented the British government with a variety of problems that required the deployment of a significant number of troops. In April 1919 General Wilson set out these problems in a lengthy memorandum to the War Cabinet headed 'The Military Situation Throughout the British Empire With Special Reference to the Inadequacy of the Numbers of Troops Available'.[1] The memorandum began: 'I feel compelled to bring to the notice of the War Cabinet the grave possibilities which confront us'. Wilson was clearly anxious about the heavy demands on Britain's military resources: 'apart from the numberless requests for British troops that are constantly being received from all parts of Europe, our liabilities in vital portions of the British Empire have increased rather than diminished'. Wilson had ample cause to be concerned.

At home, with the revival of the Triple Alliance of miners, railwaymen, and transport workers, there was an imminent threat of major industrial and social unrest that might require some degree of military intervention. However, it was recognized that the use of soldiers to control strikes and riots and maintain services would be a last resort. An official pamphlet set out the government's attitude:

> It is not that we wish to maintain a Regular Army for use in industrial disputes at home. The notion of a body of trained gladiators to stand at the call of Capital is abhorrent to every English instinct. The British Army has always been part and parcel of the nation from which it springs: so much so that such small attempts at the employment of troops in case of civil emergency as have been thought necessary in the past have almost always ended in an appeal to common-sense backed by a mere show of force … [an] armed force has never been used to coerce the orderly striker.[2]

However, it was considered prudent to have soldiers available in adequate numbers should a serious crisis occur. In the event, soldiers were deployed during the railway and coal strikes of 1919–21, but only to preserve public order, not to break the strikes.

Ireland was a sore that continued to fester. In the General Election of 1918 Sinn Fein had won every seat outside Ulster except four, and, of its successful candidates, half were in prison. In January 1919 a separate Irish parliament was set up in Dublin – the Dáil Éireann – and Ireland declared itself an Independent Republic. There were spasmodic outbursts of severe IRA violence. FM Bernard Montgomery, who had served in Ireland as a young brigade major, wrote later that the experience was worse than that of the First World War and described the situation as 'a murder campaign'.[3] In April 1919 Wilson reported to the War Cabinet that while there were 19,800 troops in Ireland, 'the Sinn Fein organisation controls some 100,000 well-organised, though indifferently armed, men. It is therefore necessary to contemplate not mere police measures, but active military operations of a serious nature.' Wilson informed the Cabinet that the Viceroy in Ireland had requested eight additional battalions immediately 'to deal effectively' with the situation.[4] By May 1919 the number of troops in Ireland had increased to 53,000.

There was even discussion about the value of keeping Ireland in the Empire – there were more troops needed to keep the peace in Ireland than were recruited from there to serve abroad. But the prevailing argument was put by the Unionist MP Sir Edward Carson:

> If you tell your Empire in India, in Egypt and all over the world that you have not got the money, the men, the pluck, the inclination and the backing to restore order in a country within twenty miles of your own shore, you may well begin to abandon the attempt to make British rule prevail throughout the Empire at all.[5]

Even in Scotland there were signs of nationalist agitation. On 16 May 1919 the House of Commons debated the issue of Home Rule for Scotland. The debate petered out and it was reported that: 'The House showed its profound contempt for the proposal by calmly counting itself out. This is a blow to those who affirm that Scotland is hungering for self-determination'.[6]

In terms of nationalist activity, India was following the same course as Ireland. The 1919 Government of India Act conceded limited powers to central and provincial governments, but they were insufficient for Gandhi's Congress Party. The effect of the April 1919 Amritsar Massacre, when troops commanded by a British commander, General Dyer, dispersed a mob by shooting 379 Indians and wounding about a thousand more, was to ensure that the threat of local disruption and violence was always present. In April the Viceroy sent a telegram to Wilson outlining what was a seriously uneasy position and requesting reinforcements – four British divisions and four British cavalry brigades – 'in the event of the situation taking an unfavourable turn'.

In Egypt, a British protectorate, there was a growing pressure for independence and a revolt against British rule took place in March 1919. General Allenby reported that, while the disturbances had been suppressed, the necessary action was only successful through stopping the demobilization of all British troops and remobilizing the Dominion mounted troops who were on the point of returning home. Allenby's assessment was that 'this quiet can only be considered temporary, and that an outbreak on a far more serious scale is in preparation. In this it is anticipated that the Egyptian Army and Police may join forces against us and attempt to release the 90,000 Turkish prisoners of war now in Egypt'. In his despatch, Allenby noted that 74,000 men who were waiting to be demobilized had been retained to put down the riots and 'they are discontented'. There was now an urgent need for reinforcements – one British division, a replacement for the Anzac Mounted Division that was to be demobilized, and an additional Indian division.

The situation in Palestine, now liberated from the Turks, was aggravated by the Arab-Jewish question. To the Jews the Balfour Declaration of November 1917 had promised a home for the Jewish people in Palestine; to the Palestinian Arabs the November 1918 declaration by both Britain and France to set up a national government meant Arab predominance. As a result of the Versailles Treaty of June 1919 Britain gained 'mandates' to administer not only Palestine but also Iraq and Mesopotamia. Britain consequently became embroiled in the continuing political upheavals in the Near East. The situation in Mesopotamia was 'comparatively quiet' even though the number of troops had been reduced. However, the Commander in Chief in that area had made it clear that 'no more pivotal men or demobilizers can be released, as he is down to bed-rock'.

In Turkey and the Caucasus, where Britain was providing an Army of Occupation, the number of troops had already been halved, and the Commander in Chief, General Milne, pointed out that '40,000 of his men were entitled to demobilisation whilst the great majority have had no leave for a long period'. The Army in France and Belgium had already been reduced to strengthen the forces in Egypt and Italy and General Wilson considered that there were no further reductions to be made without incurring considerable risk: 'Should the contemplated military emergency arise in India it will be imperative to draw on this source regardless of consequences'.

Wilson's April 1919 memorandum to the War Cabinet, which covered all the above areas of military activity, came to the conclusion that 'should the contingencies arise which are considered as possible by the highest authorities in England, Ireland, Egypt and India then, in my opinion, we have not the military force to ensure the safety of the Empire'.[7]

In addition to these problems, Wilson also had to maintain a British army on the Rhine – an obligation arising from the Armistice discussions between the Allies. For the first six months of 1919 this Army of Occupation, commanded by Sir William Robertson, was on the alert to move forward into Germany should the German government fail to sign the Treaty of Peace. The Armistice was extended on three occasions – 13 December, 17 January and 16 February. The February extension was 'prolonged for a short period, without, however, any date for its expiration'.[8] Even in mid-June 1919 Marshal Foch, the commander of the Allied forces, was making plans to march into Germany and occupy Berlin, and Wilson was unclear 'whether or not we have to take further military action'.[9]

In one sense it was fortunate that the Armistice continued to be extended. In April Robertson estimated that, of his total force of ten divisions and one cavalry division, only six divisions were ready to move forward if called upon to do so. Even those six divisions were limited as to the distance they could advance because of a shortage of technical services – artillery, engineers, railwaymen, signallers and mechanical transport.[10]

The great irony was that while Britain had no option but to accept these military pressures, the highly charged process of demobilization was diminishing the size of the British Army at a considerable rate. Wilson's understandable concern was evident in his cryptic diary entry of 6 January 1919: 'the war is not over, we are demobilising quite fast enough'.[11]

Just how many soldiers did Britain need to carry out these diverse military obligations? In November 1918 various general statements were made indicating the possible role and size of the British Army. At a Cabinet Meeting on 5 November:

> The Chief of the Imperial General Staff [Wilson] stated that he understood Marshal Foch was going to ask the British Government for 16 infantry divisions, as well as 3 cavalry, to act as an Army of Occupation in Western Germany. With lines of communication this would mean the retention under Marshal Foch's command of half a million British troops in the Rhenish Provinces.[12]

Less than two weeks later, on 18 November, the Director of Military Operations, Major General P.P. de B. Radcliffe, informed the Cabinet that he 'understood that Marshal Foch was likely to ask that thirty British divisions should be allowed to remain as part of the army of occupation'.[13] Foch's demands on Britain seemed to be growing and Lloyd George, well aware of the wider demands on British military resources, 'urged the desirability of the Army Council working out alternative schemes for the maintenance of the Army. They would have to consider not only the maintenance of the Army of Occupation, but also the retention of the necessary garrison troops after the war'.[14]

On 5 December Wilson presented a paper to the Cabinet in which he gave his estimate of the number of troops required: in Germany 14 to 20 divisions; in Italy 1 brigade to 1 division; in the Bosphorous area 1 division; in Russia 1 division. Taking account of the numbers required in Britain and in Egypt, Palestine and India, Wilson's estimate totalled between 19 and 25 divisions which meant an army of 750,000 to 1,000,000 men.

Shortly after Winston Churchill became Secretary of State for War in January 1919, he wrote a memorandum 'Note on Armies of Occupation'. In this Note Churchill defined further the scope and size of the Army: 'The Armies of Occupation will be as follows – Home Army, Army of the Rhine, Army of the Middle East, Detachments of the Far North [Russia], and Garrisons of the Crown Colonies and India'. Churchill went on: 'Our Military Commanders say that in their opinion not more than 900,000 men of all ranks will be sufficient to guard our interests in this transition period'. The Note ended: 'The above arrangements seem to be the best that can be devised for the year 1919'. Churchill added somewhat patronisingly: 'I wrote an explanation for the Armies of the whole position in language which they would understand'.[15]

Of all the areas of military concern for Britain, Russia, in terms of the number of troops involved, was disproportionately contentious. Opinion, both within and outside the Cabinet, was divided – was it worth supporting the anti-Bolsheviks? There was little doubt that the War Office and the Cabinet believed that Bolshevism was a pernicious evil. On 22 October 1918 Charles Sackville-West, the British Representative on the Allied Military Committee at Versailles, wrote to General Wilson: 'Russia is the great danger – I dread Bolshevism for Europe'.[16] Weekly reports from the War Office to the Cabinet included comments on the latest Bolshevik activities. The report dated 9 January 1919, stated: 'Bolshevism is taking the place of discredited Kaiserism as a world menace'.[17]

Within the Cabinet, Churchill made clear his hatred of Bolshevism and his fear of its possible effects not only in Britain and the rest of Europe, but also in the Baltic States and those parts of Russia not yet committed to Bolshevism. In his Mansion House speech of 19 February 1919 he praised those anti-Bolshevik Russian forces who 'were called into the field originally during the German war to some extent by our inspiration and who are now engaged in fighting the baboonery of Bolshevism'.[18]

The division of opinion within the Cabinet over Russia was not caused by differences about the possible evil effects of Bolshevism. It arose because there was uncertainty as to what action should be taken and how effective any such action would be.[19] At the time of the Armistice Britain already had soldiers stationed in Russia. The first British troops – a detachment of 150 Royal Marines – arrived in Murmansk in March 1918. It was the task of the Marines, who were shortly to be joined by other troops, to safeguard war materials sent from Britain to help the Russia Army and prevent them falling into German or Bolshevik hands. For the same reason an Anglo-Japanese force had landed at Vladivostok in April 1918. Within weeks, however, the role of the British troops had changed from simply guarding armaments to taking military action. This change was brought about by two events. Following the Russian Revolution of February 1917 the Eastern Front began to crumble. A succession of German victories led to the Treaty of Brest-Litovsk which took Russia out of the war. The Bolsheviks had neither the inclination nor the resources to fight the Germans and it was now in the interests of Britain and its Allies to support the anti-Bolshevik and anti-German White Russians. A second event was also critical. In May 1918 70,000 Czechoslovak prisoners of war, positioned along the Trans-Siberian railway, revolted against German control and Britain, as part of an International Force, sent troops in support. By the end of 1918, some 30,000 Allied troops were stationed in Murmansk, Archangel, Siberia, the Caucasus and Trans-Caspia. Britain's contribution to this force was 14,000 troops. The White Russians were commanded by General Kolchak in Siberia and General Deniken in South Russia.

Among the British troops sent to Russia in 1918 was Private Walter Wright of the 2/7 Battalion, the Durham Light Infantry who arrived in Archangel via Murmansk on 23 October. Both the weather and the military situation deteriorated rapidly. In his diary, Wright recorded that on Saturday 23 November 'D Company made a raid on a neighbouring village as it was thought that the Bolsheviks had ammunition stored there and of course you cannot tell who are Bolshies and who are not. Fifty of the DLIs went in with rifle and Lewis gun'. Three weeks later, on 13 December, Wright noted that 'the Royal Scots had a good few casualties. Two hundred I think. One thousand two hundred Russians that had been enlisted and trained by the British mutinied when they found that they had to go up the line to fight the Bolsheviks. We were at once stood ready'. The mutiny was put down, but Wright remarked: 'If ever the Ruskies join together and attack us we shall not have a ghost of a chance as the Expedition, counting all nationalities, French, British, American, Serbian and Italian, does not consist of a handful of men. There are enough Ruskies hanging about to eat us ... Still freezing like blazes.'[20]

The Armistice with Germany served to focus the attention of the Cabinet on its future policy towards Russia. H.A.L. Fisher, the Minister of Education, made a thoughtful contribution – not least in putting forward to the War Cabinet his opinion of the attitude of the British public towards intervention in Russia:

> I am most impressed with the evidence that flows in from many sides of a general feeling of uneasiness with respect to the character and design of our military commitments in the Russian Empire. There is no doubt whatsoever that the continuance of military operations in Russia, now that the Armistice has been signed with the Central Powers and their Allies, is extremely unpopular with the working man and women of this Country … Working people do not understand why we are fighting in Russia at all unless it be, as they are informed by the Independent Labour Party, to assist in the restoration of an Autocracy. Probably only a small minority of working men in this country sympathise with the Bolshevik regime, but a very much larger number consider that the constitution of the Russian Government is an affair to the Russians themselves and that Russia should be left to stew in her own juice.

Fisher concluded his memorandum:

> I take it that I am correct in assuming that our original military intervention in the Russian Empire was prompted by three motives – first, the restoration of the Eastern Front against the German powers; second, the protection of the Czecho-slovaks; and third, the deliverance of the Russian people from the tyranny of a Government of Revolutionary malefactors. Of these motives, the first has now disappeared with the signature of the Armistice and the second is not, I take it, an operative consideration in view of the fact that the Czecho-Slovaks can now be returned to the Czecho-Slovak Republic … To this extent then, the problem has been simplified by the course of events, and we can now confine our enquiry to the extent to which the continuing presence of the Allied forces on the soil of the Russian Empire is likely to contribute to a better order of things in Russia.[21]

On 29 November 1918 Lord Balfour made clear his view on this issue: 'This country would certainly refuse to see its forces, after more than four years of strenuous fighting, dissipated over the huge expanse of Russia in order to carry out political reforms in a state which is no longer a belligerent Ally. We have constantly asserted that it is for the Russians to choose their own form of government'.[22]

Both Fisher and Balfour were correct in believing that sections of the public were against intervention in Russia. In August 1918 the British

Socialist Party had appealed to trade unionists to protest against Allied interference in Russian affairs and meetings held at Glasgow, Wigan, Blackburn, Openshaw and at Finsbury Park endorsed this appeal. On 1 December 1918 a militant group of shop stewards held a mass meeting at the Holborn Empire in London. The meeting condemned 'the appalling sacrifice of members of our class involved in the continued campaign against the Russian Socialist Republic by the international capitalists, and demand the immediate withdrawal of the Allied forces from the country'. The meeting also called for a general strike 'to compel the governing class to cease violating Russia'.[23] This opposition among working men and women, even if loudly expressed, was not widespread nor particularly effective, but its effect was to bolster the efforts of those opposed to action against the Bolsheviks.

Despite the strength of opinion voiced both for and against intervention in Russia, the effect of the Armistice was to place the issue in limbo. Referring to the troops in North Russia, the War Cabinet decided on 31 December 1918 that 'no demobilisation measures are to be taken for the present' and that 'no further reinforcements were to be ordered to North Russia until the question can be dealt with [during the Peace negotiations] in Paris'. As far as the British War Cabinet was concerned, Russia was a matter not just for Britain, but for all the Allied governments.[24] On 2 January 1919 General Wilson, frustrated by this decision, sent a résumé of the North Russian situation to the Secretary of the War Cabinet. Wilson stressed that a lack of reinforcements could mean that a withdrawal might have to take place 'which will expose considerable numbers of the Russian population, who have supported the Allied forces, to massacre by Soviet troops'. Wilson summed up: 'I would earnestly draw the attention of the War Cabinet to the present unsatisfactory situation of our forces in North Russia, and to the urgent necessity of coming to a decision on the policy to be adopted without delay'.[25]

Government policy was finally determined by practicalities. Churchill's proposal that the Allies should supply soldiers and substantial assistance to the White Russians was opposed by both Wilson and Lloyd George. Wilson was under constant pressure from all quarters to provide troops and, from a purely practical point of view, he was reluctant to allocate manpower to an area where outright victory was highly unlikely. Moreover, there was gathering evidence to suggest that British troops were unwilling to be posted to Russia. Wilson told the Cabinet on 10 January that within the army 'the prospect of being sent to Russia was immensely unpopular'.[26] At Park Royal on 7 January one of the demands of the RASC protestors was that no drafts should be sent to that area. In February 1919 Wilson wrote:

'After careful and detailed examination [of the proposal to overthrow the Bolsheviks] I have come to the distinct conclusion that the Allies do not dispose of sufficient forces to warrant the attempt to be made. I therefore rule it out'. Instead, Wilson proposed a strict delineation of the Russian state, treating it as a neutral power. Wilson also proposed that the countries that had seceded from Russia – Finland, Esthonia, Latvia. Lithuania, Poland, Ruthenia and the Caucasus – should be protected as a barrier to the spread of Bolshevism.[27]

Lloyd George threw his weight against involvement in North Russia. He considered it too costly – one estimate was £73 million;[28] he assessed that the British people were either unconcerned about or against intervention; and he also thought that it might be counter-productive. As he said to Churchill in February 1919: 'an expensive war of aggression against Russia is a way to strengthen Bolshevism in Russia and create it at home'.[29] Churchill was obliged to give way and, in September 1919, the last British soldier left North Russia. Churchill's reputation as a War Minister, which had been strengthened as a result of his swift actions in dealing with the demobilization problems, was now weakened because of his insistent wish to be involved in North Russia. His failed efforts in both North Russia and the Dardanelles painted Churchill as something of a wayward adventurer.

Britain's involvement in South Russia and the Caucasus had a stronger strategic justification. These areas were adjacent to Afghanistan and India and, as Wilson wrote to Lord Curzon: 'A combination of Bolsheviks and Afghans would be a serious menace in the first place to Persia and, in the second place, to India.'[30] This might have been so, but the Deniken/Kolchak White Russian forces in the region, which included only two British battalions, were clearly inadequate to overcome Trotsky's revolutionary army. Wilson's view was forthright: 'I am perfectly clear that our proper course is to clear out bag and baggage. I do not believe in these small missions or small forces – neither one thing or the other ... There is no middle course – there never is in these sorts of countries'.[31] The matter dragged on into the 1920s and ended in an inevitable withdrawal.

It was a consolation to the government that, by that time, the threat of a serious Bolshevik movement in Britain had virtually disappeared. In July 1920 the British Socialist Party and the Socialist Labour Party of Glasgow, together with shop stewards from Glasgow and Sheffield, set up the Communist Party of Great Britain. Its aim was to repeat Lenin's success in Russia and establish a proletarian dictatorship. Support was thin and the movement failed to gather momentum. Both the Independent Labour Party and the Labour Party refused to come under the influence of Moscow.[32] The outbreaks of disorder in the British Army which took place in late 1918 and through much of 1919 have been interpreted by some commentators as manifestations of a widespread class uprising.[33] But these disturbances, disruptive though they were at the time, petered out. The circumstances behind them were spasmodic and reflected local frustrations and the slow pace of demobilization rather than a growing Bolshevik-inspired political take-over. With demobilization the army was dispersed thus reducing any opportunity for concerted action. The main concern of the soldier was to get home and find work rather than making an attempt to overturn the government.

In April 1919 General Wilson informed the War Cabinet of the number of British troops required in each theatre and these are set out in Table 2, below. The total establishment amounted to 903,000.[34] Given the rate of demobilization and the eagerness of soldiers to return home, this was a daunting figure. However, it represented, in the considered opinion of Wilson and his generals, the estimated number required for the greater part of 1919. It was anticipated that at various points during the year the demand for troops would reduce – for example, after the evacuation from North Russia. And the requirement for troops in the Army of the Rhine would lessen once the Peace Treaty had been signed. Nevertheless, in spring 1919 an army of 903,000 was considered essential.

Table 2: Required Numbers of British Troops, April 1919

Command	**Establishment**
Home	220,000
Defended ports	5,000
Army of the Rhine	260,000
Troops in France and Flanders	120,000
Italy	11,000
Army on the Black Sea	45,000
Egypt and Palestine	70,000
India	135,000
Mesopotamia and Persia	23,000
North Russia	14,000
TOTAL	903,000

Where were these men to come from? As Wilson had noted in December 1918, no machinery existed for the provision of these forces.[35] Remobilization was becoming as big a problem as demobilization. At midday on 11 November 1918 compulsory enlistment under the 1916 Military Service Act was suspended. From that date until 15 January 1919 recruitment under that Act was confined to those who were in the process of being called-up and had already reported themselves. There was still the option for young men, aged 18–25 to enlist voluntarily so long as they signed on for a full twelve-year period. The number of recruits from these sources between 11 November 1918 and 15 January 1919 totalled 1,139. Serving soldiers were able to re-enlist for periods of two, three, or four years and they were encouraged to do so by the offer of bounties of £20, £40 and £50 respectively which would be in addition to any amounts due to them because of their war service. As a result, 74,930 men were recruited in this way.

Efforts were made to enlist men for special service. For example, a Relief Force was required to provide reinforcements in North Russia prior to the general withdrawal from that area. This Relief Force was particularly in need of tradesmen and, in this connection, on 28 June the RASC advertised in the national press for men with mechanical or horse transport experience stating that the period of service would be 'for one year or such shorter service as might be required for this special service'.[36] A total of 5,344 demobilized men, from a variety of corps and regiments, volunteered for the North Russian Relief Force.

In April 1919 there was a recruitment drive to attract men, aged 38 or older, for the Stores Section of the RE. By 23 June 4,667 men had enlisted for these duties. In May recruitment opened for special duties with the Labour Corps. The particular task was to exhume the bodies of dead soldiers in France and Flanders and create centralized cemeteries. For each day that they carried out this work there would be an additional payment of 3*s*. for NCOs and 2*s*. 6*d*. for Other Ranks. Under this scheme 15,445 joined the Labour Corps. Also in May an advertisement appeared stating: 'There are a large number of vacancies in the Tank Corps for men between the ages of 18 and 27 … to enlist for seven years with the colours and five years in reserve. The scale of pay is that now in force, with a minimum bonus of 10*s* 6*d* a week.'[37] Men who had previously served in the Tank Corps could enlist for shorter periods of service – two, three or four years.

Early in 1919 the War Office decided to recruit boys of 17 or 18 years on a man's rate of pay so long as they had parental consent and they were prepared to enlist for nine years with the colours and three years in reserve. By 30 September 1919, a total of 7,195 boys were recruited under this scheme. Boys were also encouraged to receive training in several of the technical corps which increased the number of training places above 1914 levels. The number of trainees in the Royal Artillery increased from 182 to 450 and in the RE from 72 to 420. The RASC, which had not previously taken trainees, offered 500 places in the Motor Transport section and 230 with Horse Transport.

All of these devices were helpful in building up the new army, but the numbers involved were small in relation to the hundreds of thousands that were required. Other measures of a more substantial kind were necessary. It was decided that the system of recruitment would have to revert to the pre-war arrangements. There would be centres in all the large cities and towns and in existing infantry depots. Staff officers, reporting to the War Office, were appointed in each location to administer the process. In June 1919 a poster campaign was introduced to boost recruitment. As many as 20 different designs were used and 300,000 posters were distributed to recruiting offices, post offices, railway stations and regimental depots. Ireland received 6,500 posters. The campaign was supported by lantern slide shows of the posters in cinemas in London and the provincial cities and the authorities declared that they were 'entirely satisfied' with the results. In the period 15 January to 30 September 1919 the number of new recruits from all sources reached 347,438. Of these, 120,205 were ex-soldiers and 38,586 joined for at least 7 years' service.[38] Within the total number of recruits, 126,693 entered directly from civilian life – a surprisingly high figure when set against the annual average enlistment of 28,800 during the 5-year period before the war. The success of the recruitment policy was attributed to attractive levels of pay and the uncertainties of post-war life.[39]

Despite the recruitment efforts of the army the in-flow of new recruits, especially in the early days of 1919, was slow, and long-serving soldiers were often obliged to forego a quick demobilization. The British Army in India was an example of this. Churchill explained the position:

> Many of the Territorial and garrison battalions who left England in the autumn of 1914 to guard our Indian Empire or our Overseas possessions have served four hot weathers in the East without either relief or the excitement of battle. Up to the present hardly any volunteers have come forward to take their places ... It is therefore necessary while this 'after-war' or 'Old British Army' is being reconstituted that these men should remain abroad for another hot season.[40]

Two volunteers who did serve in India were Billie Picton and his friend Ralph Cheetham. They were typical of the new ex-civilian recruits. Both had left school when they were 14 and found jobs in a glass-bottling factory near Barnsley. When they were 18 they decided to enlist – it was an opportunity for them to escape their dull and monotonous work and seek some adventure. They hiked the 10 miles from their homes to the depot of the York and Lancaster Regiment in Pontefract and immediately enlisted. Both friends served on the North-West Frontier with the 2nd Battalion. Billie Picton remembered his time in the army as the best ten years of his life.[41]

Considering the numerous riots that were taking place at the time in various parts of the British Army in connection with demobilization it is noteworthy that no such disturbances took place in India. Sergeant J. Davey of the RE, stationed in India, recorded in his memoirs that a soldier was given permission to question his general: 'since the war for which the men had joined up was over, didn't he, the General, think it time the troops held up in India were sent home, so that they might see how their wives and families were faring, their men folk being away in many cases up to 4 years?' Sergeant Davey's only comment was: 'The question, being a fair and politely put one, was accepted in good part'.[42]

The Army of Occupation on the Rhine was Britain's biggest commitment. The British Second and Fourth Armies began their march to the German frontier on 17 November 1918 and by 13 December the allotted British area around Cologne was occupied by the Second Army under General Sir Herbert Plumer. Most of the Second Army was made up of Canadian and New Zealand troops together with British cavalry and infantry units. However, it was not long before the demobilization process changed the situation. On 16 December, a War Office order reached Sir Arthur Currie, the commander of the Canadian Corps, detailing how the demobilization of his men should take place. They were to return home via the UK at the rate of: '400 men daily this month, 17,500 in January and 20,000 each succeeding month'. A few days later British troops received notification of demobilization plans that would affect them. Coal miners were to be released first followed by policemen and those involved in the demobilization process. By 28 December all the Canadian divisions in the Cologne bridgehead area were relieved. The last New Zealand troops left the Rhineland on 25 March 1919.[43] On 21 April Sir Herbert Plumer was succeeded as commander on the Rhine by General Sir William Robertson. The Second Army was dissolved and took on the new title of the British Army of the Rhine (BAR).

Replacements for the gradually demobilized troops of the Army of the Rhine came from the Young Soldiers battalions made up mainly of 18-year-olds who had been conscripted during the last months of the war and held back in Britain. Seasoned troops were therefore replaced by barely trained youths.

As Churchill explained on 28 January 1919:

> young soldiers now serving will be sent from home to take their turn and do their share. All these will be in relief of the older men … In particular the 69 battalions of young soldiers of 18 years of age and upwards who are now at home will be sent at once to help guard the

> Rhine Bridgeheads … They will thus enable an equal number of men, old enough to be their fathers, to come home … they will have chance to see the German provinces which are now in our keeping and the battlefields where the British Army won immortal fame.[44]

Such an arrangement did not make life easy for General Robertson. His new troops were green: 'Many of the young infantry soldiers from home had not been instructed in the use of rifles … the young artillery soldiers could neither drive nor shoot, and the cavalry regiments were so weak in numbers that they could not move from one station to another without borrowing men from other regiments to lead their spare horses'. Robertson expressed a particular concern: 'the army was for some time deficient in two classes of men – cooks and commanding officers – without which it is impossible to have efficiency and contentment'.[45]

Fortunately, the German population, including ex-soldiers, gave little trouble. Life for the British troops in the Cologne area was made as pleasant as possible. An officers' club was opened in March; a theatre was taken over for soldiers to organize their own performances; swimming baths were reserved; and sports grounds were prepared. There was even a golf course. Equipment comprising: '2,300 sets of boxing gloves; 37,000 pairs of gym shoes; 8,000 gym vests; 224 football pumps; 17,200 football jerseys; 840 pairs of football hose; 52,700 football boots; 530 hockey sticks and 90 hockey balls' were provided. Education courses were organized covering the subjects required for the 1st Class Army Certificate. Two newspapers appeared and a musical society was formed. As the Official Historian was able to note: 'There were few signs of war in Cologne'.[46]

In the mind of the general public, the end of fighting meant demobilization and the end of conscription – and the government had acted on both of these. Demobilization was taking place with some speed and the Military Service Act of 1916 had gone. But the dilemma remained. How, in 1919, was the government to balance the swift run-down of its forces through demobilization with its post-Armistice military obligations? The build-up of a new voluntary army would clearly take many months or even years. General Wilson, supported by a strong War Office faction, was all for continuing conscription. He believed that 'it would be unsafe to assume that [the new armies] will be obtainable on a voluntary basis'.[47] But such a move was politically and socially unacceptable and Lloyd George was against it.

The solution was a halfway house. The Naval, Military and Air Force Service Act of March 1919, which was to be in force until April 1920, enabled the government to retain soldiers who had enlisted after 1 January 1916, were under 37 and had fewer than two wound stripes. It therefore included the young soldiers who had been recruited just before the end of hostilities as well as experienced troops in India and other regions covered by the British Army. It was a compulsory extension of the 1916 Act, but it was not conscription and it did not preclude authorized demobilization.

When the Bill went through Parliament it was not without opposition. The labour leader, J.H. Thomas, was concerned that a conscript army would be used to crush any agitation by working men and proposed that volunteers would be quickly raised if soldiers received a decent wage. Sir D. Maclean, leader of the Independent Liberals, said that 'in 1916 the Government of the day had a measure of public support for the first Military Service Bill which did not exist for the present bill … there should be reliance on the voluntary system. It was not too late'.[48] And Mr T. Griffiths, the Labour Member for Pontypool, went as far as to say: 'We have destroyed militarism in Germany and were introducing it at home'.[49]

Many thousands of workers took part in a demonstration in Barrow and a resolution was passed protesting against conscription.[50] The Miners' Confederation, meeting on 26 March, called both for a withdrawal from Russia and an end to conscription. These demands were accompanied by the threat of industrial action. Concerns that conscription and the requirement for troops in Russia were connected were specifically dealt with by Churchill during the second reading of the Bill on 6 March 1919:

> There is not the slightest truth in saying that we want this bill for conscription … because of Russia or because we contemplate sending a large mass of conscript troops to Russia. If there was not a single British soldier in Russia, or if it was possible by a gesture to withdraw every single British soldier from Russia, or if there was no such place as Russia, I should still introduce this bill … This bill has nothing whatsoever to do with Russia.[51]

The Times of 7 February 1919 supported the government's policy: 'From now until Peace is secured we must maintain adequate military strength; in other words, we must keep forces on the Rhine and other fronts, and for garrisons in India and other vital points of the British Empire, until they can be replaced by troops voluntarily enlisted for our after-war Army'. The article ended: 'Patience, Co-operation, and an intelligent appreciation of the Nation's needs will win us the Peace'. The *Observer* of 9 March also gave its support:

> Peace is truly ratified on the day when intentions are manifest in practice. Meanwhile voluntary effort does not suffice to meet the transient emergency. The Government rightly declines to be forced

> by these circumstances into adopting conscription as a principle of peace-time defence. The right and only remaining course to take is to delay the dispersal of our forces, retaining a proportion with the colours upon just principles of selection. Voluntary recruitment, as a normal basis for the future army proceeds *pari passu*, and volunteers will be available to release men compulsorily retained.

An advertisement, published in June in a local newspaper by Veda Bakeries of Lincolnshire, reflected what most people were thinking at the time: 'Let us remember our brave lads in the Army of Occupation. They must remain for a time yet to ensure that Peace shall be permanent. They need regular Veda Fruit Cake NOW just as much as when they were in the trenches of Flanders'.[52] In Parliament the final reading of the 1919 Military Service Bill was passed 283 votes to 61.

Somewhat belatedly, the Ministry of Reconstruction published, in its series of Reconstruction Problems, a pamphlet (No. 37) justifying the government's 1919 military policy. It was entitled 'The Mission of the British Army' and it was drafted with great care and with some apparent nervousness.[53] There were at least three versions. The first draft was written by a Captain Rowe in May 1919, but it was rejected on the grounds that it was 'too parliamentary' and 'rather too philosophic' in style. A second version, this time by a Kenneth Colvile, was considered 'not suitable'. A third, and accepted version, by a Colonel de Watteville, eventually appeared in August. It sold widely for 2*d*.

The stated aim of the pamphlet was 'to educate the ordinary citizen in his conception of what the British Army is and for what it exists, and especially what are the present calls on the Army arising out of the present condition of the world'.[54] At that stage, the government's approach was well publicized and hardly needed further explanation. The pamphlet, though well-meaning, was essentially a piece of propaganda supporting the government's actions. A selection of sentences gives the flavour of the document:

> The Military Service Bill of 1919 was an extraordinary measure designed to meet an extraordinary situation ... The Act was forced upon us by the necessity of releasing three quarters of our armies of 1918 ... Conscription was not being retained as such; the term is being erroneously used ... The present is but a period of transition, and the question of our ultimate military status in the future is unsettled.

The writer considered it necessary to refer to ancient history comparing the responsibilities of the British Empire in 1919 with those of the Roman Republic of the second century BC. They both 'radiated civilisation throughout the world'. The pamphlet is certainly an interesting historical document but, coming as late as it did, it was neither educational nor inspiring.

Even while the various drafts of the 'The Mission of the British Army' were being written the numerical strength and the structure of the army was steadily changing. The dual pressures of implementing demobilization and making economies transformed the military scene. In Europe, Sir Douglas Haig's GHQ was closed down (April 1919) and at the same time the four armies stationed in France and Flanders (the First, Third, Fourth and Fifth) were reduced to one. Lieutenant General Sir J.J. Asser became the GOC British Troops in France and Belgium responsible mainly for the clearing up and disposal of equipment. The British Army of the Rhine was to report directly to the War Office. The divisions in Germany, against the advice of Sir Douglas Haig, were given new names dropping the numerical identifications used during the war. The famous 29th Division, for example, became the Southern Division.

The British Army of the Rhine was never required to advance into Germany to enforce a peace treaty. On several occasions – 20 May, 23 May, 27 May and 20 June – General Robertson was ordered by Marshal Foch to make the necessary preparations and was told that he would have 72 hours warning of an advance. At the last moment the Germans agreed to the peace terms in entirety and the British troops returned to their normal stations.[55]

The signing of the Versailles Peace Treaty on 28 June 1919 was a watershed. The threat of armed intervention in Germany receded. In August four of the Army of the Rhine's ten divisions in Germany were sent back to the UK and a fifth division returned in September. In October 74,269 men were demobilized from Germany, in November 66,366 and in December 24,038. By the end of 1919, apart from five brigades, the British Army of the Rhine had virtually disappeared.[56]

The process of demobilization and efforts to reduce costs applied in all theatres where the British Army operated. The Ministry of Reconstruction pamphlet on 'The Mission of the British Army' pointed out, in August 1919, that the Army of the Rhine had already been heavily reduced and that: 'Italy, and the Balkans have virtually been evacuated; the Caucasus has been handed over to the care of the Italians; and, but for the unsettled state of the Middle East, a large reduction might have been effected in that region also.' Table 3, below, shows the geographical distribution of the British Army at the end of October 1919, when the total Regimental strength was 1,064,743.

Table 3: Geographical Distribution of Forces, October 1919

Home 543,561	Black Sea 33,163
Colonies 14,860	Egypt 66,882
India 67,235	Mesopotamia 28,102
France 181,619	Russia 7,747
Italy 5,184	East Africa 536
Rhine 115,854	TOTAL 1,064,743

The total Regimental strength of the army, including the Territorials, fell from 3,676,473 at the beginning of January 1919 to 698,000 in December 1919 – a reduction of 80 per cent. (See Chart II below.)[57]

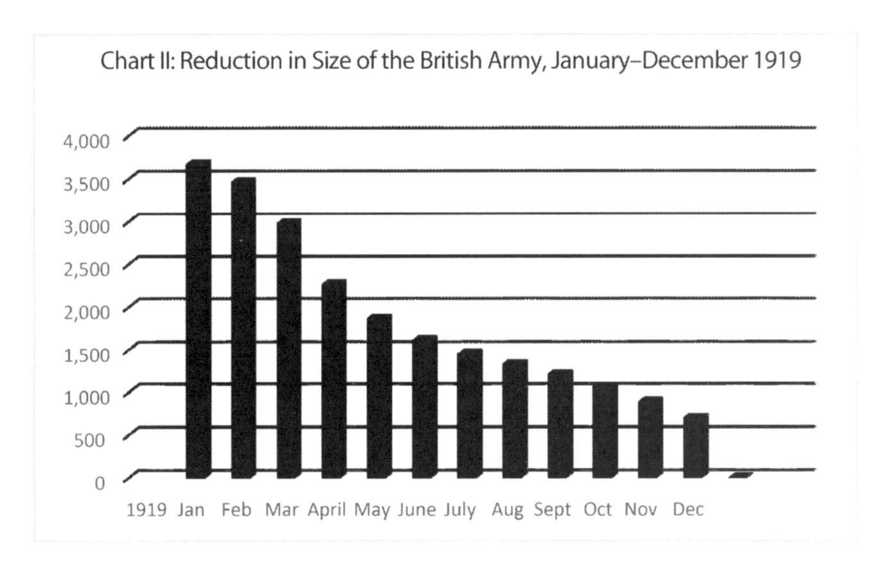

'The Mission of the British Army' set out four stages that the army would follow immediately after the war. It repeated a framework outlined by Churchill in a speech of 3 March 1919:

> The first period is covered by the end of the war in which we maintain our great national armies. The second period covers the demobilisation of those great national armies and the constitution 'out of their remains' of our present armies of occupation. The third period covers the creation of a standing Regular Army and the ultimate disbandment of the Armies of Occupation … The fourth period will cover the institution of the military system to be adopted in the future.[58]

Looking back over 1919, the government could take some satisfaction in the extent to which it had achieved the aims of the first three periods. By the end of 1919 the greater part of the 1918 army had been demobilized, not in the manner that was first planned and not without considerable unrest, but, in the end, effectively. Following the Armistice, the British Army, although stretched for numbers, had carried out its obligations, both within its Empire and through its Armies of Occupation. And the process of enlisting fresh troops to form a new Regular Army was well underway. The fourth period, the institution of a new military system, was for the future.

Postscript

The story of the soldiers' peace does not end with the demobilizing of the British Army in 1919. Certain related developments continued well into the 1920s, are of particular importance and they should be recorded.

Considering the number and size of the problems that faced the British government in 1919 it can reasonably be said that, in connection with the army, good progress had been made. However, there were many who thought that the country's political and social scene was far from satisfactory. *The Times* published a letter on 1 January 1920:

> If there is any word more than another which sums up the year 1919, it is surely 'disillusionment'... The ideals we were bidden to slave and die for seem to be very much at a discount now ... Did the war really take place in the same world and only end just over a year ago? And then there is Ireland, and Egypt, and India, and all the rest'.[1]

On the same day a leading article in the *Manchester Guardian* made a similar point: 'Few people would deny that 1919 has been a most disappointing year ... Everybody looked for all sorts of good things in the year after hostilities ceased. None of which seem to have been realised.'

The CIGS, Sir Henry Wilson, who had been at the centre of the military scene since the Armistice and who was a staunch champion of the British Army and the Empire, took a similar view. He also assessed 1919 as being 'disappointing ... the Frocks [politicians] have muddled everything, peace with our enemies, Ireland, Egypt, India, Trade Unions, everything ... we are certain to have trouble in Ireland, Egypt and India, possibly even with the Bolsheviks'. He was of the opinion that 'there is absolutely no grip anywhere'.[2] In December 1920 he wrote to General Rawlinson complaining of 'this miserable Government' and its Irish policy.[3] Everywhere he looked Wilson could see problems brought about by what he considered to be weak government. He regarded the fortunes of the army and the Empire to be inextricably linked and he was particularly concerned about the state of the army:

> owing to the Frocks having flung the British Army out of the window the day after the Armistice, the British Empire at the present moment has no Army worth the name, and in addition such semblance of troops as we have are scattered in a most scandalous manner … Now the picture that I see is this that if we are not careful we shall lose Ireland. If we lose Ireland we have lost the Empire … the whole Treaty of Versailles is going to crash right under our eyes.[4]

Some of Wilson's comments were prophetic. By February 1922, when Wilson moved out of the War Office, an Anglo-Irish Treaty had been signed and the Irish Free State had been given Dominion status. As a consequence, eighteen Irish battalions were no longer part of the British Army. British troops were withdrawn from southern Ireland in 1922. Formal independence had been granted to Egypt. The British influence in the Middle East was much reduced when Feisal was installed as King of Mesopotamia. Wilson was appalled and he directed his dismay at the government and Lloyd George in particular: 'But in truth the outlook in our poor country is exceedingly bad … With Ireland gone, with Egypt going, the date for India is not far removed … it is not the problems that have ever frightened me … but it is the nerveless, cowardly hands of those who sit in 10 Downing Street'.[5]

Wilson's preferred approach to the problems in Ireland, India and Egypt was to establish strong military control and put down any disturbance. He wrote in June 1921, in connection with Ireland, that he would: 'crush out the murder gang with ruthless hand'.[6] It was a policy that did not appeal to the government and, in the light of growing nationalism, it was a policy that was hardly likely to succeed in anything but the very short term.

It was especially likely to fail because of the government's defence policy in the 1920s – a policy brought about by Britain's difficult financial situation. The government decided that the economic plight of the country necessitated heavy cost reductions. The National Debt had risen from £677 million in 1910 to £7.8 billion in 1920 which was higher than the country's GDP of £6.2 billion.[7]

In such circumstances some drastic action needed to be taken. Lord Rothermere, the proprietor of the *Daily Mail*, took it upon himself to set up an Anti-Waste League which attacked what he considered to be excessive government spending. Candidates standing under this banner won three by-elections in 1921. Lloyd George's reaction was to form, in August 1921, a Committee of National Expenditure, headed by Sir Eric Geddes with the brief 'to recommend all possible reductions in the National Expenditure on Supply Service'. Such were the swingeing cuts proposed by this Committee that the process became known as the 'Geddes Axe'.

For the financial period 1921–2 Geddes proposed savings of £87 million. After some debate the government accepted reductions amounting to £52 million. To achieve this figure the planned expenditure on education, health, housing, pensions and unemployment was cut thus effectively repudiating the post-war promise of 'a land fit for heroes'. In February 1918 the Minister of Reconstruction, Christopher Addison, had drawn up a list of social reforms including a housing programme, the acquisition of land for soldiers' settlements, and the rebuilding of roads and railways. To Addison, the post-war priority was not the servicing of the massive debt, but further expenditure to increase national productivity and carry out the promise of improving the living conditions of the returning soldiers. But Addison's view was not accepted by the government.

Even as early as June 1919 there were signs of disillusion: 'Tommy went out to fight for his home, but had none to return to'.[8] The Geddes proposals confirmed such dissatisfaction. Business leaders tended to applaud the Geddes plans and called him a 'superman'; the more liberal-minded, such as the *Manchester Guardian* newspaper, commenting particularly on the cuts to education, condemned the proposals as 'going back to the 1870s'.[9]

Financial constraint determined the government's policy towards the armed forces which it set out in December 1920: 'The Cabinet are convinced of the necessity of curtailing military expenditure to the utmost extent compatible with the fulfilment of Imperial obligations and national safety'.[10] During the early 1920s the Defence Budget suffered the largest reductions – from £189.5 million in 1921–2 to £111 million for 1922–3 – a 42 per cent cut. Within these numbers the army estimates were reduced from £75 million to £55 million.[11] Eventually the War Office managed to maintain a budget for 1922–3 of £62 million, though actual expenditure, as shown in Table 4, below, was less. Army expenditure as a percentage of total government expenditure fell steadily from 37.7 per cent in 1918–19 to 5.5 per cent in 1922–3.[12]

Table 4: Government Expenditure, 1918–22

Year	**Amy Annual Expenditure, £m**	**Total Government Expenditure, £m**
1918–19	974.0	2,579
1919–20	521.5	1,665
1920–1	216.8	1,195
1921–2	95.1	1,079
1922–3	45.4	812

These cuts were accompanied by the Ten Year Rule, adopted by the Cabinet on 15 August 1919, which stated that:

> It should be assumed that the British Empire will not be engaged in any great war during the next ten years, and that no Expeditionary Force is required for this purpose ... the principal function of the Military and Air Forces is to provide garrisons for India, Egypt, the new mandated territories (other than self-governing) under British control, as well as provide the necessary support to the civil power at home ...[13]

It was a decision taken because it was considered that Britain had no sizeable enemies to guard against. It was taken also in the hope that the newly formed League of Nations, an off-spring of the peace discussions, would control any international conflict that might occur. The purpose of the British Army, therefore, was to be essentially the same as it was before the war, but without the element of Haldane's Expeditionary Force. Once more it was to be a police force for the Empire. The Ten Year Rule was renewed every year until 1932.

General Wilson considered the Geddes proposals as 'simply terrifying'.[14] As he wrote to General Allenby in January 1922: 'I presume the Government will swallow all Geddes proposals and probably ask for more, but as they stand they are sufficiently drastic. We are to start with a reduction of 28 Battalions, 8 Cavalry Regiments, and a lot of Batteries, etc. and then we are expected to be able to make further and considerable reductions!'[15] An embittered Wilson relinquished his office as CIGS in February 1922 and became a Unionist MP for North Down. He was shot dead on 22 June 1922 outside his home in London by two Irish republicans.

The government's austerity policies of the early 1920s brought about a series of reductions in the size of the British Army – from 1,064,743 in October 1919 to 205,095 in October 1923. The pre-war (1913) size of the Regular Army was 247,250.[16] The War Office Staff was reduced from 4,114 to 2,561 in the years 1922–5 – though this was generally agreed to be a removal of dead wood.

The Territorial Force, renamed the Territorial Army in 1922, did not escape the cuts. As the then Secretary of State for War, Sir Laming Worthington-Evans, pointed out in August 1921: 'A Territorial battalion costs £19,500 per year and by adopting a policy of amalgamation, or failing that, disbandment, a saving of over £400,000 a year can be effected'.[17] The War Office considered the part-time Territorials to be the most expendable part of the army – unsuitable for garrison roles in the Empire and unnecessary at home if invasion and war were unlikely.[18] The numbers in the Territorial Army fell by 42 per cent from its pre-war level of 245,779 to 140,626 in 1923. The Territorials were to provide home defence and be liable for service abroad only in emergencies.[19]

The government pamphlet of 1919, 'The Mission of the British Army', which aimed at explaining to the British public why the army existed, stated that: 'a well-trained national army on a larger scale might have prevented the war', and 'if we judge from the experience of the past five years, it would have been well worth the sacrifice of leisure and money to form a great National Army before 1914'. If that had been done, the pamphlet continued, 'the war might never have taken place'.[20] It was therefore ironic that only two years later the same government pursued policies that depleted the British Army to pre-1914 levels. The policy-makers bowed to financial pressures, introduced strict economy measures and were content to adopt the view that the war was something of an aberration and could never happen again. When, in 1926, the then CIGS, Sir George Milne, addressed his Chiefs of Staff, he described the war as 'abnormal'.[21]

The repetition of another global war was unthinkable particularly because of the heavy cost in lives and an aspect of the peace that touched every community in the country was the memory of those who had been killed. Some 750,000 British military personnel died in the war and 1919 saw the development of both national and local forms of commemoration. Peace may have come to those who were fortunate enough to survive the conflict, but, even so, many survivors suffered emotionally and physically as a result of their wartime experiences. Some carried a sense of guilt for having survived while their comrades had died. The families and friends of the dead continued to mourn their loss. The Armistice Day Silence was a profound act of mourning and remembrance. It was based on the practice in South Africa where a 3-minute silence had taken place at noon every day of the war. King George V, supported by the Cabinet, made a personal request that the Silence should take place on the first anniversary of the Armistice – 11 November 1919. In 1946 Remembrance Sunday became the main day of commemoration, but since 1995 the Silence has been increasingly observed on 11 November.[22]

In 1920 the two major British symbols of remembrance were unveiled – the Cenotaph in Whitehall and the Tomb of the Unknown Soldier in Westminster Abbey. These memorials demonstrated a public and national commitment never to forget those who had given their lives and they became a powerful and unifying force that brought together both the survivors and the dead. At a local level there was a natural movement to commemorate the dead servicemen of a village, a town or a city and this spread to cover local organizations such as places of work, schools, social clubs and sports centres.

Following the South African War it became customary for the names of the fallen to be inscribed on a memorial or a tablet regardless of rank, social standing, race or religion and this practice was continued. War memorials were special places of mourning where families and friends could remember in a very personal way. They became a feature of the British landscape. They took many forms – stone crosses or monuments, bronze or marble figures, stained glass windows, lych-gates, hospitals, gardens, village halls and clock towers. They were erected in churches, churchyards, schools, market squares and on public buildings and village greens. Most were unveiled in the early 1920s. It was only in a relatively few communities – around fifty-four – that all the serviceman who went to war returned. They are the Thankful Villages.

Even before the end of the war there were discussions in towns and villages throughout the country concerning the possible form of a war memorial. In the village of The Lee in Buckinghamshire, for example, the discussion began in February 1918 and continued for a further eighteen months. The villagers put forward a variety of suggestions: the restoration of a chapel; a simple structure in marble; an endowed bed at the local hospital; a drinking fountain; a gateway; an almshouse; a war museum. These suggestions were often hotly debated – the idea of a Church of England restored chapel was not acceptable to the Baptist community who threatened to erect a memorial of their own. Finally, in June 1919, the lady of the manor offered to contribute £50 if her suggestion of a granite Celtic cross was adopted. The village accepted this proposal and the war memorial, inscribed with the names of the thirty men of the village who were killed, was erected on the green at a cost of £350. Apart from the £50 donation, the cost was covered by the subscriptions of local people. The memorial was unveiled in January 1921. There are some 100,000 such war memorials in the UK generally paid for by local communities in a great and democratic tribute to the soldiers who died.[23]

The Imperial War Graves Commission was founded by Fabian Ware in 1917. Its aim was to care for the graves of all members of the Imperial Forces who had 'died from wounds inflicted, accident occurring or disease contracted, while on active service whether on land or sea'.[24] The policy adopted was that there would be no repatriation of bodies and there would be no distinction of treatment between officers and men. The dead had served together and they would lie together.

By May 1920 the Commission controlled 750 cemeteries tended by over 400 gardeners, many of whom were ex-soldiers. The graves were marked by headstones of Portland stone. They were of a uniform design showing the regimental badge, details of the dead soldier and with a short inscription chosen by the next of kin. The first cemetery to be completed was at Forceville in France. *The Times* described it as: 'The most perfect, the noblest, the most classically beautiful memorial that any loving heart or any proud nation could desire to their heroes fallen in a foreign field'.[25] Those who had no known grave – there were 350,000 in Belgium and France alone – were commemorated on imposing memorials such as the Menin Gate at Ypres, Tyne Cot near Passchendaele, the Thiepval Memorial on the Somme and the Helles Memorial in Gallipoli.

In 1919 the beginnings of battlefield tourism were seen. Visitors were considered to be either pilgrims (who were visiting the grave of a relative) or tourists (who were simply wishing to view the front-line areas). In 1922, when King George V, together with Rudyard Kipling whose son had been killed at Loos in 1915, visited cemeteries in Northern France, the official record was published as 'The King's Pilgrimage'.[26] The St Barnabus Society was formed by the Revd Michael Mullineaux, an ex-army padre, specifically to help the bereaved as they visited cemeteries. The Church Army and the YMCA prioritized their services and reserved their accommodation for relatives in search of graves. Battlefield guide books, notably those issued by Michelin, were produced to help both the pilgrim and the tourist. Guiding organizations, such as the Franco-British Travel Bureau, multiplied in numbers offering personally conducted tours, sometimes in 'a high class private motor'. Such tours were clearly for the wealthy and the Church Army was prompted, in 1919, to offer subsidised tours for bereaved relatives who paid what they could afford. In 1920 the government gave money to the Church Army and the YMCA to help poorer travellers. Even so, only a minute proportion of the relatives of dead soldiers had the money or the opportunity to take advantage of these tours. The experience of visiting the grave of a loved one was no doubt cathartic for the few, but most of those who mourned did so with their families and friends at their local war memorial.[27]

* * *

The soldiers' peace in 1919 was made up of many forms of individual experience. Some soldiers found themselves back in civilian life within weeks. Some, the fortunate majority in 1919, found work easily, at least in the short term, while others, particularly many of the disabled, became a statistic of unemployment. A large, but diminishing number of soldiers had to remain in the army for many months – in Germany or Egypt, Mesopotamia or India – until replacements could be found. But, eventually, and generally within the year of 1919, those soldiers who wished to leave the army did so following a process that, through their own protests, had achieved a measure of acceptability. Nevertheless, it can only be considered as lamentable that the life awaiting the demobilized soldier frequently fell short of his expectations as the promises made by the politicians failed to materialize and as economic conditions and work opportunities deteriorated in the 1920s. During the war prices had escalated with the Retail Index moving from 100 in July 1914 to 233 in November 1918. Real wages in mid-1918 were 75 per cent of their 1914 level.[28] The short-lived economic boom of 1919–20 was followed by the slump of 1921 during which unemployment reached 2.2 million. Among those out of work were thousands of ex-soldiers.

In 1919 the British Army had been dismantled. Over 3 million soldiers had been demobilized and much of the redundant military hardware had been scrapped or sold off. It was an undertaking of immense proportions. A remarkable feature of the whole dismantling process was the persistent effort of the politicians and public servants who, even from the early months of the war in 1914, conscientiously carried out their task of devising schemes that, in their honest opinion, best fitted the needs of the soldier and the country. Mistakes were made, but their dedication was unquestionable. Montagu, Llewellyn Smith, Brade, Addison and their colleagues on the numerous Reconstruction and Demobilization Committees, together with thousands of faceless administrators, spent countless hours proposing, debating, refining and recording the details of how and when and under what terms a soldier would re-enter civilian life and how the army would be broken up. What is particularly striking is that in all the vast amount of committee minutes, files and discussion papers there is no hint or suggestion that the demobilization process would be carried out other than in a context of victory. Even in the disappointing days of 1915, by which time the old Regular Army had virtually disappeared; even when British soldiers were killed in their thousands on the Somme and at Passchendaele; even when the Germans almost won the war in the spring of 1918, there was never any talk of the possibility of defeat or of how a defeat might affect the dismantling of the British Army. By any standards, it is a remarkable indication of the patriotism and professionalism of those who took on an almost impossible task. Their efforts should not be forgotten.

Appendix I

Soldiers' Strikes, 1918–19

Date	Place	Involved	Grievances/ Demands	Outcome
6 Dec. 1918	Taranto, Italy	West Indian troops	Equal pay with white soldiers and conditions of work	Ringleaders arrested
9 Dec. 1918	Le Havre	Miners from various Artillery units	Poor food and accommodation	Groups of miners shipped home
Dec. 1918	Falmouth	25 Garrison Battalion, Rifle Brigade	Unfair demobilization scheme Training regime to be reduced	Battalion demobilized within three weeks
Dec. 1918	Kantara, Egypt	Various Infantry units	Poor food and conditions Concerns about demobilization	Concessions on living conditions but no undertakings on demobilization
14 Dec. 1918	Wargnies le Petit, France	Units of RE	Refusal to march and carry full equipment	Concessions made
17 Dec. 1918	Nivelles, Belgium	7th Canadian Brigade	Objection to marching in full kit	9th Brigade arrested protesters Ten soldiers imprisoned

Date	Place	Involved	Grievances/ Demands	Outcome
18 Dec. 1918	Calais	RAOC workshops	Demand for shorter working week Longer holidays and better food	Concessions made
21 Dec. 1918	Le Havre	RASC workshop men	Hours of work	Hours reduced
3 Jan. 1919	Calais, Boulogne and Le Havre	RASC and RAOC workshop men	Hours of work Demobilization quotas	Hours reduced Quotas increased
3 Jan. 1919	Folkestone	10,000 men from RASC, RE and Infantry	Refused to return to France Pivotal men and demobilizers to return home	Contract men and others return home
4 Jan. 1919	Dover	2,000 soldiers	Pivotal and slip men to be released	Demands agreed
4 Jan. 1919	Bedford	RE, large group	Trivial work to stop Quicker demobilization	Pivotal and slip men to be released Promise to address demobilization issue
5 Jan 1919	Upper Norwood, SE London	Hospital discharge camp	Quick demobilization	Not stated
5 Jan. 1919	Salisbury Plain	Men to be sent to Russia	Objected to be part of compulsory draft	Demobilized
6 Jan. 1919	Shortlands, Grove Park, Sydenham	1,500 RASC men	Delays in demobilization Carrying out civilian work	Demobilization began 10 Jan.

Date	Place	Involved	Grievances/ Demands	Outcome
6 Jan. 1919	Osterley Park	3,000 RASC men plus troops returning to Salonika	Slow demobilization Poor food	From 8 Jan. 200 per day to be demobilized
6 Jan. 1919	Uxbridge	400 men from Armaments School	Slow demobilization Poor food	Grievances to be dealt with
6 Jan. 1919	Shoreham and Southwick	7,000 men march to Brighton	Delays in demobilization Telegraph sent to the PM	PM replies that demobilization to be speeded up
6 Jan. 1919	Winchester	150 soldiers	Quicker demobilization Better food	Men resume duties after talks with CO
6 Jan. 1919	Freshwater, IOW	Groups of men	Better food	Spokesmen arrested and later released
7 Jan. 1919	Park Royal	4,000 RASC	Quicker demobilization Better conditions and reduced hours No drafts to Russia	Demands agreed
7 Jan. 1919	Aldershot	Several hundred RASC, RAOC and RE	Quicker demobilization	Demobilization began 8 Jan.
7 Jan. 1919	Longmoor Camp	Various units	No details recorded	
7 Jan. 1919	Kempton Park	About 600 men with lorries to War Office	Slow demobilization Poor food	Grievances to be dealt with

Date	Place	Involved	Grievances/ Demands	Outcome
7 Jan. 1919	White City	100 RASC men	Slow demobilization Fewer hours	Demands to be addressed within a week
7 Jan. 1919	Maidstone	1,000 men of Glosters, Queen's and Wiltshires	End of unnecessary duties and drill	Demands agreed
7 Jan. 1919	Biggin Hill	700 technicians	Delays in demobilization Bad food Officers using troops for personal duties	Grievances to be dealt with Men sent on ten days' holiday
7 Jan. 1919	Leeds	700 in RASC MT	Quicker demobilization Better rations No sentry duty	Unknown
7 Jan. 1919	Bristol	100 men in Bedfordshire Regiment	Quicker demobilization Better pay	Unknown
7 Jan. 1919	Falmouth	600 Rifle Brigade men	Reduced drill and night manoeuvres	Demands met
7 Jan. 1919	Blackpool	7,000 RAMC men	Better pay and conditions Fewer parades	Drafts of men demobilized
8 Jan. 1919	Richborough Camp	Demonstration	Better conditions	Unknown
8 Jan. 1919	Edinburgh	100 men HLI	Immediate demobilization	Promises to speed demobilization
8 Jan. 1919	Belfast	3rd Battalion, Somerset LI	Quicker demobilization Fewer parades	One parade per day only Look into demobilization

Date	Place	Involved	Grievances/ Demands	Outcome
8 Jan. 1919	Cromarty	700 Seaforth Highlanders	Quicker demobilization	Unknown
8 Jan. 1919	Felixstowe	Several thousand soldiers and RAF	Protest against retaining men over 41	Grievance to be considered
9 Jan. 1919	Heaton Park	600 soldiers	Demobilization system wrong Better food	Complaints sent to War Office
9 Jan. 1919	Leith	200 Scottish Rifles	Poor food Refused to carry out drill	Unknown
9 Jan. 1919	Witley	Canadian soldiers attack a police station in Godalming	Poor conditions and victimization of a comrade	Unknown
9 Jan. 1919	Étaples	Various infantry	Petty restrictions	Demands met
9 Jan. 1919	Kilnsea	Group of RE and KOYLI	Bad work conditions	Demands met
Mid-Jan. 1919	Southampton	5,000 soldiers	Various	Dispersed by armed troops
Mid-Jan. 1919	Newport and Swansea	Group of soldiers	Quicker demobilization	Unknown
Through Jan. 1919	Calais, Valdelievre workshops	RASC plus 5,000 infantry plus QMRAC	Quicker demobilization 36-hour week Leave to find a job Reduced hours of work Better food	Demobilization began Reduced hours Improved rations

Date	Place	Involved	Grievances/ Demands	Outcome
10 Jan. 1919	Stirling Castle	455th Agricultural Company	Quicker demobilization Working for farmers at low pay	Demonstrators penalized
11 Jan. 1919	Yate, Bristol	700 RAF and RASC	Protest against demobilization of short-service men	Told that the men were pivotal
13 Jan. 1919	Harlaxton, Lincs	400 soldiers attached to RAF	Protest against demobilization system. Pivotal men not allowed to leave Parades to stop	CO to represent their grievances
13 Jan. 1919	Dannes, Calais	RAOC labourers	Reduced hours of work	Unknown
15 Jan. 1919	Calais	RE	Working hours	Hours reduced
16 Jan. 1919	Kettering	Groups of soldiers	Better food More free time	Promises to improve matters
23 Jan. 1919	Sinderland, Altrincham	250 RASC	Shorter hours	To be give consideration
23 Jan. 1919	Crystal Palace	Soldier clerks at discharge centre	Prevented from taking bribes to hasten procedure	Grievances on pay to be investigated
24 Jan. 1919	Dunkirk	Marines and crane drivers	Quicker demobilization	Demands agreed
27 Jan. 1919	Calais	Various troops at No. 6 Leave Camp	Extra leave to find a job	Disturbance ended by show of force
27 Jan. 1919	Calais, Vendoux	RASC and RAOC	Reduction in hours of work	Hours reduced
7 Feb. 1919	Victoria Station	Scottish, Canadian Australian and British troops	Shortage of boats to return soldiers home	Guards stopped riot

Date	Place	Involved	Grievances/ Demands	Outcome
15 Feb. 1919	Witley, near Guildford	Canadian soldiers raided a canteen	Poor food	One rioter killed by sentries
22 Feb. 1919	Archangel Area	RASC, RAOC and Yorkshire Regiment	Protest that missing out on jobs at home No wish to advance on Archangel front	Ringleaders arrested
Feb.–May 1919	Kantara, Egypt	Various troops	Grievances over working conditions Petty restrictions	Grievances to be investigated
4/5 March 1919	Kinmel Park, Rhyl	Canadian soldiers	Delays in promised demobilization	Demobilization speeded up Five rioters killed
March 1919	Gosport	300 British ex-prisoners of war	Refuse orders to guard German POWs	Grievances to be taken up
3 May 1919	Seaford	Canadian soldiers	Canadian Military Police arrest a black soldier	Police office attacked
10 May 1919	Guildford	Canadian and British soldiers and ex-servicemen	Fighting	Police stood by. Canadians moved back to camp
7 June 1919	Epsom	Canadian ASC	Release of soldiers in prison	Riot One man killed
6–9 June 1919	Plymouth	British troops returning from Egypt	Refused to go into quarantine following outbreak of smallpox	Allowed home

Date	Place	Involved	Grievances/ Demands	Outcome
14 June 1919	Witley	Canadian soldiers' gambling gang imprisoned	Riots and arson	Forty rioters arrested
17 June 1919	Ripon	23rd Canadian Battalion	Sailing cancelled 200 soldiers raided canteen	Fifteen men convicted
19 July	Luton	Soldiers and locals	Riot on Peace Day arrangements and pensions	Town hall burnt down
22 Aug. 1919	Southampton	200 West Country and Midlands soldiers	Protest at demobilization system Refused to board ship to 'distant theatre'	Offer to discuss grievances

Appendix II

Industrial Classes and Groups

1. Agriculture
2. Seamen and fisherman
3. Coal and shale mining
4. Other mining
5. Slate mining
6. Quarries
7. Food
8. Explosives
9. Indiarubber
10. Printing
11. Woollen
12. Cotton
13. Other textile trades
14. Dyeing
15. Boot makers
16. Leather tanning
17. Other leather trades
18. Clothing
19. Sawmilling
20. Furniture
21. Coach building
22. Shipbuilding
23. Iron and Steel manufacture
24. Tinplate manufacture
25. Iron foundry
26. Engineering
27. Other metal trades
28. China
29. Brick
30. Building
31. Railway
32. Dock labourer
33. Carters
34. Motor drivers
35. Public employees
36. General labourers
37. Commercial
38. Warehouseman
39. Domestic
40. Other occupations
41. Employers

Source: TNA, WO 106/344, April 1917.

Appendix III

Demobilization – Questions and Answers

Extract from Reconstruction Problems, No. 3, Demobilisation – questions and answers (source TNA, RECO 1/879).

1 Q. *How soon after the end of the War shall I personally get home?*
A. That depends principally upon the nature of your employment in civil life and whether there is a definite job waiting for you on your return.

2 Q. *Will not demobilisation take place then by military units?*
A. No. The Government has adopted the general principle of demobilisation by individuals in accordance with the requirements of industry and commerce.

3 Q. *How will the authorities know what my employment in civil life is and whether there is a job waiting for me?*
A. Your Army Book 64, which every soldier carries, gives the number of your Industrial Group and your Trade or Calling. In addition, as long before the probable date of demobilisation as possible, you will be required to fill up a form stating your home address, whether you are married or single, and, if you require employment after the War, particulars of your previous employment, your Trade union, if any, and as to any promise on the part of your employer to keep your place open for you.

IT IS OF THE UTMOST IMPORTANCE, IF YOU WISH TO GET YOUR DISCHARGE AS EARLY AS POSSIBLE AND OBTAIN THE BEST CHANCE OF IMMEDIATE EMPLOYMENT IN CIVIL LIFE THAT, WHEN THE TIME COMES, THIS FORM SHOULD BE FILLED UP FULLY, LEGIBLY AND ACCURATELY.

4 Q. *But will not some of us have to be left behind with our unit to deal with guns, stores, horses, ammunition, etc?*

A. Yes. 'Cadres', or skeleton units, will be required for this purpose and these will be made up of men who have not got a definite job waiting for them and whose work in civil life is not of urgent national importance.

Arrangements will be made for men who are continuing with the colours in the Post-bellum army and men enlisted on attestations under which they have still more than two years to serve to have furlough before recommencing military duties, the majority being required for service abroad. The actual order of demobilisation will be as follows:-

(1) 'Demobilisers', i.e., those required in their military or civil capacity to enable the work of demobilisation to be carried out.
 'Pivotal Men', *i.e.*, those men in the various industries without whom the bulk of the men to be employed cannot get to work effectively.
 The numbers to be demobilised in these two classes will be very limited, and only absolutely indispensable men will be included in them.
(2) Men who have definite jobs waiting for them on their return – hereafter referred to as 'Slip' men (see Question 7), in the order of the priority of their Industrial Groups.
(3) Men who have not got definite jobs waiting for them, but whose employment in civil life is in an industry which, because it is of high national importance from the point of view of reconstruction, is likely to be able to provide work for them immediately.
(4) Other 'Non-Slip' men in the order of importance of their civil employment.
(5) The Cadres, some of which will, however, be returned concurrently with the above groups.

5 Q. *Is no preference to be given to married men or to men with long service at the front?*

A. Yes, *within each group* preference will be given to married men over single, and a certain proportion of each draft will be men with a long period of service in the field and men who are time-expired soldiers enlisted on normal attestations before the War.

6 Q. *Can you explain exactly how my Commanding Officer would make up a draft of, say, one hundred men?*

A. After the 'demobilisers,' the 'pivotal men' and the men engaging for, or liable to serve in, the new Regular Army have gone home, he will make up his draft from men for whom he has received release slips, *i.e.*, men for whom definite jobs are known to be waiting. If he had 100 'slips' left in his battalion those 100 men would go. If, however, he had, say 120, he would give preference to men whose Industrial Groups stood highest on the list of priority and to married men. In the same way, if he had only 90 slip men he would make up the other ten from 'non-slip' men according to the priority of their Industrial Groups. In both cases he would include a proportion of men with a long period of service in the field and men who had enlisted on normal attestations before the war, if he had them, whether they have jobs waiting for them or not, or whether they belong to priority Groups or not.

7 **Q.** *What exactly are those slips of which you speak?*

A. In the answer to Question 3 it was stated that, before demobilisation began, every man would be required to fill up a form giving particulars of his previous employment, etc. These forms will be collected and forwarded to the Employment Department of the Ministry of Labour at the Claims and Record Office, Kew, where they will be sorted according to the Employment Exchanges, within the areas of which the men's pay address lie. In the cases where the man states that his employer has promised to keep his place open for him, this statement will be checked, and if it is found to be correct, the tear-off 'Slip' at the bottom of the form will be returned to the man's commanding officer. That man, then, becomes a 'slip' man. The same thing will happen where a job is found for the man, although it had not been previously promised.

8 **Q.** *How will the Government know what are the trade requirements referred to in the answer to Question 2?*

A. The trades and occupations in the country have been divided into groups, and a 'Priority List' of these Industrial Groups will be prepared, placing them in the order of their national importance from the point of view of the re-establishment on a peace basis of the essential industries of the country. Industries that it is vital to re-establish immediately will be placed high up on the list, which may be altered from time to time according to the season of the year (which would affect the claims of some) and the available supplies of raw material, shipping, etc. (which would govern the amount of employment in others). It must be remembered that it is not only of importance to the nation that the essential industries should be re-established first, but that it would be to the disadvantage of the individual to give him priority of discharge and thereby return him to a trade that had not had sufficient time to adapt itself to peace conditions and where unemployment was consequently inevitable and widespread.

9 Q. *Is the order in which these Industrial Groups are now numbered the order in which they will be demobilised?*

A. No, the present numbering is merely for reference purposes and bears no relation to their national importance or the order in which they will stand in the eventual Priority List.

10 Q. *Are any steps being taken to prevent all the available jobs being obtained by the Army at Home?*

A. The Armies at Home and abroad will, as far as possible, be demobilised by equal numbers daily so that neither portion of the Forces shall get an unfair advantage. It must be remembered in this connection that the Home Army contains, at any particular moment, large numbers of men who have served long spells in theatres of active operations.

11 Q. *At what average rate is it expected that demobilisation will be carried out?*

A. The rate of demobilisation must be dependent on the means of transportation available, *e.g.*, ships, and railway trains. No doubt use will be made of march route and mechanical transport, both Overseas and at Home. The limiting factor will probably be the amount of dock and wharf space available. The estimated daily rate is a high one, and there is no intention of keeping any man in the Army longer than is absolutely necessary. Prisoners of War, Sick and Wounded in medical care will be demobilised as they are repatriated and physically fit for return to civil life, irrespective of any other consideration.

12 Q. *In the answer to Question 5 you said that units would be reduced to cadres who would be required for the care and transportation of stores, etc. How large will those cadres be?*

A. About one-third of War Establishment in some cases and less in others. *All* cadres will not necessarily be retained until all the individuals in the first four classes (see answer to Question 4) have been disbanded. Those required for the re-organisation of the new Regular Army will be brought home concurrently with parties for dispersal. The first to be brought home will be those detailed for foreign reliefs. The personnel of these cadres, if not continuing in the

Service, will be demobilised in the ordinary course. A stream of cadres will be repatriated concurrently with the stream of dispersal drafts.

13 Q. *Supposing that I am detailed by my Commanding Officer for a particular draft, can you explain exactly what will happen to me from the time I leave my unit until I reach my home?*

A. If you are abroad your draft will be sorted out into parties for various Concentration Camps at suitable points behind the front which serve certain Dispersal Areas at Home. For instance, if your home is in Bradford you would be sent from your unit to the Concentration Camp for the West Riding of Yorkshire, where you will meet other men from other units, all of whom are going to the West Riding. From the Concentration Camp (or Collecting Place in the case of units serving at Home) there will be mapped out a particular route – sea, road or rail – by which parties will travel direct to the Dispersal Stations in their particular area at Home. On leaving your unit you will be provided with a Dispersal certificate which will give you all the information required en route together with a list of the arms, equipment, etc., that you will carry with you.

14 Q. *How long shall I be kept at the Dispersal Station, and what will happen to me there?*

A. Experiments have been carried out which show that it will only be necessary for men to be kept at Dispersal Stations for a few hours. You will hand in there your arms and equipment, and will be liable to be charged for any deficiencies as shown by the list on your Dispersal Certificate. If you are in a unit serving in the United Kingdom you will not take your arms and equipment to a Dispersal Station. You will then receive:-

(1) A protection Certificate,
(2) A Railway Warrant to your home,
(3) A Cash Payment,
(4) An Out-of-Work Donation Policy (See Question 20),
(5) A Ration Book, and will be at liberty to proceed to your home. There will be no further reporting or formalities except such as can be done through the post.

15 Q. *Will that be the time of my final discharge?*

A. No, you will be entitled first to 28 days furlough, during which time you will receive your pay and ration allowance, and the separation or family allowance to your wife or dependants will be continued. At the expiration of your furlough you will be finally demobilised. You should not, however, wait for this before beginning work in civilian employment.

16 Q. *What will be the cash payment that I shall receive at the Dispersal Station?*

A. It will be a part payment on account of the following:-

(1) Any credit balance of your accounts.
(2) Pay and ration allowance during your 28 days furlough.
(3) Any Service or other gratuity you have earned.
(4) An allowance for the purchase of plain clothes.

The balance of the total due to you on the above, with the exception of any war gratuity, which will be placed to your credit in the Post Office Savings Bank, will be forwarded to you through the post in three weekly payments during your period of furlough. The money or postal orders will only be cashable on production of the Protection Certificate that will be issued to you at the Dispersal Stations.

17 Q. *What shall I have to do with my uniform?*

A. You will be allowed to retain it (except your great-coat), together with your boots and underclothes, as your private property. You will be permitted to wear uniform during your 28 days furlough, at the expiration of which you will be expected to have re-clothed yourself in plain clothes and your great-coat will have to be returned.

18 Q. *Supposing that I am not a 'Slip' man – i.e., that I have no definite job waiting for me – what assistance shall I get in obtaining work?*

A. In the first place every effort will have been made by the local Employment Exchange, working in conjunction with the Local Advisory Committee (see Question 23) and the appropriate trade organisations, to make you into a 'Slip' man, that is, to find a definite job for you before you come home. On the form that you will have filled up before demobilisation you will have stated whether, if your previous employer had not promised to keep your place open for you, you would like that employer to be asked to re-engage you, and if that cannot be arranged what precise nature of work you require. You will also have been asked for the names of other previous employers and to state any special experience you have gained while serving with the colours – *e.g.*, as a signaller or artificer – which would be likely to be useful to you in obtaining civil employment. These employers and, if necessary, others will then be communicated with. In the second place you will yourself apply to the Exchange on your return and to your Trade Union if you belong to one.

19 Q. *Will not most of the available jobs be already filled by munition workers and women?*

A. In a large number of cases employers have undertaken to reinstate their former employees now serving with the Forces, and there is every reason to think that they will gladly fulfil their obligation. Even where no promise has been made, it may be anticipated that the discharged man will generally be given consideration. Moreover, in many of the organised industries formal agreements or undertakings exist between the employer and the Trade Unions under which priority of employment is to be given to men who have served in the Forces. As regards controlled establishments in munitions industries the Munitions Acts provide that in any readjustment of staff which may have to be effected after the War, priority of employment will be given to workmen in the owner's employment at the beginning of the war who have been serving with the Colours or who were in the owner's employment when the establishment became a controlled establishment.

20 Q. *Supposing that I fail to get a job, or that I am successful in obtaining one, but lose it again owing to bad trade or other causes, is any provision being made for me during unemployment?*

A. Yes you will receive before your discharge a free Out-of-Work Donation Policy which will remain in force for one year from the date of your discharge, and will be payable for not more than 20 weeks in the year. The weekly payments under this policy will be at a higher rate than under the National Unemployment Insurance Scheme of 1911, and the benefits will be on a graduated scale according to the number of children under 14.

21 Q. *Has any alteration been made in the ordinary procedure of the Employment Exchanges to meet the special needs of demobilisation?*

A. Yes, working in close co-operation with the Employment Exchange there will be Local Advisory Committees to whom the ex-soldier will be able to apply for any information and advice in connection with demobilisation, employment or training.

22 Q. *Of whom will these Local Advisory Committees consist?*

A. They will be representative of all the industries of the district and of employers and workpeople in equal numbers, with a small number of members who are for various reasons likely to be able to give special help during the demobilisation period.

23 Q. *But will such a body be able to deal in sufficient detail with any particular Trade?*

A. It has been realised that some sub-division will be necessary, as representatives of agriculture, for instance, might not be sufficiently acquainted with the conditions in, say, Engineering, and for this purpose Trade Sub-Committees will be set up where necessary, consisting of representatives of the employers and workpeople in equal numbers, to deal only with details in connection with their own trade. It is to these bodies of experts that the individual ex-soldier will be able to make personal application for assistance and advice in any difficulty.

24 Q. *In the reply to Question 21, you mentioned training. Can you tell me what help will be given to a man who finds himself unable through wounds or ill-health to follow his previous employment.*

A. The Local War Pensions Committee set up by the Ministry of Pensions will advise the partially disabled man on this and other points, will consider what other employment he might be fitted for, and will assist him in obtaining training for it.

25 Q. *What will be the position of the man who was still an apprentice at the time he joined up?*

A. The whole question of interrupted apprenticeship has been gone into very carefully by the Government, in consultation with the Employers and the Trade Unions, and a scheme has been prepared. Further information on this question will be made public before demobilisation begins.

26 Q. *Is any provision being made to give the men any opportunity of improving their educational training during the period of demobilisation?*

A. Yes it is hoped greatly to extend the scheme of Educational Training that, after being in operation at Home for some time, was started in France in March 1918, and which has been received with enthusiasm by all ranks.

27 Q. *Can you give me an idea of the sort of subjects in which instruction will be given?*

A. Classes are already being held in no less than eleven languages, in economics, political economy, mathematics, chemistry, electric lighting and power, art and design, the principles of machines, accountancy, agricultural science, and many other subjects, and it is intended to make the whole scheme much more comprehensive during the time following the cessation of hostilities, and to place facilities of real value at the disposal of all who may wish to take advantage of the period before their own discharge to improve their education and their equipment for civil life.

28 Q. *What will happen to men who came from abroad to join the Army for the War?*

A. They will be repatriated, at the public expense, as soon as their services can be dispensed with. This facility will be extended to all who can prove that their home is Overseas, whether they joined the Army abroad, or came to the United Kingdom after the outbreak of War for the purpose.

The above description of the scheme shows how it applies to Forces in the United Kingdom or in France.

It is found that it applies with but slight alteration, not only to Expeditionary Forces in other Theatres of War than France, but also to Commands abroad which during the war have been garrisoned by troops for its duration.

In the case of these it will not be a hard-and-fast rule that all units are to be reduced to cadres before being embarked for the United Kingdom. In fact, the proportion of drafts of individual men for dispersal to the number of cadres to be embarked will almost entirely depend on the class and quantity of shipping available.

The repatriation of Dominions and Overseas contingents direct from Theatres of War or the United Kingdom, according as they are situated when demobilisation occurs, will be in accordance with the express wishes of their own Governments and will be as expeditious as transport facilities allow.

Appendix IV

Disabled Officers' Gratuity, etc.

Extracts from Disabled Officers' Gratuity, Retired Pay, etc. on Discharge from Service. (source TNA, PIN 15/398).

An Officer, disabled in consequence of his war service may, according to the circumstances of his case, be awarded any or all of the following:-

(1) War service gratuity from the War Office, paid to Officer whether disabled or not.
(2) Wound gratuity or pension from the War Office.
(3) Retired pay or gratuity (corresponding to the disablement pension or gratuity awarded to non-commissioned ranks) from the Ministry of Pensions.

Of these the Officer may receive the War service gratuity and the wound gratuity or pension while still in the service. The retired pay will only be awarded after he is invalided out of the service or demobilised.

WAR SERVICE GRATUITIES

General Conditions. – Re-employed retired Officers, Officers of the Special Reserve and Territorial Force, and most Officers holding temporary commissions receive from the War Office a gratuity in respect of service during the war. In the case of re-employed retired Officers, the gratuity is reckoned at 31 days' pay for each year or part of a year of war service. In other cases it amounts to 124 days' pay for the first year and 62 days' pay for each further year or part of a year.

Officers holding permanent commissions on the active list of the Regular Army receive a war gratuity as laid down in A.O.85 of 1919. No service rendered subsequent to the 3rd August, 1919 reckons towards the gratuities. The gratuities referred to in this and the preceding paragraph are payable on the 4th August, 1919, or on the cessation of employment, if it occurs before that date.

Gratuities, wounds and disablement pensions are exempt from Income tax, gratuities from the 4th August, 1914, and wound and disablement pensions from the 5th April, 1918.

Ill Health. – Gratuities may be granted by the War Office to Officers who are otherwise eligible and who relinquish their commissions, or are demobilised, or revert to unemployment, **owing to ill-health** *except* in cases where the disability is attributable to or aggravated by the Officer's own negligence or misconduct.

Resignation. – Normally the gratuity is not admissible in the case of an Officer who voluntarily resigns his commission but it is allowed to an Officer so resigning after 1st June, 1918, provided he has performed at least two years' commissioned service during the present war. An Officer whose voluntary resignation is accepted since the signing of the Armistice (11th November, 1918) would not lose the gratuity by reason of his having asked for his discharge.

Misconduct and Other Causes. – An Officer discharged for misconduct or inefficiency, or as the result of the finding of a Court Martial, is ineligible for gratuity.

No application is necessary for these gratuities. They will be credited to Officers' accounts by the Army Agents.

WOUND GRATUITIES AND PENSIONS

An Officer who has lost a limb or eye in action, or suffered a wound equivalent to the loss of a limb, is granted a gratuity, which varies with rank. It is £250 for a captain or subaltern, and at higher rates for higher ranks. At the end of 12 months the Officer may become entitled to an annual pension (minimum £100), which is permanent for actual loss of a limb or eye and *may* become so in the other cases according to the ultimate condition of the case.

If the Officer has suffered a 'very severe' wound in action he may have a gratuity at the above mentioned rate for the first year following the date of his wound, the amount varying according to the period for which he is incapacitated for general service. At the end of that period he may, if the wound is still 'very severe' and likely to be permanent, be awarded a wound pension at a rate varying with rank (£50 for captains and subalterns and at higher rates for higher ranks).

If an Officer loses a limb or eye through performance of military duty (not in action) or suffers very serious and permanent injury, he may have an injury pension (maximum £100 a year for a captain or subaltern). If less seriously injured through the performance of military duty, he may be granted a gratuity if the injury is severe and likely to be permanent.

Officers should apply in writing for wound gratuities, wound pensions, and injury pensions to the Secretary, War Office, S.W.1.

RETIRED PAY

An Officer who retires or relinquishes his commission or is placed in the Territorial Force Reserve *on account of medical unfitness*, which is certified to be either *attributable to or aggravated by* Military Service in consequence of the war may be awarded retired pay according to the degree of his disablement, provided that his disablement was not due to his own negligence or misconduct. Medical unfitness may be the result of wound, injury, or disease.

Once it has been determined that the Officer's disablement is due to his War Service, the amount of his retired pay will depend on the estimate of the Ministry of Pensions, based on a medical examination of the Officer by a Medical Board, as to the extent of the injury which the Officer has sustained. This does not mean the extent to which his earning power in relation to any particular occupation is reduced, but simply *the amount of the loss of general physical capacity* which he has sustained by the injury or disease for which he is invalided.

The grant of retired pay will be either temporary or permanent according as the Officer's medical condition is susceptible of improvement or likely to be permanent. On the Officer's discharge from the Army a temporary award is made in nearly all cases, and the amount of the award will depend on a medical estimate of the disablement at the time that the Officer is examined. The retired pay awarded on the first occasion will be subject to review at intervals according to the period for which the Ministry of Pensions consider the condition in which they find the Officer is likely to last. It is important to remember that *before the period of award expires the Officer may apply* to the Ministry of Pensions for a further medical examination and renewal of his retired pay if he considers that his condition requires this. Once fixed it will not be reduced on account of anything the Officer may earn by his work, though it may be increased temporarily or permanently if his condition at a later date becomes worse.

When the disability is deemed to have been aggravated and not entirely caused by service, the retired pay is fixed at a rate corresponding to the full disablement of the Officer, although only a small part of the disablement may have resulted from service; but the duration of the retired pay depends on the period during which the effects of the aggravation continue.

Statutory Right. – Under a recent Act of Parliament every Officer is now Statutorily entitled to the pension (retired pay) gratuity or allowance awarded to him by the Ministry of Pensions in respect of disability due to or aggravated by war service, subject to the conditions contained in the Royal Warrant.

Rates of Retired Pay. – The extent of disablement is reckoned in percentages and the amount of retired pay for each degree of disablement will vary according to the rank of the Officer. For this purpose temporary or acting rank is reckoned as substantive rank provided the Officer was actually holding the temporary or acting rank when injured or removed from duty in consequence of disablement. The rates of retired pay are shown in the following table:-

Degree of Disablement	Percentage Degree of Disablement	Retired Pay on Account of Disablement											
		Officers Not Holding Permanent Commissions in Regular Forces										Officers Holding Permanent Commissions in Regular Forces	
		Major-General	Brigadier-General		Colonel		Lieutenant-Colonel	Major		Captain, Lieutenant or Second Lieutenant		All Ranks	
(1)	(2)	(3)	(4)		(5)		(6)	(7)		(8)		(9)	
	Per cent.	£	£	s.	£	s.	£	£	s.	£	s.	£	
1	100	350	325	0	275	0	250	225	0	175	0	100	In addition to retired pay under Royal Warrant of 1st Dec. 1914
2	80	280	260	0	220	0	200	180	0	140	0	80	
3	70	245	227	10	192	10	175	157	10	122	10	70	
4	60	210	195	0	165	0	150	135	0	105	0	60	
5	50	175	162	10	137	10	125	112	10	87	10	50	
6	40	140	130	0	110	0	100	90	0	70	0	40	
7	30	105	97	10	82	10	75	67	10	52	10	30	
8	20	70	65	0	55	0	50	45	0	35	0	20	

In cases where the extent of disablement is assessed at less than 20 per cent a gratuity is ordinarily awarded.

The actual amount of retired pay, however, which an invalided Officer will receive may differ from the figures in the above table in cases where:-

(a) The Officer was holding a permanent commission in the Regular Army: *or*
(c) Is in receipt of a Service Pension as a soldier and not holding a permanent commission in the Regular Army; *or*
(a) Is in receipt of a wound gratuity or pension.

An Officer who comes under both (a) and (c) or (b) and (c) will be dealt with under the more favourable provision.

An Officer holding a permanent commission is entitled, if invalided from the service, to either retired pay at the rate shown in the above table, or to the amount of retired pay which he could have got under the Pay Warrant of 1914, with the additions shown in column 9, whichever is more advantageous to him. The Ministry of Pensions will see that the Officer is granted the retired pay which is more advantageous to him without the necessity of application on his part.

EXAMPLES:

Retired pay under Pay Warrant	£120
add for 80% disablement	£ 80
	£200

which is better than the scale
Rate for 80% disablement, viz: £140;

Retired pay under Pay Warrant, 3*s*. a day	£54 15 0
add for 100% disablement	£100 0 0
	£154 15 0

which is less than the scale rate
for 100% disablement. viz: £175

Officers in receipt of Service Pensions as soldiers and not holding permanent commissions may be granted retired pay on the same principle as in (a) above; '*i.e.*, they may receive their soldier's service pension plus an addition as in column 9, *or* disability retired pay alone, as per previous columns, whichever is the more advantageous.'

Officers in receipt of wound pension or gratuity. – An Officer who has drawn, or is drawing, a wound gratuity or pension has already been compensated to some extent for the disablement for which he is invalided from the Service, and the wound gratuity or pension is therefore taken into account in assessing the retired pay. The wound gratuity for this purpose is reckoned as an allowance covering the first 12 months from the date of the wound. The Officer may, therefore, have *either*

(1) The wound pension or gratuity *plus* any disability retired pay under the Pay Warrant of 1914 (that is, the pre-war disability rates); *or*
(2) The appropriate rate of retired pay under the present Warrant including the wound gratuity or pension.

The Officer will have whichever of these alternatives is more favourable to him. Officers other than those holding permanent commissions in the regular forces are generally ineligible for retired pay under the Pay Warrant of 1914, unless they are disabled at least 50 per cent. The following examples will illustrate the rule:-

(1) Retired pay under Pay Warrant of 1914, £120 plus
wound pension, £100 = £220.
Rate of retired pay under Warrant of 1917, say £140
(2) Retired pay under Pay Warrant, £54.15*s*. plus wound gratuity, £250 = £304.15s.
Rate of retired pay under Warrant of 1917, say £175.
(3) Retired pay under Pay Warrant, £54.15*s*. plus wound pension, £50 = £104.15*s*.
Rate of retired pay under Warrant of 1917, say, £140

Retired pay will on discharge be awarded by the Ministry of Pensions without application on the part of the Officer, though some interval must often elapse before an award can be made because the necessary documents relating to the Officer have to be obtained from or through the War Office. For renewal of retired pay application must be made to the Secretary to the Ministry of Pensions **before the period of award expires** *and application should be made* **not less than six weeks** *before that date. Any inquiries regarding retired pay should be similarly addressed, but applications for payment should be made to the Assistant Paymaster General, Whitehall. Retired pay is payable in arrears quarterly or monthly and the Officer should inform the Assistant Paymaster General at which period he prefers to receive it.*

ALLOWANCES FOR CHILDREN

In addition to retired pay a disabled Officer may be granted an Education Allowance for each child above the age of 8 in any case where there is pecuniary need. The existence of need will be determined by the Ministry of Pensions according to the circumstances of the case on the application of the Officer. For the purpose of an Education Allowance the term 'child' includes any legitimate child born before or within 9 months after the Officer's discharge, on account of disablement, from military service. The maximum amount granted will depend on the needs of the case and the actual expenses incurred for each child, as vouched by receipted bills, and will not be granted to an Officer receiving alternative pay.

Pay is designed, speaking generally, to place the Officer in the same position financially, within reasonable limits, as he enjoyed before the War, after making allowance for his remaining capacity to earn a living. In order to obtain Alternative Retired Pay, it is necessary for an invalided Officer to show that his retired pay (and wound gratuity or pension, if he has been awarded either) *plus* the amount which he can still earn, amounts in the aggregate to less than he earned before the War. In calculating pre-war earnings account is taken of the full amount of the Officer's pre-war earnings up to £300 per annum; and of one half of his pre-war earnings between £300 and £600 per annum. The maximum amount of Alternative Retired Pay is therefore £450, since above the limit of £600 pre-war earnings are not taken into account. Two examples will illustrate the plan on which Alternative Retired Pay is awarded:-

a. Where pre-war earnings were not more than £300 a year –

	A Year	A Year
	£	£
An Officer who was earning before the war	250	
who is now capable of earning	100	
and is now receiving a wound pension of	50	
would receive as alternative retired pay		250
less £100+£50		150
His alternative retired pay would therefore be		
(excluding wound pension)	£100	
b. Where pre-war earnings exceeded £300 a year -		
An Officer who was earning before the war	500	
and is now capable of earning	150	
would receive as alternative retired pay		300
plus one-half of the difference between		
£300 and £500		100
		400
less what he is capable of earning		150
His alternative retired pay would therefore be		250

Application should be made to the Director General of Awards, Ministry of Pensions, New North St., W.C.1.

WAR BONUS

From the 1st January, 1919, a War Bonus of 20 per cent is added to the disability retired pay or alternative retired pay of disabled Officers, and will, it is expected, remain in force for three years.

The bonus is given under the following conditions:-

(1) The bonus has effect from 1st January, 1919. It is reckoned at the end of the financial quarter, and, subject to the next sub-paragraph, upon the actual amount payable for the quarter, and is issued quarterly, in arrear.

(2) In cases of:-

(a) Regular Officers and
(b) Temporary Officers in receipt of Service Pension

whose retired pay is a composite rate covering service and disablement, it is necessary to make a special calculation in order to eliminate the service element, and the bonus is reckoned on the rate which would be awarded to a temporary Officer of the same rank similarly disabled.

(3) In cases of Officers in receipt of wound pensions or gratuities, the bonus is reckoned on the sum of the wound compensation and the retired pay; the wound gratuity being reckoned as an allowance for 12 months. Bonus is not payable on wound pension if unaccompanied by disability retired pay.

(4) All ranks are eligible, but there is a money limit of the annual rate of pension and bonus combined, namely £300 a year.

Thus, where an Officer is already in receipt of a rate equal to or in excess of £300 a year no bonus is granted, and only such bonus may be allowed on a lower rate as will not bring the total above that limit.

Application for the bonus is not necessary. It will be paid by the Paymaster-General after the end of each quarter.

GRATUITY FOR NON-ATTRIBUTABLE DISABILITY

If an Officer is invalided for a disability which the medical authorities of the Ministry are not able to certify as attributable to or aggravated by military service, he may (provided the disablement was not due to his own fault) be granted a gratuity, the amount of which is decided with reference to all the circumstances of his case, including the degree and nature of disablement. In very exceptional cases the gratuity may amount to £300. *This gratuity will be awarded without application on the part of the Officer.*

RIGHT OF APPEAL

Where the claim of an Officer is rejected on the ground that the disability on which the claim is based

(a) is not attributable to or aggravated by service during the present war, *or*
(b) is due to the serious negligence or misconduct of the claimant;

or where such disability, although admitted to be aggravated by, is certified not to be attributable to such service;

the Officer has under a recent Act of Parliament the right of appeal to the Pensions Appeal Tribunal. The Tribunal will be composed of independent persons, not officials, appointed by the Lord Chancellor. No Court fees will be charged on the hearing of any case before the Tribunal.

The Tribunal will not be competent to hear appeals against the degree at which disablement has been assessed, but arrangements are being made under which such appeals will be considered by a Medical Appeal Board of the Ministry of Pensions.

Appeals, either to the Tribunal or the Board, should be addressed to the Secretary, Ministry of Pensions, New North Street, London, W.C.1.

NOT GAZETTED FOR ILL-HEALTH

An Officer who is *gazetted out for reasons other than ill-health* but is disabled by his service may have his case specially considered, provided his resignation is not for inefficiency or misconduct, or for his personal convenience only; but Officers wishing to resign because of their health would do well to indicate if they wish their resignation to be conditioned by its being gazetted as for ill-health, and to ask for a Medical Board.

On general demobilisation Officers, not on sick leave or under treatment, will be invited to state (on A.F. Z. 22) whether they claim to have a disability due to their service, and all claims will be given consideration as soon as may be possible.

Advances on account of Retired Pay. – Owing to the great number of claims dealt with by the Ministry of Pensions, and to other causes, it is not always possible to decide an Officer's claim to retired pay within a month of his relinquishing his commission or being demobilised. Temporary arrangements have, therefore, been made for granting to disabled Officers with a *prima facie* claim to retired pay, interim payments on account of such retired pay.

The War Office pass to the Ministry of Pensions at as early a stage as practicable a provisional record in each case, and if this justifies it, an advance is made dated one month after the date of discharge and is repeated, if necessary, until such time as it seems likely the award will be settled. Advances are paid by draft from the Ministry of Pensions, and will be recoverable from the retired pay or gratuity ultimately awarded. Where the disablement is slight, or probably not attributable to service, no advance can be made, as a future award is too uncertain.

Such advances will be authorised without application by the Officer, but if any disabled Officer has not received an advance or other communication after six weeks from the date of his dispersal or gazetting, he may write to the Ministry of Pensions stating briefly the essential dates and facts of his case.

After Demobilisation. – An Officer who, when demobilised, is not found to have been impaired by his military service may, if he finds at any later date that he is suffering from an incapacity which he considers due to his war service, apply for a Medical Board after retirement, and if the disability is held to be attributable to or aggravated by service in the present war he may be granted retired pay from the date on which his claim is established.

Applications should be addressed to the Director General of Awards, Ministry of Pensions, New North Street, London W.C.1.

MEDICAL TREATMENT

An Officer suffering from injury or disease receives the full medical or surgical treatment necessary at the time, and, as a rule, convalescent treatment also before being discharged from service. But in some cases further treatment is required after discharge, and the necessity for treatment may recur at a subsequent date.

An Officer who is awarded Retired Pay or a gratuity in lieu of Retired Pay, can be assisted by the Ministry of Pensions to obtain necessary treatment for the disability or disabilities for which retired pay or gratuity has been awarded. (Article 6 of the Royal Warrant). This assistance is given in one of the following ways:-

(1) If the Officer is medically certified to require treatment in a hospital or other institution, and the arrangements are made through the Ministry of Pensions

  (a) his retired Pay is raised to the maximum and
  (b) the cost of treatment and maintenance in the institution is defrayed by the Ministry in full, except that a deduction of £1 11*s* 6*d* per week towards the expense of his maintenance is made

from the Officer's Retired Pay. This is the only contribution he is required to make.

(2) If the Officer is medically certified to require treatment in an institution and, with the approval of the Medical Advisers to the Ministry, makes his own arrangements for it,

(a) his Retired Pay is raised to the maximum, and

(b) the cost of treatment and maintenance will be defrayed up to the amount which would have been incurred if the arrangements had been made by the Ministry. A deduction of £1 11*s* 6*d* per week is made from the Officer's Retired Pay, and he will be required to pay any excess over the charge accepted by the Ministry. The authorised charges vary at present from £2 2*s* to £6 6*s*, according to the special character of treatment.

(3) If an Officer is receiving medical treatment approved by the Ministry in an institution his wife may, provided there is pecuniary need, be granted an allowance not exceeding £50 a year, or his dependent relative an allowance not exceeding £40 a year.

(4) If an Officer is undergoing treatment approved by the Ministry otherwise than in an institution, and is certified to be unable to work in consequence, his retired pay may be raised to the maximum, and, in addition, whether he is unable to work or not, actual necessary medical and other expenses incidental to treatment may be defrayed. If the course of treatment is authorised in advance by the Ministry and the terms are fixed, the whole cost will be defrayed by the Ministry.

ALLOWANCE FOR CONSTANT ATTENDANCE

An invalided Officer in receipt of retired pay at the maximum rate for his rank, whose disablement renders it necessary that he should have a person constantly in attendance on him may be given an additional allowance ranging, according to circumstances, from £39 to £78 a year. This does not apply to cases where temporary nursing is necessary as an incident of medical treatment, but where, as in cases of paralysis, the Officer is not in a condition to look after himself. Payments are made by the Paymaster General, Whitehall, S.W.1.

Applications for an allowance in cases where a constant attendant is required should be addressed to the Secretary, Ministry of Pensions, New North Street, London, W.C.1

ARTIFICIAL LIMBS AND APPLIANCES

An Officer who requires an artificial limb in consequence of wounds or injuries received in action or on military duty will be provided with it at the public expense at one of the Special Fitting Hospitals for Officers, where he will receive advice as to the type of limb most suitable for the amputation stump, and will be instructed in the use of the artificial limb when completed. Fitting Hospitals for Officers are:-

Queen Mary's Convalescent Auxiliary Hospital, Dover House, Roehampton, S.W.15
5th London T.F. General Hospital (St. Thomas'), Lambeth S.E.1.
The Prince of Wales' Hospital, The Walk, Cardiff
Edenhall Limbless Hospital, Musselburgh, N.B (as out-patients only)
Ulster Volunteer Force Hospital, Belfast, Ireland

An Officer can attend a Special Fitting Hospital either as an in-patient or as an out-patient, except at Edenhall, Musselburgh, N.B

The first artificial limb is supplied to an Officer free of charge. Subject to regulations which can be ascertained by reference to the address given below, a second or spare artificial limb is supplied at the cost of the Ministry of Pensions for use on occasions when the other is in need of repair. All repairs and renewals that become necessary *after the retirement of the Officer from the servic*e are carried out or paid for by the Ministry.

Readjustments of artificial limbs rendered necessary by changes in the condition of the stump should be carried out by the original maker of the limb either at a Fitting Hospital or at the limb maker's premises, and will be paid for by the Ministry of Pensions according to a scale of recognised charges. Limb makers' accounts should be submitted for payment to the address given below. Stump socks and arm mitts may be obtained on application to the same address.

Officers desirous of obtaining any information regarding artificial limbs, charges for readjustments and repairs, or admission to Fitting Hospitals should communicate with the Director of Artificial Limb Supplies, Ministry of Pensions, 14, Great Smith Street, Westminster, London, S.W.1. Envelopes should be marked 'L.Branch, Officers.' Various types of artificial limbs and appliances may be inspected at this address.

Appliances other than limbs (*e.g.*, crutches, surgical boots, abdominal belts, etc., etc.) are supplied at the public expense when required in consequence of injuries or disease attributable to service. Mechanical chairs and hand-propelled tricycles are provided (1) in paraplegic cases when medically recommended, and (2) in all double amputation cases. Bath chairs and spinal carriages may also be supplied when needed.

Applications in respect of these appliances should be addressed to the Appliance Branch, Ministry of Pensions, 14, Great Smith Street, Westminster, London, S.W.1.

TRAINING AND EMPLOYMENT

Training

Substantial provision has been made by the government for training of disabled, as well as able-bodied, officers on discharge or demobilisation in the following cases:-

(1) For Officers to whom it is considered in the national interest to afford further opportunity of training, and whose education or career has been interrupted by their war service.
(2) For disabled Officers, the degree of whose dependence could be diminished by training for a suitable occupation, especially in the case of those whose disability prevents them resuming their old occupation, or whose health or prospects are likely to be prejudiced if they do resume it.
(3) Concurrent treatment and training

Class (3) is referred to under Medical Treatment. Classes (1) and (2) can be dealt with under the Government Education Scheme announced on December 14th, 1918, but class (2) is also provided for to some extent under the Royal Warrant of the Ministry of Pensions.

Under the Government Scheme. – The scheme for State financial assistance for higher education and training of ex-officers and men of similar educational qualifications is now in operation. It is a condition of assistance that the Officer is of sufficient educational promise to justify a grant for training being made to him from public funds. The object of the scheme, broadly speaking, is to restore the supply of men of high general, scientific, professional, and business attainments whom the nation needs for the professions and industry, and in the cases of such of these as are disabled to diminish the degree of their dependence. The following are the main principles of the assessment of grants under the scheme.

The annual sum granted will be assessed with a view to covering the fees for the course, and the cost of maintenance during the period of education or training includes term time and vacation. The sum for maintenance will not exceed £175 per annum in the case of a single, nor £200 per annum in the case of a married candidate, and in either case may be substantially less. The maximum annual allowance for fees is £50. In the cases of married candidates an allowance not exceeding £24 per annum may also be made towards the maintenance of each child under 16 years of age, and up to a maximum of £96. The extra allowances which apply to married candidates are irrespective of the date of marriage. A special scheme has been arranged for candidates who are selected for residential farm training in the United Kingdom. These receive maintenance allowance at the rate of £125 per annum; in the case of married men this will be increased to £150 per annum in addition to children's allowances.

No account is taken of service gratuities, wound gratuities, wound pensions, disability retired pay, or disablement pension. A candidate is required to declare his own, and, if married, his wife's income, and account will be taken of this, and of any assistance accruing from scholarships and grants from public or voluntary funds other than the war payments mentioned above. Account will also be taken of the extent to which the applicant's parents, relatives, or friends who would in ordinary circumstances have borne the whole or part of the charges involved.

Appendix V

Principal Office Holders, 1916–22

PRIME MINISTER
Herbert Asquith, 1908–16
David Lloyd George, 1916–22

CABINET SECRETARY
Maurice Hankey, 1916–38

SECRETARY OF STATE FOR WAR
Lord Kitchener, 1914–16
David Lloyd George, 1916
The Earl of Derby, 1916–18
Viscount Milner, 1918–19
Winston Churchill, 1919–21
Sir Laming Worthington-Evans, 1921–2

PERMANENT UNDER SECRETARY OF STATE FOR WAR
Sir Reginald Brade, 1914–20

CHANCELLOR OF THE EXCHEQUER
Bonar Law, 1916–19
Austen Chamberlain, 1919–21
Sir Robert Horne, 1921–2

PERMANENT SECRETARY OF BOARD OF TRADE
Sir Hubert Llewellyn Smith, 1907–20

CHIEF OF THE IMPERIAL GENERAL STAFF (CIGS)
General Sir William Robertson, 1915–18
General Sir Henry Wilson, 1918–22

COMMANDER in CHIEF THE BRITISH EXPEDITIONARY FORCE (BEF)
Field Marshal Sir Douglas Haig, 1915–19

THE BRITISH ARMY OF OCCUPATION IN GERMANY
General Sir Herbert Plumer, 1918–19
General Sir William Robertson, 1919–20
General Sir Thomas Moreland, 1920–2

CHAIRMAN OF THE RECONSTRUCTION COMMITTEE
Herbert Asquith, 1916
David Lloyd George/Edwin Montagu (Deputy), 1917

MINISTER OF RECONSTRUCTION
Dr Christopher Addison, 1917–19
Sir Auckland Geddes, 1919–20

SECRETARY TO RECONSTRUCTION COMMITTEE
Vaughan Nash, 1916–19

CHAIRMAN OF THE RECONSTRUCTION DEMOBILIZATION SUB-COMMITTEE
Sir Edwin Montagu, 1916–17
General Smuts, 1918

CHAIRMAN OF THE WAR OFFICE DEMOBILIZATION COMMITTEE
Sir Reginald Brade, 1917

DEMOBILIZATION CO-ORDINATOR
Sir Eric Geddes, 1918–19

CHAIRMAN OF THE COMMITTEE OF NATIONAL EXPENDITURE
Sir Eric Geddes, 1921–2

Appendix VI

Timeline, 1914–19

1914 – December. Brade and Llewellyn Smith prepare first demobilization proposal – 'Demobilisation and the Labour Market'. Accepted by the Asquith Cabinet and then shelved until 1916.

1916 – 18 March. Asquith establishes the first Reconstruction Committee.
24 March – First Meeting of Reconstruction Committee. Montagu and Hankey raise question of demobilization.
19 May – First meeting of the Demobilization sub-Committee chaired by Montagu.
19 May–2 September – five meetings of the Demobilization Committee.
9 October – First Interim Report of the Demobilization Committee. Accepted by Cabinet.

1917 – 15 February – Lloyd George announces that the Demobilization Committee will continue.
16 March – First meeting of Second Reconstruction Committee. Lloyd George to chair with Montagu as deputy.
4 April – First meeting of new Demobilization Committee.
4 April–1 August – Five meetings of the Demobilization Committee.
16 April – Brade's War Office Demobilization Report. Basis of demobilization to be industrial needs.
6 June – Priority list of Industrial Classes drawn up.
17 July – Formation of a Ministry of Reconstruction chaired by Addison. Montagu becomes Secretary of State for India and Brade appointed chairman of the Demobilization Committee.
27 October – Second Interim Report of the Demobilization Committee. Accepted by the Cabinet on 16 November.

1918 – 19 February – General Wilson appointed CIGS.
18 March – A report by the Ministry of Labour confirms industry priorities for demobilization with 'pivotal' and 'slip men'.

October – General Smuts joins the War Cabinet.
11 November – Armistice.
December – General Election. Lloyd George remains Prime Minister of a Liberal/Conservative government. Start of post-Armistice disturbances/riots for improved demobilization system and better conditions of service and pensions. Disturbances continue through most of 1919. General Plumer appointed Commander in Chief of British Army of the Rhine.
9 December – Smuts becomes chairman of Demobilization Committee. 'Contract' men demobilized.
19 December – Eric Geddes appointed to co-ordinate the government departments involved in demobilization.

1919 – January – Auckland Geddes appointed Minister of Reconstruction.
3 January – Mutinies at Folkestone, Calais, Boulogne and Le Havre.
10 January – Churchill replaces Milner as Secretary of State for War.
24 January – Churchill introduces a revised demobilization procedure based on 'First Out, First Home' principle.
22 February – Wilson's term as CIGS ends. Replaced by Lord Cavan.
March – The Naval, Military and Air Force Act extends period of conscription service.
21 April – Robertson appointed Commander in Chief of the British Army of the Rhine.
28 June – Treaty of Versailles signed.
August – Publication of 'The Mission of the British Army'.
11 November – prototype of Cenotaph erected in Whitehall and the Silence introduced.

Bibliography

UNPUBLISHED PRIMARY SOURCES

Centre For Buckinghamshire Studies
The *Lee Magazine*
Imperial War Museum
M'Ewen, D. and Dallas, J., *From Trench to Bench*, The Royal Philosophical Society of Glasgow, 1917
Papers of Major A.E. Bundy
Papers of F.H. Kibblewhite
Papers of Sergeant Major G. Lipscombe
Papers of Field Marshal Sir Henry Wilson
Papers of Lieutenant James Worthington
Podcast 48, *Homecoming*
The Problems of Demobilisation, Joint Committee on Labour Problems After the War, Co-Operative Printing Society, London, 1916
The National Archives
RECO 1/ series. Particularly 1/663-667, 1/832-837
WO 32, 33, 73, 95 and 106
CAB 23, 24, 27, 33 and 37
MEPO, MUN, LAB and PIN files

PUBLISHED PRIMARY SOURCES

Ashbourne Telegraph
Blake, R., *Private Papers of Douglas Haig*, Eyre and Spottiswoode, London, 1952
Buxton Advertiser
Buxton Herald and Visitors Gazette
Daily Mirror
Derby Mercury
Eade, Charles (ed.), *The War Speeches of the Rt Hon Winston S Churchill*, 3 vols, Cassell & Co., London, 1952

General Annual Reports on the British Army, prepared by the Army Council, HMSO, London, 1920
Gorton and Openshaw Reporter
High Peak News
History of the Eight Battalion of the Queen's Own West Kent Regiment 1914–1919, Hazel, Watson and Viney, Aylesbury, 1921
History of the Ministry of Munitions, 12 vols, HMSO, London, 1922
Keevil Papers, in possession of the Wiltshire and Swindon History Centre, Chippenham, in the *Bulletin* of the Western Front Association, March 2016
Labour Market Trends, Government Statistical Section, Unemployment Statistics from 1881 to the Present Day
Manchester Evening Chronicle
Manchester Evening News
Manchester Guardian
Manchester Weekly Times
Mansfield Chronicle and Advertiser
The Military Correspondence of Field Marshal Sir Henry Wilson 1918–1922, ed. Keith Jeffery, Army Records Society, Bodley Head, London, 1985
The Mission of the British Army, HMSO, London, 1919
Nottingham Evening Post
Observer
Official History of the Great War: The Occupation of the Rhineland 1918–1929, ed. Brigadier General Sir James Edmonds, Naval and Military Press Ltd and the Imperial War Museum, Uckfield, n.d.
Reconstruction Problems, HMSO, London, 1918
Sheffield, G. and Bourne, J. (eds), *Douglas Haig, War Diaries and Letters 1914–1918*, Weidenfeld & Nicolson, London, 2005
Statistics of the Military Effort of the British Empire in the Great War, 1914–1920, Naval and Military Press, London, 1997 edn
Surrey Advertiser
The Times

PUBLISHED SECONDARY SOURCES

Memoirs and Biographies

Addison, Christopher, *Politics from Within 1911–1918*, Herbert Jenkins Ltd, London, n.d.
Callwell, C.E., *Field Marshal Sir Henry Wilson. His Life and Diaries*, Cassell & Co., London, 1927

Carrington, Charles, *Soldier from the Wars Returning*, Hutchinson, London, 1965
Churchill, Winston S., *The World Crisis 1916–1918*, Thornton Butterworth Ltd, London, 1927
Churchill, W.S., The *Aftermath*, Thornton and Butterworth Ltd, London, 1929
Duff Cooper, A., *Haig*, 2 vols, Faber & Faber, London, 1934
Dunn, Captain J.C., *The War the Infantry Knew 1914–1919*, Cardinal, London, 1987 edn.
Gilbert, Martin, *Winston S. Churchill*, 8 vols, Heinemann, London, 1966
Jenkins, Roy, *Churchill*, Pan Books, London, 2003
Killick, Alf, *Mutiny*, Militant Pamphlet, 1976
Lloyd George, David, *War Memoirs*, 2 vols, Odhams Press Ltd, London, 1936 edn
Richards, Frank, *Old Soldiers Never Die*, Kirijnen and Langley, Peterborough, 2004 edn
Robertson, Field Marshal Sir William, *From Private to Field Marshal*, Constable & Co., London, 1921
Rothstein, Andrew, *The Soldiers' Strikes of 1919*, Journeyman Press Ltd, London, 1985

Monographs

Andrews, E.M., *The Anzac Illusion*, Oxford University Press, Oxford, 1922
Arthur, Max, *Last Post*, Phoenix Paperbacks, London, 2006
Atkinson, C.T., *The Queen's Own West Kent Regiment 1914–19*, Simpson, Marshal, Hamilton, Kent and Co., London, 1924
Babbington, A., *For the Sake of Example, Capital Courts Martial 1914–18, the Truth*, Leo Cooper, London, 1983
Beckett, Ian F.W., *The Great War*, Longman, London, 2001
Beckett, Ian F.W. and Simpson, Keith (eds), *A Nation in Arms, The British Army in the First World War*, Pen & Sword Military, Barnsley, 2014
Bishop, James, *Social History of the First World War*, Angus and Robertson, London,1982
Blythe, Ronald, *Akenfield*, Allen Lane, London, 1969
Bond, Brian, *British Military Policy Between the Two World Wars*, Clarendon Press, Oxford, 1980
Bowman, Timothy, *Irish Regiments in the Great War*, Manchester University Press, Manchester and New York, 2003
Brereton, J.M., *The Horse in War*, David & Charles, London, 1976

Brown, Malcolm, *IWM Book of 1918, Year of Victory*, Sidgwick & Jackson, London, 1998

Dallas, G. and Gill, D., *The Unknown Army. Mutinies in the British Army in World War I*, Verso, London, 1985

de Groot, Gerard, *Back to Blighty. The British at Home in World War I*, Vintage Books, London, 2014

Ewing, Major J., *The Royal Scots 1914–19*, 2 vols, Oliver and Boyd, Edinburgh, 1925

Farwell, Byron, *The Great War in Africa 1914–1918*, Viking, Harmondsworth, 1987

Ferguson, Niall, *The Pity of War*, Penguin Books, London, 1999

Forbes, Major General A., *History of the Army Ordnance Services*, Medici Society, London, 1929

Garrett, Richard, *The Final Betrayal*, Buchan and Enright, Southampton, 1989

Hetherington, Andrea, *British War Widows of the First World War. The Forgotten Legion*, Pen & Sword Books Ltd, Barnsley, 2018

Holmes, Richard, *Tommy, The British Soldier on the Western Front 1914–1918*, HarperCollins, London, 2004

Jenkinson, Jacqueline, *Black 1919 – Riots, Racism and Resistance in Imperial Britain*, Liverpool University Press, Liverpool, 2009

Lamb, David, *Mutinies 1917–1920*, Solidarity, London, 1979

Lewis, Jon E., *The First World War*, Constable & Robinson Ltd, London, 2003

Lewis-Stempel, John, *The War Behind the Wire*, Phoenix Press, London, 2014

Lloyd, T.O., *Empire to Welfare State*, Oxford University Press, Oxford, 1991 edn

Longworth, Philip, *The Unending Vigil*, Pen & Sword Books Ltd, Barnsley, 2003

Macdonald, Lyn, *1914–18, Voices and Images of the Great War*, Michael Joseph Ltd, London, 1988

Moore, W., *The Thin Yellow Line*, Leo Cooper, London, 1974

Mowat, Charles Loch, *Britain Between the Wars 1918–1940*, Methuen and Co. Ltd, London, 1956

Nicolson, Juliet, *The Great Silence*, John Murray, London, 2009

Panikos Panay, *Prisoners of Britain*, Manchester University Press, Manchester, 2012

Putkowski, J., *The Kinmel Park Camp Riots, 1919*, Flintshire Historical Society, Hawarden, 1989

Putkowski, J. and Sykes, J., *Shot at Dawn, Executions in World War One*, Leo Cooper, London, 1993

Senior, Michael, *Fromelles 1916. The Loss of a Village* Pen & Sword Books Ltd, Barnsley, 2004

Sheffield, Gary, *The Chief. Douglas Haig and the British Army*, Aurum Press Ltd, London, 2011

Tatchell, Peter, *The Hidden Story of Soldiers' Mutinies, Strikes and Riots*, Good Society, London, 2014

Taylor, A.J.P., *English History 1914–1945*, Book Club Associates, London, 1977 edn

Thomson, David, *England in the Twentieth Century*, Penguin Books, Harmondsworth, 1965

van Emden, Richard, *Prisoners of the Kaiser: The Last POWs of the Great War*, Pen & Sword Books Ltd, Barnsley, 2000

Vansittart, Peter, *Voices from the Great War*, Pimlico, London, 1998

Weetman, Captain W.C.C., *Sherwood Foresters in the Great War 1914–19*, Thomas Forman and Sons, Nottingham, 1920

Wilson, Trevor, *The Myriad Faces of War*, Polity Press, Cambridge, 1988 edn

Winter, D., *Death's Men*, Penguin Books, Harmondsworth, 1979

Wintringham, T.H., *Mutiny*, Stanley Nott, London, 1937

Journal Articles and Chapters

Aiden, Michael, 'Rudyard Kipling and King George V. The 1922 Pilgrimage to Flanders Cemeteries', *Stand To!*, the Journal of the Western Front Association, No. 85, April/May 2009

Connelly, Mark, 'Visiting and Revisiting the Battlefields, 1919–21', *Bulletin* of the Western Front Association, August/September, 2017

Dallas, G. and Gill, D., 'Mutiny at Etaples Base in 1917', *Past and Present: A Journal of Historical Studies*, Oxford, 1975

Davies, Ross, 'Prisoners of War', *Stand To!*, the Journal of the Western Front Association, No. 45, January 1996

Graubard, Stephen Richards, 'Military Demobilisation in Great Britain Following the First World War', *Journal of Modern History*, XIX, 1947

Gutteridge, Herbert, 'One Man's War', *Stand To!*, the Journal of the Western Front Association, No. 23, Summer 1988

Jeffery, Keith, 'The Post War Army', in *A Nation in Arms*, eds Ian F.W. Beckett and Keith Simpson, Pen & Sword Military,Barnsley, 2014 edn

Long, S.S., 'Right and Wrong Methods of Demobilisation', *The Nineteenth Century and After*, No. CCCCLXXVI – October 1916

Marples, Pauline, 'Clipstone Camp and the Mansfield Area in World War One', Forest Town Heritage Group, 2013

Morton, Desmond, 'Kicking and Complaining: Demobilisation Riots in the Canadian Expeditionary Force, 1918–19', *Canadian History Review*, 61, 1989

Oram, G., 'Pious Perjury. Discipline and Morale in the British Force in Italy 1917–1918', *War in History*, Vol. 9, 4.

Reid, Fiona, 'Not Ordinary Lunatics', *Stand To!*, the Journal of the Western Front Association, No. 78, January 2007

Walsh, J., 'The Durham Light Infantry in Archangel', *Stand To!*, the Journal of the Western Front Association, No. 56, September 1999

Notes

Introduction

1. Quoted in Lyn Macdonald, *1914–18, Voices and Images of the Great War*, Michael Joseph Ltd, London, 1988, p. 307.
2. Major J. Ewing, *The Royal Scots 1914–19,* 2 vols, Oliver and Boyd, Edinburgh, 1925, p. 759.
3. Reported in the *Daily Mirror*, 12 November 1918.
4. Winston S. Churchill, *The World Crisis 1916–1918*, Thornton Butterworth Ltd, London, 1927, p. 542.
5. TNA, CAB 23/8/23, War Cabinet Meeting, 14 November 1918.
6. *Buxton Advertiser*, 16 November 1918.
7. Quoted in *The First World War*, ed. Jon E. Lewis, Constable & Robinson Ltd, London, 2003, p. 455.
8. The *Lee Magazine*, December 1918.
9. Churchill, *The World Crisis*, pp. 542–3.
10. Reported in *The Times,* 25 November 1918.
11. The Liberals who supported Asquith gained only twenty-eight seats.
12. *The Military Correspondence of Field Marshal Sir Henry Wilson 1918–22*, ed. Keith Jeffery, Army Records Society, Bodley Head, London, 1985, p. 72.
13. TNA, RECO 1/879, *The Aims of Reconstruction.*
14. See A.J.P. Taylor, *English History 1914–1945,* Book Club Associates, London, 1977 edn, pp. 122–4.
15. Parliamentary Papers, 1917–18, Cd. 8668, p. 23.
16. David Lloyd George, *War Memoirs*, 2 vols, Odhams Press Ltd, London, 1936, Vol. II, p. 1587.
17. TNA, RECO 1/854.
18. Ian F.W. Beckett, *The Great War*, Longman, London, 2001, p. 262.
19. W.S. Churchill, *The Aftermath*, Thornton Butterworth Ltd, London, 1929, p. 71.
20. Ibid., pp. 171–2.
21. India constituted two-thirds of the population of the British Empire.

22. See T.O. Lloyd, *Empire to Welfare State*, Oxford University Press, Oxford, 1991 edn, Ch. 4 and Taylor, *English History*, pp. 132–4.
23. Richard Garrett, *The Final Betrayal*, Buchan and Enright, Southampton, 1989, p. 62.
24. TNA, RECO 1/853, GT 6408.
25. See Trevor Wilson, *The Myriad Faces of War*, Polity Press, Cambridge, 1988 edn, p. 651.
26. Churchill, *World Crisis*, p. 542.
27. TNA, RECO 1/837, Board of Trade, 14 December 1914. At that stage of the war the British Army numbered 1.3 million men.
28. TNA, RECO 1/837, Memo from H. Llewellyn-Smith and R.H. Brade,. November 1916.
29. TNA, RECO 1/832.
30. IWM, 66 (41) 3.89, *The Problems of Demobilisation*, Joint Committee on Labour Problems After the War, Co-Operative Printing Society, London, 1916.
31. IWM, 33 (41) 8/3, K 4524. D. M'Ewen and J. Dallas, *From Trench to Bench*, The Royal Philosophical Society of Glasgow, 1917.
32. IWM 66(41) 3.89, *The Problems of Demobilisation*.
33. *General Annual Reports on the British Army For the Period from 1 October 1913 to 30 September 1919*, Tables 5E and 5F, prepared by the Army Council, HMSO, London, 1920.
34. IWM, Podcast 48, *Homecoming*.
35. TNA, RECO 1/832, September 1916.
36. Charles Carrington, *Soldier From the Wars Returning*, Hutchinson, London, 1965, p. 247.
37. Major J. Ewing, *The Royal Scots 1914–19*, Oliver and Ward, Edinburgh, 1925, Vol. II, p. 760.
38. TNA, RECO 1/832, September 1916.
39. Malcolm Brown, *IWM Book of 1918, Year of Victory*, Sidgwick & Jackson, London, 1998, p. 308.
40. Captain J.C. Dunn, *The War the Infantry Knew 191419*, Cardinal, London, 1987 edn, p. 572.
41. IWM, Podcast 48, *Homecoming*.
42. Ibid.
43. IWM, 33 (41), 8/3. K4524. M'Ewen and Dallas, *From Trench to Bench*.
44. TNA, First World War Web site, Catalogue ref. 30/30/8, n.d.
45. TNA, RECO 1/832.
46. TNA, RECO 1/837, 22 July 1917.
47. TNA, RECO 1/660.
48. See Wilson, *Myriad Faces of War*, pp. 520–2.

49. Taylor, *English History*, p. 90.
50. TNA, RECO 1/837.
51. TNA, RECO 1/698.
52. See Martin Crick, *History of the Social-Democratic Federation*, Keele University, Ryburn Publishing, 1994.
53. *Statistics of the Military Effort of the British Empire in the Great War 1914–1920*, Naval and Military Press, London, 1997 edn, p. 93.
54. See www.redcross.org.uk.
55. *Statistics of the Military Effort*, p. 333.
56. *General Annual Reports on the British Army For the Period From 1 October 1913 to 30 September 1919.*
57. *Statistics of the Military Effort*, pp. 396–7 and 861.
58. Ibid., pp. 869, 405.
59. Taylor, *English History*, p. 122.
60. *Statistics of the Military Effort*, p. 1595.
61. TNA, RECO 1/832.
62. TNA, RECO 1/837.
63. TNA, RECO 1/879, *Reconstruction Problems*, HMSO, London, 1918.
64. *Mr Punch's History of the Great War*, Cassell & Company Ltd, London, 1919, p. 281.

Chapter 1

1. TNA, RECO 1/837.
2. Ibid.
3. TNA, CAB 37/127/37.
4. TNA, RECO 1/834, Interim Report of the War Office Demobilization Committee, 16 April 1917.
5. TNA, CAB 37/27/37.
6. TNA, CAB 37/144/44.
7. TNA, RECO 1/655.
8. Ibid., Secret Memorandum to the Reconstruction Committee, 22 June 1916.
9. House of Commons Debates, 10 July 1916, Vol. 84 cc33-4.
10. *The Times*, 30 June 1916.
11. TNA, RECO 1/655, Secret Memo, June 1916.
12. TNA, RECO 1/664.
13. TNA, RECO 1/837.
14. TNA, RECO 1/832, memorandum, dated 21 July 1916.
15. TNA, RECO 1/832, Appendix VI of the First Interim Report of the Demobilization Sub-Committee, October 1916.

16. TNA, RECO 1/832.
17. TNA, RECO 1/832, see undated note from Brade.
18. TNA, RECO 1/832.
19. Ibid., Appendix II of the First (Interim) Report of the Army Demobilization sub-Committee, October 1916.
20. Ibid., Appendix VII.
21. IWM 66(41)/3.89, *The Problems of Demobilisation*, Joint Committee on Labour Problems After the War, Co-operative Printing Society, London, 1916.
22. TNA, RECO 1/832, First (Interim) Report, p. 2.
23. Ibid., p. 4.
24. TNA, RECO 1/837, letter, dated 12 September 1916.
25. TNA, RECO 1/837.
26. TNA, RECO 1/832.
27. Ibid., Appendix V of the First (Interim) Report.
28. Ibid., p. 5.
29. Lloyd George, *War Memoirs*, Vol. I, p. 556.
30. A list of sub-Committees can be found in TNA, RECO 1/664. These sub-Committees were made up of 242 members and secretaries.
31. TNA, RECO 1/656, memo from Nash to Hankey, 27 December 1916.
32. Ibid., memo from Nash to Hankey, 8 February 1917.
33. Lloyd George, *War Memoirs*, Vol. II, p. 1160.
34. Apart from the Prime Minister and Montagu, the members were: Professor W.G.S. Adams, Sir A. Duckham, P.H. Kerr, J. Jones, B. Seebohm Rowntree, Leslie Scott, Sir J. Stevenson, D.H. Thomas.
35. TNA, RECO 1/664.
36. TNA, RECO 1/663.
37. TNA, RECO 1/657, undated memorandum, but early 1917.
38. TNA, RECO 1/665.
39. TNA, WO 106/344, Interim Report of the War Office Demobilization Committee, 16 April 1917, p. 4.
40. TNA, RECO 1/833.
41. TNA, WO 106/344, Interim Report of the War Office Demobilization Committee, 16 April 1917, pp. 7 and 9.
42. TNA, RECO 1/664, Labour Problems after the War – Demobilisation, January 1917.
43. Ibid., Part II, Scheme of Demobilization.
44. TNA, RECO 1/833, Army Demobilization sub-Committee meeting, 4 April 1917.

45. TNA, WO 163/23, minutes of the Proceedings of the Army Council, Precis 932, 31 July 1918.
46. TNA, WO 32/5240, see the Second (Interim) Report of the Army Demobilization Committee, 27 October 1917.
47. TNA, WO 32/5239, Ministry of Labour – Employment Department Report on Demobilization Procedure, 7 May 1917, p. 10.
48. TNA, RECO 1/833, minutes of Sixth Meeting of the Army Demobilization sub-Committee, dated 4 April 1917.
49. TNA, WO 32/5240.
50. TNA, RECO 1/833.
51. TNA, RECO 1/588.
52. TNA, RECO 1/834, Interim Report of the Demobilization Priority Committee of the Ministry of Labour.
53. TNA, RECO 1/837.
54. TNA, WO 32/5239, Appendix II to the Minutes of the Tenth Meeting of the Demobilization Committee, 1 August 1917.
55. TNA, RECO 1/833, Army Demobilization sub-Committee meeting of 28 June 1917.
56. TNA, RECO 1/833, Army Demobilization sub-Committee meeting of 1 August 1917.
57. TNA, WO 32/5240, Second (Interim) Report on the Demobilization of the Army, October 1917, pp. 5, 6.
58. TNA, RECO 1/656, memo, dated September 1917.
59. TNA, WO 32/5240, minutes of a meeting of the War Cabinet, 15 November 1917.
60. There were committees for: the Machinery of Government; Local Government; Civil War Workers; Adult Education; Army Demobilization; Coal Conservation; Relations between Employers and Employees; Women's Employment; and Acquisition of Land. See TNA, RECO 1/239, 27 September 1917.
61. TNA, RECO 1/834, May 1918.
62. TNA, RECO 1/853, memorandum by the Minister of Reconstruction to the War Cabinet, 19 November 1918.
63. TNA, CAB 27/41, minutes of a meeting, dated 7 November 1918.
64. TNA, RECO 1/854, memorandum from the Home Office to General Smuts' Committee, 30 November 1918.
65. TNA, RECO 1/853, minutes of meeting, 10 December 1918.
66. TNA, WO 106/344, paragraph headed 'Publicity', April 1917.
67. TNA, RECO 1/879, Pelican Press, London, December 1918.
68. TNA, WO 32/5240, The Second (Interim) Report of the Demobilization Committee, memorandum from Addison to War Cabinet, 17 October 1917.

Chapter 2

1. TNA, RECO 1/832, 19 May 1916.
2. TNA, RECO 1/832.
3. TNA, RECO 1/837, First (Interim) Report of the sub-Committee on Demobilization, October 1916.
4. TNA, RECO 1/834, Interim Report of the War Office Demobilization Committee, Part I, April 1917.
5. TNA, WO 106/344, Scheme of Demobilization, Part II, April 1917.
6. TNA, CAB 24/30/46, 27 October 1917.
7. TNA, RECO 1/833.
8. TNA, RECO 1/832.
9. TNA, RECO 1/833.
10. TNA, WO 32/5241.
11. TNA, CAB 23/4/48, 15 November 1917.
12. British Library, S.S. Long, 'Right and Wrong Methods of Demobilisation', *The Nineteenth Century and After*, No. CCCCLXXVI – October 1916.
13. M'Ewen and Dallas, *From Trench to Bench*.
14. TNA, RECO 1/837, February–April 1916.
15. TNA, LAB 2/286/DF 16983/19/1918.
16. TNA, WO 106/344.
17. TNA, WO 32/5241.
18. Ibid., 5 December 1917.
19. TNA, WO 32/5240, Lloyd George claimed that he had not been informed about Haig's letter.
20. TNA, RECO 1/854, War Cabinet Meeting Sub-Committee on Demobilization, 9 December 1918.
21. TNA, WO 106/329.
22. Forms required in the demobilization process included: W 5065 (Soldier's Demobilization Account); Z 11 (Protection Certificate and Certificate of Identity); Z 18 (Certificate of Employment during the War); Z 21 (Certificate of Discharge); Z 22 (Medical Examination Form); Z 44 (Plain Clothes Form); Z 50 (Returned Great Coat Certificate).
23. TNA, WO 32/5242.
24. Ibid.
25. Ibid.
26. TNA, WO 32/5248.
27. Ibid.
28. TNA, WO 32/5242.

29. Ibid.
30. TNA, WO 106/344.
31. TNA, CAB 27/41 and Cab 27/42, 9 and 10 December 1918.
32. Frank Richards, *Old Soldiers Never Die*, Krijnen and Langley, Peterborough, 2004 edn, p. 229.
33. See Max Arthur, *Last Post*, Phoenix Paperbacks, London, 2006, p. 114.
34. *Military Correspondence of Field Marshal Sir Henry Wilson*, ed. Jeffery.
35. IWM, War Diary of Major A.E. Bundy, entry for 8 July 1919.
36. *Military Correspondence of Field Marshal Sir Henry Wilson*, ed. Jeffery, p. 73.
37. Reported in the *Observer*, 12 January 1919.
38. *Military Correspondence of Field Marshal Sir Henry Wilson*, ed. Jeffery, 10 January 1919, p. 77.
39. TNA, CAB 24.74.21.
40. *Mansfield Chronicle and Advertiser*, 16 January 1919.
41. Information on the race riots has been taken largely from Jacqueline Jenkinson, *Black 1919 – Riots, Racism and Resistance in Imperial Britain*, Liverpool University Press, Liverpool, 2009.
42. TNA, WO 32/5248, Weekly Appreciation No. 2.
43. TNA, WO 32/5248, Weekly Appreciation No. 3.
44. Quoted in Andrew Rothstein, *The Soldiers' Strikes of 1919*, Journeyman Press, London Ltd, 1985, p. 24.
45. Quoted in C.E. Callwell, *Field Marshal Sir Henry Wilson. His Life and Diaries*, Cassell & Co., London, 1927, p. 148.
46. Quoted in Martin Gilbert, *Winston S. Churchill,* 8 vols, Heinemann, London, 1966, Vol. IV, 1917–22, p. 226.

Chapter 3

1. During the War only 10.8 per cent of those who were sentenced to death by courts martial were actually executed.
2. See Richard Holmes, *Tommy, The British Soldier on the Western Front 1914–1918*, HarperCollins, London, 2004, p. 558.
3. Timothy Bowman, *Irish Regiments in the Great War*, Manchester University Press, Manchester and New York, 2003, p. 14 and p. 204. For other discussions of discipline in the British Army see also: A. Babbington, *For the Sake of Example, Capital Courts Martial 1914–18, The Truth*, Leo Cooper, London, 1983; G. Oram, 'Pious Perjury. Discipline and Morale in the British Force in Italy 1917–1918', *War in History*, Vol. 9, 4, pp. 412–30. J. Putkowski and J. Sykes, *Shot at*

Dawn. Executions in World War One, Leo Cooper, London, 1993; W. Moore, *The Thin Yellow Line*, Leo Cooper, London, 1974.

4. Bowman, *Irish Regiments in the Great War*, p. 206.
5. See Oram, 'Pious Perjury'.
6. TNA,CAB 24/79.
7. TNA, WO 106/401.
8. The Sources for Appendix I are national and local newspapers, particularly several in the Manchester and Buxton area; various documents in The National Archives (WO and MEPO series); and a selection from G. Dallas and D. Gill, *The Unknown Army. Mutinies in the British Army in World War I*, Verso, London, 1985 and Rothstein, *Soldiers' Strikes*. J. Putkowski describes the Kinmel Park disturbances in *The Kinmel Park Camp Riots, 1919*, the Flintshire Historical Society, Hawarden, 1989.
9. IWM 75/28/1, Lieutenant James Worthington, *Worthington's War*, 2008.
10. IWM, War Diary of Major A.E. Bundy, Box 371, p. 21.
11. The abbreviation RASC is used throughout this chapter, although the pre-fix 'Royal' was awarded after the Armistice in recognition of the outstanding services of this corps.
12. TNA, CAB 23/9, Cabinet minutes for the meeting on 8 January 1919.
13. TNA, WO 95/59.
14. Ibid.
15. TNA, WO 95/3992.
16. TNA, WO 95/60.
17. TNA, WO 95/3992.
18. TNA, WO 95/3994.
19. TNA, WO 95/26.
20. Ibid.
21. TNA, WO 95/522; WO 95/23; WO 95/2486.
22. TNA, WO 95/522.
23. TNA, WO 95/23.
24. TNA, WO 95/26.
25. IWM 75/28/1, Lieutenant James Worthington, 2008.
26. T.H. Wintringham, *Mutiny*, Stanley Nott, London, 1937, pp. 320–1.
27. TNA, WO 95/60.
28. Reported in the *Manchester Weekly Times*, 26 January 1919.
29. TNA, WO 95/4483.
30. TNA, WO 95/4470.
31. *Military Correspondence of Fields Marshal Sir Henry Wilson*, ed. Jeffery, pp. 98–9.

32. Ibid., p. 102.
33. TNA, WO 95/5459, 3rd Reserve Battn, KOYLI.
34. TNA, CAB 23/9.
35. *Military Correspondence of Field Marshal Sir Henry Wilson*, ed. Jeffery, p. 73.
36. R. Blake, *Private Papers of Douglas Haig*, Eyre and Spottiswoode, London, 1952, p. 350.
37. Ibid., p. 74.
38. Reported in the *Manchester Guardian*, 8 January 1919.
39. Churchill, *The Aftermath*, p. 54.
40. Eade, Charles (ed.), The *War Speeches of the RT Hon Winston S Churchill*, 3 vols, Cassell & Co., London, 1952, Vol. iii, pp. 114–15.
41. TNA, CAB 33/19.
42. TNA, CAB 23/9.
43. TNA, CAB 24/74/9.
44. Taken from Gilbert, *Winston S. Churchill*, Vol. IV, 1917–22, pp. 180–9, 234.
45. Eade (ed.), *War Speeches of the Rt Hon Winston S Churchill*, Vol. I, pp. 114–15.
46. Malcolm Brown, *IWM Book of 1918, Year of Victory*, Sidgwick & Jackson, London, 1998, p. 310.
47. Reported in the *Manchester Guardian*, 8 January 1919.
48. *Ashbourne Telegraph*, 10 January, 1919.
49. Reported in the *Ashbourne Telegraph*, 6 June 1919.
50. TNA, WO 32/11337.
51. TNA, MEPO 2/1962. It is worth noting that on 4 and 5 July 1945 Canadian troops were involved in a serious riot in Aldershot. It started with attempts to release three Canadian comrades from the cells in the High Street. Shops and the amusement park were destroyed. Boredom and the slow rate of demobilization were considered to be the main causes of the riot. I am indebted to Mr Malcolm Allen for this information.
52. See Charles Loch Mowat, *Britain Between the Wars 1918–1940*, Methuen and Co. Ltd, London, 1956, p. 22.
53. Figures derived from those provided by the War Office to the Cabinet in the Summary of Weekly Events, WO 106/329.
54. Brian Bond, *British Military Policy Between the Two World Wars*, Clarendon Press, Oxford, 1980, p. 10.

Chapter 4

1. TNA, WO 32/5243, memo from Director General of Mobilization, dated 17 January 1919.
2. TNA, RECO 1/850, memo to War Cabinet, dated 1 February 1919.
3. See E.M. Andrews, *The Anzac Illusion,* Oxford University Press, Oxford, 1992, p. 183.
4. See TNA, WO 32/5243.
5. Ibid., 'Demobilisation of Dominion Contingents' among Papers Laid Before the Conference, March 1917.
6. Ibid., memo, dated 14 January 1919.
7. Ibid., letter from Hughes to Churchill, dated 15 February 1919.
8. Idbid., see note from the Director General of Mobilization, 17 January 1919.
9. TNA, RECO 1/850, see the memo to the War Cabinet, dated 1 February 1919.
10. TNA, CAB 24/82.
11. For this section on Canadian demobilization I am indebted to the article by Desmond Morton, 'Kicking and Complaining: Demobilisation Riots in the Canadian Expeditionary Force, 1918–19', *Canadian History Review*, 61, 1989, pp. 334–60.
12. Reported in the *Buxton Herald and Visitors Gazette*, 8 January 1919.
13. Numbers taken from *Statistics of the Military Effort*, p. 93 and TNA, CAB 24/74/45.
14. See Gerard de Groot, *Back in Blighty, The British at Home in World War I*, Vintage Books, London, 2014, p. 340.
15. TNA, WO 162/41.
16. TNA, WO 162/41.
17. *Derby Mercury*, 23 May 1919.
18. The *Manchester Guardian*, 25 January 1919.
19. Ibid.
20. The *Observer*, 5 January 1919.
21. *Statistics of the Military Effort.*
22. See John Lewis-Stempel, *The War Behind the Wire*, Phoenix, London, 2014, p. xxi.
23. Ross Davies, 'Prisoners of War', *Stand To!,* the Journal of the Western Front Association, No. 45, January 1996, p. 6.
24. *The Official History of the Great War: The Occupation of the Rhineland 1918–1929*, ed. Brigadier General Sir James Edmonds, Naval and Military Press Ltd and the Imperial War Museum, Uckfield, n.d., p. 49.

25. Herbert Gutteridge, 'One Man's War', *Stand To!*, the Journal of the Western Front Association, No. 23, Summer 1988.
26. Reported in the *High Peak News*, 11 January 1919.
27. Ibid., 25 January 1919.
28. I am indebted to Mrs Caroline Harwood, the great-granddaughter of Mrs Stevens, for this information.
29. Ewing, *Royal Scots*, p. 760.
30. C.T. Atkinson, *The Queen's Own West Kent Regiment 1914–19*, Simpson, Marshall, Hamiliton, Kent and Co., London, 1924, p. 498.
31. *Statistics of the Military Effort*, p. 331.
32. Ibid., p. 333.
33. W.A. Tucker, 'The Lousier War', London, 1974, quoted in Lewis-Stempel, *War Behind the Wire*, p. 274.
34. *Gorton and Openshaw Reporter*, 1 January 1919.
35. Letter in the author's collection.
36. See Richard van Emden, *Prisoners of the Kaiser: The Last POWs of the Great War*, Pen & Sword Books Ltd, Barnsley, 2000. The Schofield experience is told in Lewis-Stempel, *War Behind the Wire*, pp. 283–4.
37. See Lewis-Stempel, *The War Behind the Wire*, pp. 282–3.
38. Ibid., pp. 284–7.
39. *The Occupation of the Rhineland 1918–1929*, ed. Edmonds, p. 51.
40. Ibid., title page.
41. See Davies, '*Prisoners of War*', p. 9.
42. Byron Farwell, *The Great War in Africa 1914–1918*, Viking, Harmondsworth, 1987, pp. 101 and 290.
43. Reported in the *Manchester Guardian*, 12 March 1919.
44. Ibid., 25 February 1919.
45. Churchill, *Aftermath*, p. 68.
46. Panikos Panay, *Prisoners of Britain*, Manchester University Press, Manchester, 2012, p. 279.
47. De Groot, *Back in Blighty*, p. 333.
48. IWM, Wilson Papers 2/78/23(a).
49. G. Sheffield and J. Bourne (eds), *Douglas Haig, War Diaries and Letters 1914–1918*, Weidenfeld & Nicolson, London, 2005, p. 489. In any event, Haig considered that he should receive a higher honour.
50. See A. Duff Cooper, *Haig*, 2 vols, Faber & Faber, London, 1934, Vol. II, pp. 408–10.
51. TNA, RECO 1/858.
52. IWM, HHW 2/7c/3.
53. TNA, CSC 5/85.
54. TNA, PIN 15/398.

55. The *Manchester Guardian*, 10 December 1919.
56. De Groot, *Back in Blighty*, p. 333.
57. Ibid., p. 335.
58. I am indebted to Fiona Reid's article, 'Not Ordinary Lunatics', *Stand To!*, the Journal of the Western Front Association, No. 78, January 2007, p. 10.
59. D. Winter, *Death's Men*, Penguin Books, Harmondsworth, 1979, p. 130.
60. The *Manchester Guardian*, 8 August 1919.
61. De Groot, *Back in Blighty*, p. 335.
62. The *Manchester Guardian*, 2 August 1919.
63. Reported in the *Nottingham Evening Post.*
64. Ibid., 22 August 1919.
65. TNA, RECO 1/853.
66. TNA, LAB 2/1066.
67. Gary Sheffield, *The Chief, Douglas Haig and the British Army*, Aurum Press Ltd, London, 2011, p. 354.
68. *Manchester Evening News*, 4 June 1919.
69. Ibid., 31 May 1919.
70. Ibid.
71. Ibid., 5 June 1919.
72. Ibid., 31 May 1919.
73. See Juliet Nicolson, *The Great Silence*, John Murray, London, 2009, p. 190.
74. I am indebted to Andrea Hetherington for letting me read a pre-publication copy of her book *British War Widows of the First World War. The Forgotten Legion*, Pen & Sword Books Ltd, Barnsley, 2018.
75. Unemployment figures as a result of 1911 National Insurance Act; 1916 Unemployment Insurance Act; and 1920 National Insurance Act.
76. Labour Market Trends, Government Statistical Section, Unemployment Statistics from 1881 to the Present Day.
77. The *Manchester Guardian*, 11 November 1919.
78. TNA, WO 32/5242.
79. TNA, RECO 1/858.
80. The *Manchester Evening Chronicle*, selected dates June 1919.
81. The *Manchester Guardian*, 27 February 1919.
82. Christopher Addison, *Politics from Within 1911–1918*, Herbert Jenkins Ltd, London, n.d., p. 212.
83. See Beckett, *The Great War*, p. 413.

Chapter 5

1. Ronald Blythe, Akenfield, Allen Lane, London, 1969. Quoted in Peter Vansittart, *Voices from the Great War*, Pimlico, London, 1998, p. 258.
2. Pauline Marples, 'Clipstone Camp and the Mansfield Area in World War One', Forest Town Heritage Group, 2013, p. 2.
3. The Western Front Association, *Bulletin*, March 2016. Papers of Mr Keevil in possession of Wiltshire and Swindon History Centre, Chippenham.
4. *Statistics of the Military Effort*, p. 399.
5. TNA, WO 107/69.
6. The Western Front Association, *Bulletin*, March 2016.
7. *Statistics of the Military Effort*, pp. 861–2.
8. J.M. Brereton, *The Horse in War*, David & Charles, London, 1976, p. 126.
9. TNA, WO 107/69.
10. Brereton, *The Horse in War*, p. 130.
11. IWM, 80/19/1, memoirs of F.H. Kibblewhite.
12. See Arthur, *Last Post*, p. 112.
13. Dunn, *The War the Infantry Knew*, p. 574.
14. Brereton, *The Horse in War*, p. 142.
15. *Statistics of the Military Effort*, p. 397.
16. Ibid., p. 862.
17. Ibid., p. 188.
18. *History of the Eighth Battalion the Queen's Own Royal West Kent Regiment 1914–1919*, Hazel, Watson and Viney, Aylesbury, 1921 p. 270.
19. Captain W.C.C. Weetman, *Sherwood Foresters in the Great War 1914–19*, Thomas Forman and Sons, Nottingham, 1920, p. 313.
20. TNA, CAB 24/65/71.
21. TNA, RECO 1/824.
22. TNA, CAB 24/65/71.
23. *Statistics of the Military Effort*, p. 397.
24. Major General A. Forbes, *History of the Army Ordnance Services*, Medici Society, London,1929, p. 182.
25. TNA, CAB 23/11/4.
26. TNA, WO 107/71, n.d.
27. TNA, WO 107/72.
28. *History of the Ministry of Munitions*, 12 vols, HMSO, London, 1922,Vol. VII, Part 5, p. 51.
29. TNA, WO 107/72.

30. *Statistics of the Military Effort*, p. 533.
31. Ibid.
32. *The Occupation of the Rhineland 1918–1929*, ed. Edmonds, p. 149.
33. TNA, CAB 24/78/82, memorandum of 26 April 1919.
34. TNA, WO 107/69, report by QMG Department.
35. Ibid., p. 154.
36. TNA, WO 107/70.
37. TNA, RECO 1/108, see memorandum from the War Office Demobilization Committee, dated 15 May 1917.
38. Forbes, *History of the Army Ordnance Services*, p. 183.
39. *The Occupation of the Rhineland 1918–1929*, ed. Edmonds. Also, memorandum from the Board of Trade, dated 14 January 1919 (TNA, WO 32/5148).
40. *The Occupation of the Rhineland 1918–1929*, ed. Edmonds, pp. 152–3.
41. Website of the Great War Forum, 1 November 2012.
42. *Surrey Advertiser*, 6 June 1923.
43. Impulse, 'Clipstone Camp and the Mansfield Area in World War One', p. 118.
44. IWM, Papers of Sergeant Major G. Lipscombe, 'The Peregrinations of the 34th Division (MT) Coy', p. 63.
45. See *The Occupation of the Rhineland 1918–1929*, ed. Edmonds, p. 158. £1 in 1918 would be equivalent to £50 in 2016 (RPI). The figures quoted therefore total around £10 billion pounds.

Chapter 6

1. TNA, CAB 24/78/82.
2. TNA, RECO 1/876. *The Mission of the British Army*, HMSO, London, 1919, p. 21.
3. Quoted in Bond, *British Military Policy*, p. 19.
4. TNA, CAB 24/78/82.
5. See Bond, *British Military Policy*, p. 18.
6. *Derby Mercury*, 23 May 1919.
7. TNA, CAB 24/78/82, memorandum, dated 26 April 1919.
8. See *The Occupation of the Rhineland 1918–1929*, ed. Edmonds, p. 360.
9. *The Military Correspondence of Field Marshal Sir Henry Wilson*, ed. Jeffery, p. 109.
10. TNA, CAB 24/78/82.
11. See *The Military Correspondence of Field Marshal Sir Henry Wilson*, ed. Jeffery, p. 69.
12. TNA, CAB 23/8/23.

13. TNA, CAB 23/8/24.
14. TNA, CAB 23/8/23..
15. This note is summarized in Churchill, *Aftermath*, pp. 57–9.
16. *The Military Correspondence of Field Marshal Sir Henry Wilson*, ed. Jeffery, p. 57.
17. TNA, CAB 24/150. Report 101.
18. Churchill, *Aftermath*, p. 163.
19. Rothstein in *Soldiers' Strikes* states that Britain's policy towards intervention in Russia was changed because of the 'soldiers' demands for demobilization' (p. vii). This assertion is difficult to sustain when financial factors, military obligations elsewhere and the impracticalities of waging a war in Russia were the main considerations influencing government policy. The reluctance of soldiers to go to Russia was primarily connected with their wish to go home rather than an indication of pro-Bolshevik feelings.
20. J. Walsh, 'The Durham Light Infantry in Archangel', *Stand To!*, the Journal of the Western Front Association, No. 56, September 1999, pp. 21–3.
21. TNA, CAB 24/71/44.
22. Quoted in Churchill, *Aftermath*, p. 164.
23. See Rothstein, *Soldiers' Strikes*, pp. 12–15.
24. TNA, CAB 24/72.
25. Ibid.
26. TNA, CAB 23/8.
27. *The Military Correspondence of Field Marshal Sir Henry Wilson*, ed. Jeffery, pp. 83–4.
28. Roy Jenkins, *Churchill*, Pan Books, London, 2003, p. 352.
29. House of Lords Records Office, F/8/18. Quoted in *The Military Correspondence of Field Marshal Sir Henry Wilson*, ed. Jeffery, p. 70.
30. *The Military Correspondence of Field Marshal Sir Henry Wilson*, ed. Jeffery, p. 136.
31. Ibid., p. 123.
32. See Taylor, *English History*, p. 142–3.
33. Notably Dallas and Gill, *Unknown Army*; Rothstein, *Soldiers' Strikes*; David Lamb, *Mutinies: 1917–1920*, Solidarity, London, 1979; Alf Killick, *Mutiny*, Militant Pamphlet, 1976; Peter Tatchell, *The Hidden Story of Soldiers' Mutinies, Strikes and Riots*, Good Society, London, 2014.
34. TNA, CAB 24/78/82.
35. TNA, CAB 24/71.
36. *Manchester Evening News*, 28 June 1919.

37. Ibid., 31 May 1919.
38. General Annual Reports on the British Army for the Period From 1 October 1913 to September 1919.
39. Ibid.
40. *The Occupation of the Rhineland 1918–1929*, ed. Edmonds, p. 161.
41. I am indebted to Mr Colin Picton for this information.
42. Quoted in Rothstein, *Soldiers' Strikes*, p. 81.
43. *The Occupation of the Rhineland 1918–1929*, ed. Edmonds, pp. 106–8.
44. Ibid., p. 158.
45. Field Marshal Sir William Robertson, *From Private to Field Marshal*, Constable & Co. Ltd, London, 1921, pp. 363–5.
46. *The Occupation of the Rhineland 1918–1929*, ed. Edmonds, pp. 116–19.
47. TNA, CAB 24/71.
48. Reported in the *Manchester Guardian*, 7 March 1919.
49. Ibid.
50. Ibid., 2 May 1919.
51. Ibid.
52. The *Manchester Evening News*, 30 June 1919.
53. TNA, RECO 1/876.
54. Letter from the Ministry of Reconstruction to Captain R.E. Rowe, dated 12 May 1919.
55. *The Occupation of the Rhineland 1918–1929*, ed. Edmonds, pp. 165–7.
56. Ibid., pp. 174–5.
57. General Annual Reports on the British Army1913-1919. Also, TNA, WO 73/111, General Military Returns of the British Army.
58. TNA, RECO 1/876.

Postscript

1. Letter from a Mr E.A. Burroughs.
2. Quoted in Bond, *British Military Policy*, p. 29.
3. *The Military Correspondence of Field Marshal Sir Henry Wilson*, ed. Jeffery, p. 213.
4. Ibid., p. 250.
5. Ibid., p. 335.
6. Ibid., p. 275.
7. See also Niall Ferguson, *The Pity of War*, Penguin Books, London, 1999, p. 422.
8. The *Manchester Evening News*, 9 June 1919.
9. The *Guardian*, 22 February 1922.
10. TNA, CAB 23/23.

11. TNA, CAB 24/131. Also, *The Military Correspondence of Field Marshal Sir Henry Wilson*, ed. Jeffery, p. 329.
12. *Statistics of the Military Effort*, pp. 326–7.
13. TNA, CAB 23/15.
14. *The Military Correspondence of Field Marshal Sir Henry Wilson*, ed. Jeffery, p. 324.
15. Ibid., p. 331.
16. General Annual Report of the British Army for the Year ending September 1923, p. 12.
17. TNA, CAB 24/127.
18. See Ian F.W. Beckett and Keith Simpson (eds), *A Nation in Arms, The British Army in the First World War*, Pen & Sword Military, Barnsley, 2014, p. 151, particularly Keith Jefferey, 'The Post War Army', p. 228.
19. General Annual Report of the British Army for Year ending September 1923, p. 100.
20. TNA, RECO 1/876.
21. Quoted in Bond, *British Military Policy*, p. 36.
22. Beckett, *The Great War*, pp. 429–41.
23. Michael Senior, *Fromelles 1916, The Loss of a Village*, Pen & Sword Books Ltd, Barnsley, 2004, pp. 203–7.
24. Philip Longworth, *The Unending Vigil,* Pen & Sword Books Ltd, Barnsley, 2003, p. 27.
25. *The Times*, 2 September 1920.
26. See Michael Aiden, 'Rudyard Kipling and King George V. The 1922 Pilgrimage to Flanders Cemeteries', *Stand To!,* the Journal of the Western Front Association, No. 85 April/May 2009.
27. See Mark Connelly, 'Visiting and Revisiting the Battlefields, 1919–21', *Bulletin* of the Western Front Association, August/September 2017, No. 108.
28. See Rothstein, *Soldiers' Strikes*, p. 5.

Index